Where We Have Hope

Where We Have Hope

A MEMOIR OF ZIMBABWE

ANDREW MELDRUM

ATLANTIC MONTHLY PRESS

NEW YORK

Originally published in 2004 in Great Britain by
John Murray Publishers, a division of Hodder Headline

Published by arrangement with Hodder Headline

Printed in the United States of America

FIRST EDITION

Library of Congress Cataloging-in-Publication Data
Meldrum, Andrew.
Where we have hope : a memoir of Zimbabwe / Andrew Meldrum.
p.cm
ISBN 0-87113-896-4
1. Zimbabwe—Politics and government—1980- 2. Zimbabwe—Social conditions—1980-
3. Meldrum, Andrew.   4. Foreign correspondents—Zimbabwe—Biography.
5. Americans—Zimbabwe—Biography.   I. Title.
DT3000.M45 2005
968.9105'1'092—dc22
[B]   2004065733

Atlantic Monthly Press
an imprint of Grove/Atlantic, Inc.
841 Broadway
New York, NY 10003

05 06 07 08 09   10 9 8 7 6 5 4 3 2 1

To my parents, who instilled in me
the values that have been the foundation for my work

To my wife, Dolores Cortes,
who encouraged me throughout

To the people of Zimbabwe,
who have inspired me

CONTENTS

CONTENTS

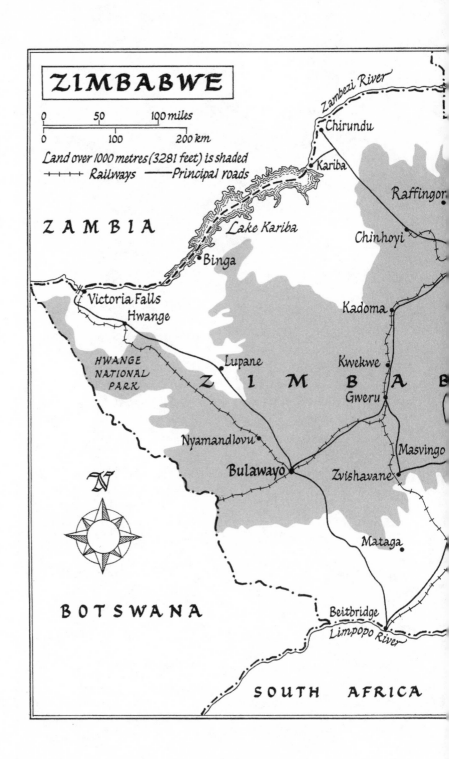

ZIMBABWE

0   50   100 miles

0   100   200 km

Land over 1000 metres (3281 feet) is shaded
+—+—+ Railways   ——Principal roads

Zambezi River

Chirundu

Kariba

Raffingor

ZAMBIA

Lake Kariba

Chinhoyi

Binga

Kadoma

Victoria Falls
Hwange

Lupane

Kwekwe

HWANGE
NATIONAL
PARK

Z I M   B   A   B

Gweru

Nyamandlovu

Masvingo

N

Bulawayo

Zvishavane

Mataga

BOTSWANA

Beitbridge

Limpopo River

SOUTH   AFRICA

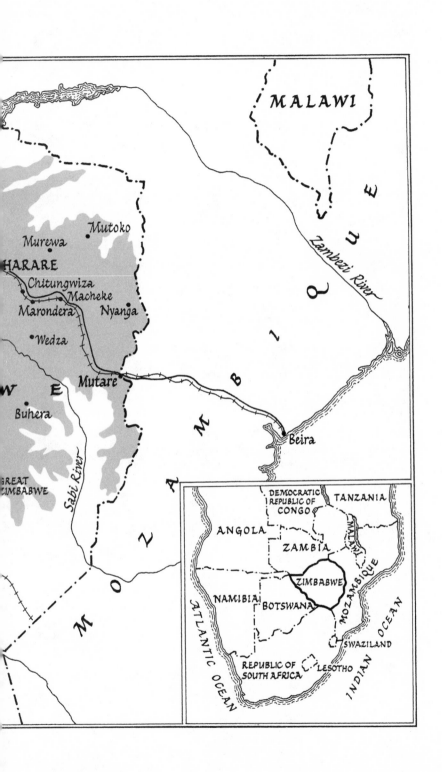

MALAWI

Mutoko

Murewa

HARARE

Chitungwiza

Macheke

Marondera

Nyanga

Wedza

WE

Mutare

Buhera

GREAT
ZIMBABWE

Sabi River

Zambezi River

M O Z A M B I Q U E

Beira

DEMOCRATIC
REPUBLIC OF
CONGO

TANZANIA

ANGOLA

ZAMBIA

MALAWI

NAMIBIA

BOTSWANA

ZIMBABWE

MOZAMBIQUE

SWAZILAND

ATLANTIC OCEAN

REPUBLIC OF
SOUTH AFRICA

LESOTHO

INDIAN OCEAN

My expulsion from Zimbabwe was physical and frightening, but the actions of Mugabe's agents could not change my deep feelings for the country. © *Aaron Ufumeli/AFP/Getty Images*

1

ETCHED IN MY MEMORY

"You are continuing to write bad things about Zimbabwe," the immigration officer says to me, leaning toward me and narrowing his eyes in a menacing way. Over the past year I have been persistently harassed by President Robert Mugabe's government. I have been arrested, jailed, put on trial, and, eventually, acquitted. Now sitting in Linquenda House, a shabby government office block in central Harare, I don't want to let the officer suggest my reporting has been less than honest and fair.

"Not about Zimbabwe," I counter. "My stories may be critical of the government, but they're not bad about Zimbabwe. I've written the truth about what's going on here. You and I both know it."

We both also know that my articles in the *Guardian* over the past three years have infuriated Mugabe and his ministers. That is what this meeting is all about. My reports have highlighted torture, rape, and murder by state agents. The government has categorically denied any such abuses, but my stories, and those of other journalists, have conclusively uncovered systematic state violence. Through my articles I have tried to hold the government accountable for its actions and to highlight the brave struggle for a return to democracy by many Zimbabweans. Supporters of the opposition party, leaders of women's groups, human rights activists, church leaders, and ordinary people have all made their own stands for democracy and have courageously faced frightening repression. Far from writing "bad things about Zimbabwe," by writing about their heroic efforts in the face of terrible threats and violence from the state, I believe I have been reporting the best of Zimbabwe.

I am aware that this is not the time for a discussion of my writing. Evans Siziba, the tall immigration officer with the threatening stance

3

of a boxer, has been hounding me for a year. Ten days ago, Siziba turned up at my house at night. The quiet residential street was especially dark because the streetlights had not worked for nearly a year. When my wife, Dolores, walked down the drive to answer the gate, she was startled to see four plainclothes officers. Behind them were four vehicles, including a large van with blacked-out windows.

It could only mean they were planning to pick me up illegally. Over the past months, I had written many stories about Zimbabweans who had been taken from their homes by plainclothes government agents who beat and tortured them. We knew from the experience of friends that such shadowy night visits meant trouble.

In fact, Siziba was not an immigration officer at all. We knew from government sources that he was really an agent of the much-feared Central Intelligence Organization, Zimbabwe's secret police, who answer directly to Mugabe and place agents in key government departments. I had interviewed many victims of CIO interrogations and seen their wounds: cigarette burns and open sores where electrodes had been placed on their fingers, toes, ear lobes, tongues, and genitals. Siziba had not come to my home to have a civilized conversation about my writing.

Siziba told Dolores that he wanted to see me. He refused to show her any identification papers, nor would he say why he wanted to speak to me. Recognizing him from our earlier encounters, she told him I was not at home. He replied that he would wait for me to return. Dolores came back to the house and immediately called our lawyer, Beatrice Mtetwa.

I was not about to comply with Siziba's illegal actions. I had to leave the house without him seeing me. Somehow I managed to finish the last paragraphs of a story I had been working on and e-mailed it to the *Guardian*. Grabbing my cell phone and some money, I went through our laundry room and out the back door. I looked at the wall behind my herb garden; it towered above me. I carried out a stepladder but it left me still short of the tiles at the top of the wall. Jumping up, I grabbed the top and then hauled myself over. Slowly I let myself down the other side. I dangled for a moment and then dropped about ten feet to the ground. My belt buckle caught on the wall, throwing me off balance, and I landed on my side. I picked myself up and stood listening. The neighboring

4

house was very close to the wall, but the people inside were playing music quite loudly so they didn't hear me, and fortunately they did not have any dogs. I hurried down their driveway unnoticed. As I let myself out at the gate, I saw a man standing at the corner near our house. I casually walked the other way until I came to a dark corner, where I used my cell phone to call a friend. He agreed to pick me up right away.

I took a deep breath and looked at the clear sky. Zimbabwe was entering its winter; it got dark early and the night air was chilly. I could see the stars of the Southern Cross and Scorpio while I watched the fruit bats fly past. The night was very still and I could hear the drumming and singing of a group of Apostolics, a religious sect that would meet in open fields nearby, dressed in white robes. This was my neighborhood, but now I was forced to hide.

My lawyer, Beatrice, arrived at our house within minutes. Later she would tell me how she had asked Siziba and the others to show their identification and state what they were doing but they refused. She insisted that it was their legal obligation, but Siziba simply said they would stay at our gate until I returned.

By then my wife had called other journalists and told them about the gang at our gate. Soon a dozen or so reporters from Zimbabwean newspapers and the international press were also at the entrance to our property, watching to see what these government agents would do. Frustrated by the presence of so many witnesses and visibly angry, Siziba announced he was leaving to get "reinforcements."

The friend who picked me up drove me to the home of another friend, where I burst in on a family dinner and was promptly invited to join it. I explained my situation and went to a quiet room to phone Dolores, Beatrice, and the *Guardian*. These good people insisted I stay with them that night, even after I described all the possible risks of a visit to their home by the CIO or the police, or even Mugabe's gangs of war veterans.

For ten days I eluded Siziba and his crew. I knew I had done nothing wrong or illegal, even by Zimbabwe's draconian laws. There was no warrant out for my arrest—in fact my lawyer had court orders protecting me. I was in the bizarre and often frightening situation of evading government agents who were acting illegally.

During the day I tried to carry on as normally as possible. I managed to file a story, cover a demonstration, and do several radio interviews. I even did some early-morning jogging along my favorite routes and met friends for lunch. But by then I had become a highly recognizable figure in Zimbabwe, especially as the government was printing stories about me in the state press, which charged that I was on the run. When people saw me they came up to congratulate me and to offer me encouragement, so Dolores insisted I wear a hat with a floppy brim, and when friends drove me into Harare's city center I lay on the floor of their cars. But these were really halfhearted gestures. I had always prided myself on doing my work openly and aboveboard and was uncomfortable about being "undercover." Dolores and I did not sleep at home.

The nights were difficult, knowing that the CIO had a way of picking people up after dark. We tried not to stay at any one place for more than a couple of days to avoid detection, so the rooms were always unfamiliar. We were in touch with a network of "safe houses" where other people had stayed when they were trying to avoid being picked up. I was just one of many people dodging government agents; others included opposition supporters, church leaders who had spoken out against government abuses, human rights activists, fellow journalists, and former police officers who had exposed torture and murder committed by uniformed officers. I was in good company.

At some of the places where we stayed people wanted to talk about what was happening in Zimbabwe and what would bring change. They would become passionate about their country and discuss different ways that Mugabe might be ousted and democracy reestablished. Everyone seemed to think that change was just around the corner.

I made a couple of strategic public appearances. On the day that the state-controlled *Herald* newspaper ran a front-page article declaring that I was in hiding and a fugitive from justice, I proved it wrong by attending a large diplomatic reception where I met with many African and European ambassadors. "I am a fugitive from *in*justice," I said, reminding them that the courts had found that I had the legal right to live and work in Zimbabwe. By evading government officers who were acting outside the law, I was merely trying to get the government to deal with my case according to its own laws.

We talked about Zimbabwe's worsening economy, with inflation at 350 percent and zooming higher, about the food and fuel shortages, and the national strike planned to shut down the country for a week. We also discussed movements that challenged Mugabe's grip on power. Other African countries were encouraging him to hold talks with the opposition party and to accept that new elections, fully free and fair, needed to be held. Many expressed optimism that things would improve. The African diplomats were friendly and frank about the need to put pressure on Mugabe, but we all knew that they would still issue public statements of support for him, in the name of African solidarity.

I ducked away from the reception, elated by the encouragement I received, but my high spirits evaporated when my cell phone rang. It was our host of the night before, fear cracking his voice, warning me not to return to his home: two men were hanging around the front of his driveway. I called Dolores and told her not to go back there. I was keenly aware that each day the CIO and the Mugabe government failed to apprehend me, the stakes were getting higher. I was worried that my colleagues, family, and friends would be attacked instead of me. "The longer this goes on, the more dangerous it becomes for you and for everyone around you," said Beatrice when we managed to meet. "It could be your life."

Beatrice generally made light of any danger, but this time she was serious. I knew that she, too, was under threat. She was followed as she went about her business during the day and when she went home at night. I was not her only high-profile client: she was also representing the mayor of Harare, Elias Mudzuri, who was fighting a battle with the government to run the city. As the candidate for the main opposition party, the Movement for Democratic Change, Mudzuri had been elected in 2002 by a whopping 80 percent majority, but the government was determined to prevent the opposition from managing the capital city. Mudzuri had been jailed for three days and then released without charge; then the judge who dropped the spurious charges against Mudzuri found himself in jail on equally questionable charges. Mugabe's toughs invaded the mayoral offices, where they beat up some city officials and locked Mudzuri out. Despite court orders stating that Mudzuri had the right to function as the mayor, police stood by and refused to take any action. Under these circumstances, merely arranging a meeting with Beatrice

was difficult. We made plans on our cell phones, which were more difficult to bug than our fixed lines. We met in an office of a large Harare
building where she went in one entrance and I went in another, but it
was becoming more dangerous as the days went on. Many people had
suggested that I simply leave the country, possibly seeking protection
from the American embassy to ensure that I got out safely. But I did not
want to give the impression that I had anything to hide or was running
away. Beatrice wanted to pursue and, if necessary, exhaust every legal
avenue to get fair treatment for me. Now we decided to go to the Immigration Department the next day. Beatrice and I tried to call Siziba but
found that he was never in his office at Immigration, his absence making us all the more suspicious that he was not a bona fide immigration
officer. Eventually I succeeded in reaching him on his cell phone. He
immediately started shouting, accusing me of hiding from him, until I
took the wind out of his sails by agreeing to come in to see him the next
morning. We knew that I could be forcibly, if illegally, expelled from
Zimbabwe at that meeting, but we could not see any better way to deal
with it than head-on.

This meeting with Beatrice lasted until dusk, and when I left I went
back to my house. I had other places to stay but I felt a burning need to
be at my own home and to sleep in my own bed. I wanted to be with my
dogs and wander through my garden. This was what the government was
trying to take away from me and I was determined not to let go of it. It
seemed there weren't any agents hanging around our street; they must
have been looking for me elsewhere.

I got a rapturous reception from our three dogs. I knew this might
be my last time with them; certainly my oldest dog, my faithful black
Labrador, was on his last legs and I would not see him again. I loved the
home that Dolores and I had made together, and I could not bring myself to accept that I would be torn away from the house, the garden, the
dogs. When friends and colleagues phoned, I explained in a matter-of-
fact tone that I was going to Immigration the next day, but I could not
bring myself to suggest that this might be good-bye. I found it much
easier to do an interview with a radio station, describing my situation
and legal status in detail and declaring that I was determined to remain
in Zimbabwe. The moon was full that night and my garden was bathed

8

in the lunar glow. I wandered through it, admiring the new growth, especially of the acacia trees I had planted. I made mental notes of things I wanted to do: tend some young palm trees, put in some seasonal flowers, and add more goldfish to the little pond. This was still my home. Dolores and I cooked dinner in our own kitchen and ate at our own table. I slept well that night.

The following morning Beatrice and I were in determined spirits when we walked into Linquenda House, the tall, increasingly shabby office block in central Harare which houses Immigration and many other government departments. The well-maintained government building that I had encountered when I first arrived in Zimbabwe in 1980 had become run-down, with long rows of missing floor tiles and peeling wall coverings. Fluorescent lights flickered uncertainly overhead and others were just burned out. Only one of the four elevators was in service. The dilapidated state of the building was a symbol for how things had changed in Zimbabwe.

In contrast to the corridor outside, the office of Elasto Mugwadi, the chief immigration officer, was well appointed and spacious, with a large couch and comfortable chairs. We were met by Mugwadi himself, together with Siziba. A trained lawyer, Mugwadi took pains to show he was proceeding legally. Prior to the meeting, Beatrice had told me he would try to show that he was going by the rules, because he knew he could be struck off the list of legal practitioners if it were proved he did anything illegal. Mugwadi was pleasant and cordial and maintained a business-like atmosphere. "We just want to clarify a few points about your residence permit," he said. "We want to make sure that everything is in order."

"If it is just a matter of clarification, then why did your officers come to my client's house after dark?" asked Beatrice. Mugwadi claimed not to know anything about that matter, and Siziba remained silent. Mugwadi repeated that he simply needed some information about my residence permit. Beatrice insisted that I had a valid permanent residence permit and the courts had ruled I had the right to stay in the country. Mugwadi said he just wanted to check a few details. He asked to see copies of some of my articles and we agreed to bring them to his office later that day. The negotiation seemed so smooth that I actually began to think that Beatrice and I could answer Mugwadi's questions satisfactorily, provide the stories and paperwork he wanted, and put the difficulties of the past week behind us.

But then I asked for my passport. Mugwadi turned to Siziba and said I must get it from his deputy. My hopes dissolved. Mugwadi suddenly declared he had a meeting elsewhere in town. I thought he looked nervous as he grabbed his briefcase. Quickly, very quickly, he left his office.

The atmosphere changes immediately. Siziba is now in charge. Beatrice and I follow him across the hall to his small office. A portrait of Robert Mugabe glares from the wall and in the background a radio plays the state mouthpiece, the Zimbabwe Broadcasting Corporation. Another officer sits next to Siziba. Where Mugwadi was amiable and civil, Siziba glowers. In a voice full of menace he begins to accuse me of criticizing the government. He refuses to listen to my rejection of his charge. He simply tells me I have been declared a prohibited immigrant and will be deported.

At this Beatrice leaps up, as if she were in court. "You can't call this a deportation. This is completely illegal," she says. "You know I have court orders saying this is illegal."

Siziba shrugs and says, "This is what we are going to do."

"When will you expel him? Where will he be taken?" Beatrice demands. It is not for nothing that she is called "the rottweiler" in court circles. "He must go home and pack his bags. He has lived in this country for more than twenty years; he needs at least twenty-four hours to get ready."

"That's not possible," says Siziba, raising his voice. "He will be in our custody."

"Where will you take me—to the airport?" I ask, struggling to suppress a rising panic. I always knew something like this might happen, but it is alarming to feel it actually taking place. I was thrown in jail in Zimbabwe a year ago. The thought of being in the custody of these men is not pleasant.

"Is that where you want to go, to the airport?" asks Siziba's assistant, leaning forward with a sinister grin. "We might have some other place to take you. Where else do you think we could take you?"

"The airport is the only place you could take me," I reply, knowing full well that it is not.

"Then you have nothing to worry about," he says in a sneering way that is far from reassuring.

"My passport should be returned to me," I insist.

"We'll give it to you later," says Siziba, who gets up abruptly and with his assistant walks out of his office.

Beatrice and I are now alone, sitting in front of his empty desk. I am stunned. It is left to my lawyer to say what I still cannot believe. "They're kicking you out illegally," says Beatrice. "No wonder Mugwadi left so quickly: he didn't have the guts to do this himself." Beatrice tells me she will go back to the courts and get a fresh order to stop this action. She has already prepared the affidavit.

When we step out of the office, the corridor is no longer empty. We are immediately surrounded by police officers. Beatrice stands right next to me, steadfastly refusing to let the men push her away. We crowd into the ramshackle elevator, which shudders to the ground floor. I am pleased, at least, that we are going out through the main foyer onto Harare's bustling Nelson Mandela Avenue. Word has spread that I am at Immigration and outside a band of reporters, photographers, and cameramen, all colleagues and friends, jostles to get a clear view of what is happening to me. Each face is familiar and I can recognize even those obscured by their cameras. After being part of that crowd for many years, it is a shock to realize that I am not free to join them. I am on the other side of the news line. They are my protection now. If the government is going to throw me out illegally, I am determined to let them know what is going on.

"I have been declared a prohibited immigrant and the government is expelling me," I tell the press pack, who begin scribbling notes and taking photos. "This is not the action of a government—" and at that the police grab my arms and shoulders and brusquely drag me away from Beatrice and the crowd. I know this is my only chance to say anything to the press, so I struggle to regain my balance and continue, now shouting: ". . . that is confident of its own legitimacy. It is a government that is afraid of a free press—" The officers nearly lift me off my feet and the scuffling becomes more intense. I somehow manage to keep shouting, "It is a government that is afraid of independent and critical reporting!"

By now I have been dragged to a waiting car. I try to resist as the police shove me into the car and they punch, hit, and kick me. Soon I find myself in the back seat, flanked on either side by plainclothesmen wearing dark glasses. Outside the window I see the reassuring figure of cameraman Michele Mathison, whom I have known since he was a boy, recording the fracas.

Tires squeal as the car zooms off at high speed, fighting through the busy traffic. I straighten my rumpled blazer and try to gather my thoughts but the passenger in the front seat turns around and throws a dark jacket over my head. I push it away and struggle to keep my head free. The two men beside me pin my arms down and hold the jacket firmly around my neck. The man on my right thumps me hard on the back. "The time for games is now over," he says. Suddenly I feel vulnerable and frightened.

I am very familiar with Harare's roads and attempt to follow where we are going, but after several quick turns I am disorientated. Peering through my shroud, I can just make out the shapes of cars and trucks as we speed by. Just take me to the airport, I keep thinking, just don't take me anywhere else. In the past month I have interviewed several prominent Zimbabweans, including four opposition members of Parliament, who had been seized by CIO agents and had hoods put over their heads. Invariably they were taken to rural police stations and severely beaten and subjected to electric shocks to the point of convulsions. If the CIO can take an M.P. from the steps of the Parliament building and torture him, maybe they will do it to me.

Suddenly our car makes a sharp turn. From the bumps and potholes I can tell that we are on a dirt road. As if in answer to my fears, the driver says, "We're going to a special place." The others snigger ominously.

It is stifling under the jacket and I am sweating, from the heat or fear or both. I wipe my clammy palms on my jeans. I straighten my shoulders and take a deep breath. I must not let them know I am scared. But I begin to imagine bruising blows to my body and the singeing sting of electric current. Stop that, I tell myself. You can get through this. I remind myself that others who have been abducted suffered torture but they were not murdered. Eventually they were released, bloodied and traumatized but alive. Whatever might be inflicted upon me, I tell myself, I'll just have to endure it.

After what seems like an eternity the car swings sharply and we are back on a smooth, tarred road. Through the jacket I glimpse the fleeting image of white columns on each side of the road. My heart soars. It is the Independence Arch! The airport lies ahead of us!

I am led into the airport with the hood still on, groping unsteadily to find my way, and taken to a small room in the basement. When the hood comes off I see I am in a little cubicle with three chairs and in one corner some empty bottles, one of cheap local brandy and two Coke bottles. The men from the car shove my arms over to two other men. I cannot find any sign of their intentions in their blank faces. I take a deep breath and try to remain calm.

We wait in that tiny space for hours. When I stand up to stretch my legs, they order me to sit down. Later they allow me to go to the toilet, following me closely. We begin talking and I keep the conversation bland, centering on the weather and sports. I gather they intend to go out tonight, so I figure I might be released by then. They realize I know a bit of the Shona language and a bit more about the culture. I try to interact with them in order to find out what is going to happen. I have no illusions that a conversation will change how I am treated, but it can't hurt to connect with them in some way.

Eventually they begin asking me questions, which I answer carefully, wanting to engage them but not wanting to infuriate them. Nor do I want to provide them with any information that might be used against me or anyone else.

"You must know a lot of famous people. What do you think of Henry Olonga?" asks the bearded guard, referring to the black Zimbabwean cricket star who, together with his white teammate Andy Flower, had worn a black armband at the opening of the Cricket World Cup games in Harare a few months earlier, to mourn "the death of democracy in our beloved Zimbabwe." I give my guards a straight answer, saying that Olonga is a dedicated and principled young man of strong Christian faith who was doing what he thought was right. Amazingly, they do not contradict me.

"What do you think of Oliver Mutukudzi?" asks the younger guard about Zimbabwe's musical superstar, some of whose songs have been banned by state broadcasting for being too critical of Mugabe.

"He is a very talented and committed musician who wants to bring people together," I say. I am surprised when they nod in agreement. More questions soon follow.

"Why is everything so expensive? Why is fuel so scarce and so many other things in such short supply?" asks the bearded one.

"Because the economy is not being managed properly," I respond.

"When will the economy improve?" he asks.

"When this government changes its policies or there is a new government that runs things properly," I say, adding, "the Zimbabwean economy is fundamentally strong and all it needs is good management and it will do well."

"But would the opposition be able to run things well?" asks the younger one. "Aren't they unpatriotic?" Their questions seem genuine and their naïveté is disarming. I explain that the opposition party, the Movement for Democratic Change, is trying to bring about change through peaceful, democratic means. They ask me about opposition leader Morgan Tsvangirai: isn't he uneducated and stupid? I say many people are not able to get good educations but that does not mean they are unintelligent. Tsvangirai may not have gone to college, but I find him intelligent in analyzing Zimbabwe's problems.

These men are security agents, but it is clear they are as confused as anyone else about Zimbabwe's spiraling economic and political crisis. Even Mugabe's own henchmen can sense that everything is going wrong in their country. I have never heard CIO agents question the status quo in this way.

"What will bring change?" asks the younger, more curious one when the other has gone to the toilet.

"When the country can have free and fair elections and the people can freely choose a new government," I tell him.

The hours drag on and I realize that I might be held in the basement overnight. It is after 9 P.M. I become even more worried with the return of the men who hooded me in the car. They take me upstairs and into a room where immigration officials are taking a break and eating their

14

dinners. "We know what they are doing to you is illegal," says one official when the others leave the room. "We know your lawyer got a court order today saying you must not be deported."

Then the airport's senior immigration official comes to the room with my guards from the car. They accompany me to the departure gates.

"Andy, ANDY!" Although it is very faint, I immediately recognize Dolores's voice and I turn to see her waving to me, far down the hallway. I pull away from my guards and start toward her. And there is Beatrice, her petite figure charging through two different sets of security men, waving a sheaf of papers. "I have a court order!" she shouts. "The judge says he must not be deported. This action is illegal." One immigration officer actually deserts her desk and runs away from Beatrice. Everyone else in the passageway stops and stares.

Startled and worried by the commotion, the guards grab me and others suddenly appear and pull me toward the plane. "That's my lawyer. She says this is illegal," I shout.

"We don't care about any court order," replies the immigration officer. "Just get on the plane."

Still struggling, I am pushed over the boarding plank onto the aircraft. I tell the Air Zimbabwe crew that this action is illegal, that there is a court order prohibiting it. They refuse to give me my passport and push me away from the door, which is quickly shut and secured. The crew escort me to my seat while stewards and startled passengers stare at me. I realize there is no more I can do. I am being expelled from Zimbabwe despite the fresh court order that Beatrice obtained. Within a few minutes the Air Zimbabwe jet pulls up in the air and starts its journey to London.

I am seated in the middle aisle and cannot see Harare's twinkling lights dwindle as we fly up and away. But I do not need to. Zimbabwe is indelibly etched in my memory. I am steeped in this country; it is in my pores. More than just the physical look and feel and smell of the land, I have a deep sense of what the country stands for: liberation, majority rule, democracy, and human rights. This is what Zimbabwe meant when it won independence in 1980 and it is what so many are valiantly fighting to regain. This conviction of what Zimbabwe stands for cannot be erased simply by forcing me out of the country.

I was delighted to discover that my newly hired housekeeper, Mrs. Enista Manomano, was a lead member of one of Zimbabwe's top traditional dancing groups. Here she is jumping high in the exuberance of the dance. © *Tessa Colvin*

2

HIGH HOPES

When I first arrived in Zimbabwe, I was a young journalist with dreams of becoming a foreign correspondent. I had worked for a few years on newspapers in the United States and was searching for an opportunity to work abroad. When Zimbabwe reached independence, I saw my chance. I knew very little about the new country, but was inspired by how a multiracial, majority-rule democracy had emerged from the bloody fourteen-year war against white-minority-ruled Rhodesia.

I was impressed by the new leader, Robert Mugabe, who had transformed himself from a hard-line Marxist guerrilla leader into a statesman who called for racial reconciliation. I wanted to chronicle the new country's efforts to improve the lives of the black majority and to become a democratic model for Africa, especially for neighboring South Africa with its apartheid system. I quit my newspaper job in the States, sold my car, and bought a ticket to Zimbabwe to find work as a freelance journalist.

I landed in Zimbabwe early one morning in October 1980. As I walked from the plane, still painted in the blue and white colors of Air Rhodesia, I was struck by the fresh, sharp air with a pleasantly cool edge to it. The airport building was clean and efficient, but also quite small and somehow quaint, with old-fashioned fittings and signs. It was my first indication of the country's time warp. The Rhodesian war and international sanctions had isolated the country for more than ten years, so that much of the look and feel of the place recalled a past era. I stood and watched the bustle of people in the airport's concourse. It soon struck me that there was virtually no socializing between blacks and whites; the only interaction was that between white passengers and black taxi drivers and porters. It was not at all what I had imagined.

Taking a bus into the city, I saw long stretches of open, undeveloped land and rows of jacaranda trees with soft purple blossoms. Once in the city center I passed many high-rise office buildings, hotels, and shops, but few had any distinctive character, either of old colonial elegance or of a new African modernism. The streets were well maintained but almost empty. I soon discovered that the city center is busy during office hours, but on weekends people retire to their homes in the suburbs and townships, leaving the downtown area nearly deserted.

Arriving six months after the birth of Zimbabwe, which had been in April 1980, I could see little of the liberated country I hoped to write about. The hotel where I first stayed was comfortable, but it was in that same curious time zone I had noticed at the airport. Its decor was from somewhere in the 1960s and was absolutely devoid of any sign of Africa. Similarly, when I went for a walk around the central blocks, especially down the pleasant pedestrian mall of First Street, I saw many impressive shops, but none of the goods on display looked African in any way. Clothes, fabric, furniture, paintings all seemed to come from England. The bookshops displayed large coffee-table tomes on Irish castles and the fens of England, novels by Frederick Forsyth and James Clavell, but nothing about Africa apart from some wildlife books. The orderly downtown area and the well-watered suburbs and golf courses reminded me somewhat of the smug prosperity of a county seat in the American Midwest, which I had just left.

As I walked around the city, still called Salisbury, that first week, I gradually began to notice a few signs of the Africa I was searching for. Black women carrying babies on their backs, often with impossibly large and heavy bundles balanced on their heads. African men holding hands as they walked down a street, an unself-conscious display of friendship and kinship. Manica Road, its charming old buildings with cast-iron poles holding wide awnings over the busy procession of shoppers and sellers. The shops there catered more to the African population, the fabrics colorful and the goods basic and sturdy. Farther down the street I got into an area known as the "Cow's Guts" that was full of small shops run by Asians for the African trade. And much farther down I came across the Mbare Market, a sprawling, noisy open-air bazaar where vendors sold tomatoes, onions, carrots, car parts, batteries, beds, and just about everything else. Here I found African baskets, stools, and beaded handicrafts. I was the only white person around but, aside from a few people trying to get me to buy things, no one seemed to take much notice amid all the hustle of the marketplace.

My first impressions of the country were of a place that was still dominated by a white minority. It was disappointing, but a country cannot change overnight. Decades of racism had left a legacy that could not be erased by a new name for the country, a new flag, or even a new black leader. I found I was looking at a great deal of the old Rhodesia and getting just a glimpse of the new Zimbabwe. It was a country in transition and it was that process of change that I was challenged to cover.

There was little sign, however, of a new spirit of racial harmony. The country seemed polarized and locked in old enmities. Almost all the whites were still living in Rhodesia and carried an angry chip on their shoulder. Many continued to treat blacks rudely and arrogantly, and I cringed at ugly scenes where whites shouted at black waiters in restaurants, at black clerks in bank lines and in government offices.

This anti-African psyche explained the shop windows. These Rhodesians longed for furnishings that spoke of England, and their dress sense displayed both their time warp and their anti-African viewpoint. So many white women favored a Farrah Fawcett–type hair flip, pastel sundresses, and high heels that it seemed like a uniform. The men sported long sideburns and wore safari suits with short sleeves and short trousers paired with knee-socks. Most wore wristwatches covered by a bulky leather flap, a relic from service in the Rhodesian Army, to prevent any reflection off the crystal being detected by the African "terrorists." That word was still used a great deal, along with *terrs, gooks,* and *munts. Floppies* was another epithet for blacks, because Rhodesians said they flopped over when they were shot. The bitterness and hatred I encountered left me reeling.

These Rhodesian types latched on to me when they heard my accent. They idolized the United States, dazzled by a vision of America they saw in movies and television shows. They assumed, by virtue of my skin color, that I shared their racist views. Within minutes of meeting I would be subjected to a lengthy litany of all the hardships that had been caused by blacks. They pressed me to agree with them and when

21

I refused to endorse their views they became infuriated. I learned to spot these bitter "Rhodies" and to avoid them altogether.

Blacks were more difficult to engage and remained wary. Most were polite but distant and reserved, and in my first week in Zimbabwe the only blacks I met were hotel employees or taxi drivers. They were friendly enough, but cautious when speaking to me.

I moved to an inexpensive residential hotel that was mainly patronized by whites who were winding up their affairs and moving to South Africa. One of the guests, however, was a middle-aged black librarian who had recently returned from exile in Zambia. We sat at the same table for dinner and enjoyed pleasant conversation while many of the whites glared at our interracial socializing. One evening this lady invited me to her apartment, where she told me of her years in exile and how she studied to get her qualifications. As the conversation went on she became increasingly bitter, venting her anger at the whites who had frustrated her professionally. At one point she raised her voice and shouted as if she were angry with me. I realized that most blacks could not see who I was, let alone trust me, because of the ninety years of oppression they had endured.

I found myself retreating to the little room I had at the hotel and gazing out of my window at the cloud of purple-blue jacaranda blossoms in the trees lining the street. The area where I was staying, known as the Avenues, was just a few blocks from the downtown tower blocks. It had a pleasant mix of apartment buildings and townhouses and a scattering of old colonial-era houses with wide verandas. Until very recently it had been a whites-only area, but it was rapidly becoming mixed. From my window I watched white secretaries and black civil servants walk back from work. Young white couples sat in cars while black couples dawdled by the large jacaranda trees. At the end of the month I watched removal vans take away the furniture, refrigerators, televisions, and stereos of the whites moving out, while old cars and trucks carted in the more modest possessions of the blacks who were making their way up in the new world.

Zimbabwe's climate was one thing that did not disappoint. The mornings began cool and fresh; day after day boasted sunny, blue skies; the hot afternoons were moderated by low humidity; the nights were deliciously cool and balmy. Zimbabwe may be in the tropics, but most of it is on a plateau nearly a mile above sea level, lifting the central part of the country out of the sweltering lowlands to an unparalleled subtropical climate. People told me Zimbabwe had "champagne air," because it is dry and sparkling, and I found it delightfully intoxicating.

Soon I rented a small apartment with sunny windows overlooking the jacaranda trees of the Avenues. The building, Richmond Court, had previously been all white, but it was rapidly filling with young, upwardly mobile blacks. I set about furnishing my new pad with some tables and benches I made from kits. I bought two foam mattresses covered in blue canvas and some matching bolsters. I put them on slabs of plywood on top of cement bricks and—bingo!—I had two sofas. I stuck up some tourist posters of Zimbabwe and got some cushions in African print fabrics. It was basic but colorful and cheerful and served my purposes perfectly. I got a telephone line connected and a subscription to the *Herald* newspaper. I was settling in.

After I had been in the flat about two weeks, the building's janitor came and asked me if I wanted a servant. I had already said no, and declined again. I had never thought of having a servant: it didn't fit with my idea of independent Zimbabwe. "Ahh, but this is giving me problems," he said, leaning on his broom. "Everybody knows you don't have any servant. People come to me every day asking for work. They pester me about you. They say they will be angry with me when you hire someone else. Why don't you hire someone?" Again I explained that I did not need such help. But he persisted: "Everyone needs someone to clean their flat. Maybe just for two days a week, please? Try someone just for a month. It will save me trouble."

Finally I relented and agreed to hire someone he recommended for a trial period. Enista Manomano arrived at my apartment the next morning. She was in her fifties with a very expressive face. She spoke little English but we managed to make ourselves understood. We agreed she would do my laundry, which was getting rather dirty, and clean the sparse two rooms. When I came back later that day my clothes were clean, expertly ironed, and put away in neat piles. The furniture had been rearranged and the rooms were so clean that I realized for the first time how grime-encrusted they had been. A notebook I had been hunting for sat by the phone, with some spare change that had been in one of my pockets.

So began a long and fruitful partnership. Mrs. Manomano had been well trained in cleaning and her ironing was deft. My appearance became considerably sharper, and my apartment, especially the kitchen, sparkled. She began teaching me Shona phrases.

Employing a servant was an almost inescapable part of Zimbabwean life. Domestic work, as a housecleaner, cook, nanny, or gardener, remained an important source of employment in the country. Surveys showed that 12 percent of those employed were working as household help. And whites were not the only ones who had servants; blacks in the townships employed them too.

But I did not want to fall into the old Rhodesian mold of having servants do everything. "S&S—sun and servants—that's all we have here and that's why we stay," a Rhodesian madam told me at a cocktail party. "Frankly, I'd rather be murdered in my bed than have to make it every day, so I'm happy here." She was candid, I granted her that, but I was not in Zimbabwe to enjoy neocolonial inequality. As was the custom, Mrs. Manomano called me master or *baas* (boss). I did not like the subservience implied by such titles but it was firmly ingrained in Mrs. Manomano. She refused point-blank to call me by my name, saying, "*Handidi,*" Shona for "I don't want" or "never." Eventually we found a solution: she called me *mukoma,* "respected brother." She was happy with that and I was, too, though I needn't have worried, because her tart, flinty nature meant she never put up with anything she thought was out of place.

One morning she brought me a letter from a government ministry, which stated that Mrs. Manomano was requested to perform as a dancer at the airport for the arrival of Tanzanian president Julius Nyerere. It was news to me that Mrs. Manomano was a dancer. Of course I gave her the day off, and since I was covering Nyerere's visit, I was able to see her performance.

At the airport, a number of dancing groups was lined up. Mrs. Manomano's group, Jerusalema Number One, had a central position, and when their turn came four men pounded out a signature drumbeat that I recognized immediately as the catchy rhythm that introduced all newscasts on the state radio and television. About fifteen dancers lined up, the men on one side and the women on the other.

24

They wore bright green, yellow, and blue African print fabrics and some of the men wore animal skins. After a bit of warm-up dancing and some whistle-blowing, one man and one woman came forward. They danced to the insistent drumbeat and at the climax they performed vigorous pelvic thrusts at each other, to much laughter and approval from the crowd. The dancing carried on and became more energetic and comic, with different partners executing the key thrust with colorful variations. Many more spectators gathered around, chuckling and cheering. Some joined the dancing, but the Jerusalema members remained the most accomplished, with Mrs. Manomano one of the stars of the show.

The dance emanated from the Murewa rural area where Mrs. Manomano grew up. Colonial missionaries had been appalled by the bawdy dance and tried to ban it, but the shrewd Africans got around their objections by saying it came from the Bible and calling it the Jerusalem dance. During the following months I would watch the award-winning group perform at festivals in the central Harare Gardens park, at the annual agricultural show, and at the airport for other heads of state. Mrs. Manomano was featured on a postcard in a soaring jump. I came to know other members of the troupe, and they were a delightful bridge for me to rural Africa, showing me how traditional culture retains a key place in the westernized life of the city.

I was eager to experience more African culture, so when the popular West African group Osibisa came to Zimbabwe, I decided to go to the concert at Rufaro Stadium in Mbare township, where, just a few months before, Robert Mugabe had been sworn in as prime minister and Prince Charles had stood by as the British flag was lowered and the Zimbabwean flag was raised. For me the highlight was not the international band but the Zimbabwean opening act, Oliver Mutukudzi and the Black Spirits. I had heard his songs on the radio and liked his distinctively expressive hoarse voice, especially on the mournful but catchy "Seiko." The crowd responded enthusiastically to every song, especially to his reggae version of the new national anthem, *Ishe Komborera Africa* ("God Bless Africa").

It was not a big crowd, however. Far from filling the stadium, the concert attracted just a few thousand people who mostly stood around the stage. Few blacks could afford the entrance fee and most whites were not interested in either act. But I found those who did choose to go a very interesting bunch. The blacks were mostly upmarket, and the whites were arty types who wore hippyish clothes and the traditional, coiled copper bracelets that I had noticed people wearing in Mbare market. Many spoke Shona. These whites had obviously rejected the old Rhodesian order and were carving out a new, Zimbabwean alternative. It was the first time I saw whites and blacks interact equally and easily.

A few weeks later I found myself at a party in a flat near the center of Harare shared by three young South African exiles who had come to Zimbabwe to work as schoolteachers. Here I met other teachers who had arrived from South Africa, Britain, Canada, and the United States. I also met young black Zimbabweans who had studied overseas and had come back to their new country, and I spoke with black students at the University of Zimbabwe who were hoping to become doctors and lawyers. Zimbabwe had just experienced an education explosion, as Mugabe had opened up primary and secondary education to all. Enrollments doubled and tripled and the teachers were delighted to be working with students who were so eager to learn.

The party became an impromptu seminar when a leader from the Quaker Church who was well known in the antiapartheid movement addressed the group:

"Zimbabwe has become the focus, the center of the progressive world. The international community's dream has been realized with Zimbabwe's independence. This country has defeated racism, discrimination, and hate. You are all here to contribute to its progress. And by helping to build a successful Zimbabwe you are bringing about the downfall of apartheid in South Africa. You are helping Zimbabwe to become a new model for all of Africa. It is inspiring to see the work that you are all doing."

These were heady words for the young gathering. I was delighted at last to be meeting people with whom I shared similar values and goals. I felt I had a mission to report about this new spirit, this nascent multiracial experiment of Zimbabwe that was going to lead the way for South Africa to eradicate apartheid and show the world that an African democracy could succeed.

Many people shared my high hopes for the country. Some diplomats called it "the Switzerland of Africa" because of its excellent roads, efficient business, and sense of order. Others said that because Zimbabwe had reached independence nearly twenty years later than most African countries, it had the opportunity to learn from their mistakes. Mugabe could avoid the pitfalls of corruption, ethnic violence, and one-party government that plagued so many other African countries. I looked forward to reporting on a country that was working to establish a democracy, a multiracial society, and an economy that would provide a decent standard of living for the black majority.

At about the same time, my personal life in Harare was becoming more settled and rewarding. A great, adventurous friend came to visit from the United States. When Dolores Cortes arrived I was eager to show her every bit of the country that I found so fascinating. She appreciated each aspect that I had noticed about Zimbabwe and found many more insights of her own. We visited all my favorite spots in Harare; went camping on the banks of the Zambezi River at Mana Pools, where we walked among elephants, antelopes, and monkeys; visited a friend in the countryside and attended a *bira,* an all-night event where a spirit medium contacts a family's ancestors. Dolores added to all these adventures, made them more fun, saw perspectives I hadn't thought about, enriched my appreciation. When a friend found out that she was an experienced occupational therapist he immediately offered her a job at a home for disabled children in Harare. Dolores accepted, and I was delighted.

Robert Mugabe in his office in 1981. © *Andrew Meldrum*

3

FIRST ADVENTURES

With Zimbabwe's independence, the international war correspondents covering the Rhodesian war packed up and moved on to other world trouble spots, many to Johannesburg and others to the Middle East. Professional journalists were in demand, so I found work quickly.

It was surprisingly easy to get a temporary work permit. I walked into the center of the city and found Linquenda House, where I went to the offices of the Department of Information. A white official who had previously controlled the foreign press under Ian Smith's tight restrictions, which required journalists to submit their war reports for approval before they dispatched them overseas, looked at me with disdain and suspicion. "The big guys are all leaving; why would you want to come here now?" he asked me. I said I was interested in reporting on the new Zimbabwe and he sniffed dismissively. I showed him a letter from Associated Press Radio saying it would take pieces from me on a freelance basis, and that seemed to satisfy him that I was a professional journalist. He issued me with a form letter supporting my application for a temporary work permit.

I then went down a few floors to the immigration offices. I could see the building was modern and well maintained, but the large glass windows were covered in tape, which, I was told, was to prevent flying shards of glass in case of a bomb explosion by "the terrorists." There, on the strength of the letter from the Department of Information, I was issued a temporary employment permit.

After that I went back upstairs, along with some other foreign journalists, to Information to get my press accreditation. The old Rhodesian official could barely hide his distaste for us as he showed us into another room where we met Justin Nyoka, the new director of Information. In contrast to the cold reception from the white official, Nyoka welcomed us effusively and told us the country needed new journalists who would bring a fresh perspective.

By the time I had finished it was midday and blazingly hot. I walked out onto the street milling with shoppers and office workers on lunchbreaks. The journalists I had met were working a few blocks away and I walked with them to their offices.

Most of the foreign journalists I met there were remarkably friendly and helpful. During the next few weeks, they would tip me off to upcoming stories. The work for AP Radio got me started but it was not enough to support me. As a seasoned journalist quipped, "You can't spell *cheap* without AP and you can't spell *cheaper* without AP Radio." I had to become a jack-of-all-trades, and began filing radio pieces and taking photographs, later becoming the freelance reporter for some news organizations. I wrote stories on the first black Miss Zimbabwe and the first black mayor.

The shift in focus of the country's economy from funding a war to providing better services to the majority of its people was of interest to Jonathan Kapstein, the Johannesburg bureau chief of *Business Week* magazine, and assignments from him provided the most interesting stories in my first months. One day I went to a demonstration of ammunition originally made for use by the Rhodesian Army and for which, with peace, the manufacturers were trying to find export markets.

At a shooting range on the outskirts of Harare I found myself surrounded by white military types bristling with confidence and self-assurance. Their conversation was full of dismissive, derogatory remarks about the new government. My professional neutrality did not satisfy them; they wanted me to agree that the new government was inept and bumbling and they looked at me antagonistically. I refused to enter into any argument with them, but I thought to myself, Who won the war, anyway? These arrogant Rhodesians, or Mugabe and his black fighters?

Round after round of ammunition was shot off and the men responded like boys setting off firecrackers. Then came the demonstration of the locally made pepper spray, which they explained would be superb for crowd control. Unlike conventional tear gas, which was shot into crowds in canisters, this pepper gas was sprayed out by a hand-held apparatus with a long pipe. One of the men switched on the spray and sure enough a large cloud of the noxious gas emerged. But the blower did not propel the gas far enough away. All it took was a small gust of wind to blow the gas back at us. The stinging, choking pepper spray engulfed the entire group of manufacturers, journalists, and potential buyers. We ran helter-skelter, coughing and spluttering. It seemed they were choking on their own hot air. I didn't hear anything more about the bungling black government that day.

The black Zimbabweans, in contrast, were positive about the future. One day a Canadian journalist and I traveled with a Zimbabwean post office clerk to the fringes of Glen View township, well over twenty kilometers from the city center, where there was an innovative government housing project; we wanted to meet the people involved. We had agreed to take with us several bags of cement and a few rolls of fencing wire for Tendai, the clerk, and in return he showed us the house he was building. "There it is," said Tendai, but at first all I could see was an unpromising vista of bare fields and rolling hills. As we got closer I saw that the area was dotted with small structures and piles of bricks, bags of cement, and corrugated roof panels. It was a hive of activity, with some people delivering materials in cars, like us, and others pushing heavily laden wheelbarrows. A couple of people used donkeys and carts to transport supplies.

Tendai stood proudly in front of a small outhouse. He explained it was the "core house" that came with the plot of land he had bought from the government. The structure had running water and electricity and he could build rooms around the core. "Here is where we will build a kitchen and a lounge," said Tendai enthusiastically. "We will sleep in the lounge until we can add a bedroom." He paced off where he planned to build five rooms altogether. His wife arrived, pushing a wheelbarrow and with a baby on her back.

All around, other families were building similar dream houses. I was impressed by Tendai's vigor and the enterprising spirit of all the home builders. It seemed a great way for the government to make new housing available to the city population with the least amount of expenditure. A few years later I returned to the area to marvel at a fully developed residential area tightly packed with houses and brimming with life. It was just the type of feature story I had wanted to write about the new Zimbabwe.

My first big break came soon afterward, when United Press International sent me to cover a weekend speech by the minister of Home Affairs, Joshua Nkomo. He was a towering figure in Zimbabwe's history, widely acknowledged as the founder of African nationalism in the country, and also, literally, because he was well over six feet tall and carried a huge girth.

Nkomo was Mugabe's great rival, having led a competing guerrilla movement in the war against Rhodesia. The differences between the two leaders highlighted important divisions in the country: Nkomo was from the Ndebele people, who make up about 20 percent of the population and are concentrated in the country's second city, Bulawayo, and the surrounding Matabeleland countryside; Mugabe is from the majority ethnic group, the Shona, who are 75 percent of the population. Nkomo forged the African nationalist movement in the country and won international attention for his outspoken opposition to Ian Smith's regime. But in 1963 his party, the Zimbabwe African Peoples Union (Zapu), was split when most of the Shona members left and founded the competing Zimbabwe African National Union (Zanu).

At first the Reverend Ndabaningi Sithole had headed the new Zanu, but he was toppled by a revolt within the party. A later leader, Herbert Chitepo, had been killed by a car bomb while in exile in Zambia. By 1977 Robert Mugabe had wrested control of Zanu, and the two parties formed different guerrilla armies to fight the Rhodesian regime. Nkomo and his Zapu were given weapons and training from the Soviet Union, while Mugabe and Zanu won support from the Chinese.

Diplomats who had been at the Lancaster House independence negotiations in London in 1979 told me that the rivalry between Nkomo and Mugabe was nearly as bitter as their relations with Ian Smith. They formed an uneasy coalition, the Patriotic Front, but Mugabe went back on an agreement that the two would stand in elections together. (The party was now renamed Zanu-PF, with "PF" standing for "Patriotic Front.") Voting in the independence polls broke down along roughly ethnic lines: Mugabe's Zanu-PF won a majority of votes while Nkomo's

Zapu won about 20 percent. Displaying astute judgment, Mugabe included Nkomo and other top Zapu members as well as two whites in his cabinet in what was called a government of national unity. But the ill feeling between the two men remained palpable.

When I arrived in Zimbabwe, Mugabe's government was working to demilitarize the country by integrating the three armed forces—the former Rhodesian Army and the two guerrilla forces—into a unified Zimbabwean army. Those who were not taken into the new army were to be disarmed and demobilized. The mistrust between Mugabe's and Nkomo's forces was so intense that they had to be housed separately, at great distances from each other, and neither side wanted to see any of its troops disarmed. Now Nkomo planned to reassure his suspicious troops about the process and the press was invited to cover the event.

I went in convoy with other journalists to Chitungwiza township, about thirty kilometers from downtown Harare, where several thousand of Nkomo's men were barracked. Many of the journalists were nervous about going into the camp, as the men were armed and had only been out of the bush for a few months. A few of the cameramen and reporters had been in the Rhodesian Army and were decidedly jittery about going into a camp of armed guerrillas.

As we filed into the area for the speech, I was turned away because I did not have my government-issued press card. So much for my big break. I couldn't believe I had made such a fundamental mistake. I tried to make up for it by talking my way in and sidling through the gate, but I was promptly grabbed by two armed men who accused me of being a spy. Matters got worse when a fellow journalist said he didn't know me. The other reporters were already a distance away at the gathering where Nkomo was to speak. I was led to a little shack where I was held at gunpoint. I was again accused of being a spy, body-searched, and ordered to sit on the dirt floor.

I was ordered to take off my shirt and trousers, and all my pockets were searched. My notebook and other equipment were taken away. I realized I had lots of scraps of paper and notes with me, but no identification papers of any sort. I was furious with myself but knew I had to remain cool if I was going to get out of this fix. When I was assertive with the fighters, arguing that I was just a journalist, they became more aggressive in turn; it proved more useful to be patient and to explain myself calmly. Being an American was no asset in this situation, as my captors suspected I was gathering intelligence about their camp to send back to Washington. My best defence was to point out that if I were a spy, I would not have been so stupid as to come without any press identification. They granted me that much, but now they did not know what to do with me.

I sat on the floor throughout the sweltering afternoon. I could hear the commotion of Nkomo's arrival, the cheers of his men, the blaring loudspeaker when he spoke, the flurry of activity when he left. The fact that I had completely missed the story of Joshua Nkomo speaking to his fighters had become insignificant: I was grappling to cope with a more threatening problem.

I asked if I could leave with the other journalists, but they refused. Nor would they allow me to speak to my colleagues. My heart sank as I heard the noise of the journalists departing. The armed men said the camp commander would decide what to do with me once everyone had left.

Night fell, and through a small window I could see a star in the sky. Without thinking, I said to myself, "Star light, star bright, first star I see tonight . . ."

"What was that?" barked one of the guards. "Who were you talking to? What did you say?"

My throat was suddenly dry. "It is just a childhood saying," I rasped. "You say it to make a wish on the first star of the night."

"Say it again," ordered the guard. I repeated it. "It rhymes," he said.

"Yes," I answered warily, "it's just a little poem. It's silly."

"I am a poet," he said. "I do poetry for the soldiers in my unit. I want to hear that again."

So I taught him the little ditty and we talked about making a wish. He hoped there would be peace and that he could go back to his family. His poems were in Ndebele, but he wanted to learn more in English. I said I wanted to learn more about Zimbabwe and to write about it.

The guard in charge told us to stop talking, but the atmosphere had relaxed considerably. I was no longer viewed as a spy but an inconvenience.

Later that night I was released and the police returned me to my hotel. I was shaken by the incident, but also buoyed by my close encounter with Zimbabwe's freedom fighters, by the rapport we had developed in the most unpromising circumstances. Once we had begun talking, I found their hopes were easy to understand. And they could understand my motivation, too. Although the incident was little short of a fiasco, it gave me confidence that, under the right circumstances, I would be able to connect with Zimbabweans and effectively portray their aspirations.

I worried that my scrape with Nkomo's guerrillas would affect my reputation among my colleagues, but the incident was quickly forgotten as the press pack moved on to other stories.

Within a few weeks Robert Mugabe was shortlisted for the Nobel Peace Prize. He did not win the award, but his nomination shows how, at that moment, he was the world's darling, the hero who brought peace and reconciliation to the nation that a year ago was one of the world's festering sores. Those on the left adored him and the right granted him grudging respect.

At that time few people in Zimbabwe really knew Mugabe or his character. He had spent many years out of the country, in Ghana, Zambia, and Mozambique, and he was out of circulation during the eleven years he was imprisoned by the Rhodesians, from 1963 to 1974. The Rhodesian media had succeeded in vilifying Mugabe as a bloodthirsty Marxist, but that image was shattered by his careful, considered actions when he became prime minister and courted support from white farmers, businessmen, and others. Charges that Mugabe had engineered the deaths of rivals within his party seemed to be the bitter rants of die-hard Rhodesians; and even they would admit they had little to criticize in Mugabe since he came to power. And Mugabe was almost as much an unknown quantity for township blacks as for suburban whites. Everybody speculated about him, his motivations, his Catholic faith, why he was a teetotaler—what was he really like?

37

His painfully proper speech, with its carefully rounded vowels and stilted yet always grammatically correct sentences, was very different from the rough-hewn English spoken by most Zimbabweans. This was a bookish leader who had earned three university degrees while imprisoned by the Rhodesians. Whether speaking at rallies or press conferences, he was excruciatingly formal at all times. From his fussy manner I could believe the story that, when he was told Bob Marley would perform at his swearing-in as Zimbabwe's prime minister, Mugabe complained that he was too scruffy and suggested the perennially wholesome Cliff Richard would be a better act. For once he was overruled.

I was eager to get a closer look at Mugabe and jumped at the chance when Jonathan Kapstein asked me to set up an interview with the leader. I helped draft questions about whether he preferred a capitalist or socialist economy, the future of race relations in Zimbabwe, whether he remained in favor of establishing a one-party state. When the date was set, Kapstein invited me to accompany him as his photographer.

Mugabe's press secretary was the same white official who had served Ian Smith, and when we entered the prime minister's spacious corner office it seemed Mugabe had kept Smith's furnishings. Kapstein recognized the same large but not ornate desk and chairs, and he later confirmed with officials in Mugabe's office that the furniture was that used by Smith. The windows were cloaked in heavy maroon velvet curtains.

Mugabe gave ample time for the interview and seemed to enjoy the intellectual challenge of tackling the questions. But he remained stiff, starchy, and distant at all times. His answers were lengthy and detailed but they lacked the punchy, concise turns of phrase that journalists prize as good quotes. Furthermore he was so strictly pedantic that his responses rarely gave insight into his thinking or approach. I thought they might be similar to the essays he wrote for the degrees he earned by correspondence.

His complicated answers were often evasive. Personally he was in favor of a socialist economy but practicalities dictated that he maintain a mixed economy. His statement of support for racial reconciliation was so obviously a phrase repeated by rote that it not only lacked warmth, it appeared insincere. On the question of a one-party state I found him most cagey. No, he would never impose a one-party state, but he found

38

it an appropriate model for an African democracy, and if the people of Zimbabwe united in oneness and expressed a desire for a one-party state, then it would be achieved in the fullness of time.

I had gone into the interview excited by the prospect of interviewing a world-class statesman. I left deflated, feeling we did not capture a telling interview. More troubling was the fact that I no longer knew what to think of Robert Mugabe.

Most Zimbabweans either loved Mugabe or hated him, depending on whether they were supporters of Zimbabwe or Rhodesia. Foreign journalists were also divided: the older reporters who had covered the war generally saw Mugabe in a negative light, while the new journalists who had come in at independence, like me, saw him more positively. Mugabe had, after all, steered the war-torn country to peace, stability, and prosperity. But there was little in his cold, schoolteacher demeanor to warm to.

Robinson House is a twelve-story office block with a very central location, at the corner of Union and Angwa Streets, a block away from the First Street pedestrian mall and Linquenda House, and three blocks from the high court and Mugabe's offices. Foreign journalists had offices on the third floor where a company called News Services provided telex communications and phones. Swedish, Japanese, Nigerian, British, and French journalists worked alongside one another, sharing telex services and phone lines. I managed to rent a small office there, too, and soon got to know everyone. Being part of this community made it easier to stay on top of the news. The fellowship was great, too. Many shared my desire to see Zimbabwe succeed and my frustration at being caught between the old and the new orders. We often stayed at the office late into the night, deep in discussion about what the latest development meant, how it would play overseas, what effect it would have in South Africa.

It seemed that Zimbabwe held a special significance for the British journalists. "Rhodesia was a bit like our Vietnam," one correspondent for a British paper told me. "It was the issue that divided people.

39

For many of us, Rhodesia was something terribly wrong, for which our country was responsible. The war was a festering sore. To have it suddenly come right, and in a way which satisfied all sides, was electrifying for us. It was little short of a miracle."

The Scandinavians took great pride in the birth of Zimbabwe. Sweden, especially, refused to see the Rhodesian conflict as part of the Cold War between the Western democracies and the Soviet Union; the Swedes had supported the nationalist guerrillas on the grounds that they were fighting for basic democratic rights. "We feel vindicated by Zimbabwe. We are proud that we supported a struggle that has brought democracy to Africa and we want to be part of helping to build a just society here."

During those first few months in Zimbabwe, I always felt like a newcomer and did not feel confident about my knowledge of the country's history. At press conferences I generally deferred to more experienced journalists and let them ask all the questions, but I often came away with unanswered questions and eventually concluded that I was being lazy. If I wanted to make my way as a journalist I would have to be more assertive. I resolved to ask a question at every press conference. As I gained confidence my questions became sharper and to the point. Occasionally I would ask the question that would be the focus for the whole conference. By pushing myself to ask questions I carved out a niche for myself among the scrum of reporters.

And, as I covered daily events in Harare and beyond, I began to gain an understanding of the country I was living in.

For a while I got around on foot and by taxi, but a journalist needs a car, and after a month I decided to invest in a vehicle. As a result of years of international sanctions against Rhodesia, Zimbabwe had a restricted and aging stock of motor vehicles. The climate was kind to cars, however, and the mechanics were ingenious at coming up with homemade solutions to keep old vehicles on the road. As a result the auto market was a vintage car lover's dream. Most of the old cars were British makes, dating from before sanctions took hold in 1965. There were classic Jaguars, usually previously owned by tobacco farmers, and many makes that were not familiar to me, such as Rover, Hillman, and Anglia.

The newer models indicated which companies had evaded sanctions: there were lots of Peugeots, Renaults, and Datsuns, and immediately following independence there was a burgeoning of shiny new Mercedes. I had to go for the low end of the market, however.

Most of the country's taxis were the old Renault 4. They were high off the ground, best for the bumpy rural roads, reliable, and very economical on fuel. The front-wheel drive would take the car anywhere. I liked its boxy design and found one in relatively good repair. It was one of the best cars I have ever owned, but it was not without its quirks. The seats were like sagging lawn chairs and the doors rattled loosely on their hinges. The high suspension gave a very bouncy ride. I had to master the distinctive but tricky gearshift that protruded from the dashboard and was operated with a pump action by the left hand. The door latch stuck out and ripped my shirts and jackets with annoying regularity.

Once I had learned how to drive around in Harare, I was eager to get out and see some of the countryside. I decided to drive east, to the Nyanga Mountains which border Mozambique. Friends suggested I visit the Nyafaru cooperative, where a community was working to develop a farm and school, and I thought it would make a good feature story. As I prepared for my journey, I was asked if I would give a ride to the area's chief, Rekayi Tangwena, who was a senator in the new government. Parliament had adjourned and he wanted to go to his home in Nyanga for the break. It would be pleasant to have a companion on the long journey, I thought.

I got up at dawn, threw my small bag in the back of the car, and headed off for the house in the Belvedere suburb where Chief Tangwena was staying. He was already waiting in front of the house. Chief Tangwena had white hair and a grizzled beard befitting his seventy years. But his upright posture, firm handshake, and canny eyes told me this was a vigorous, vital man. He spoke little English but made himself understood through sheer force of personality.

I was astounded by the huge amount of goods that he wanted to take with us. There was a towering pile of luggage, food, tools, and building materials, and a box of baby chickens. I said it would not all fit, but the chief paid no attention to my protestations and began packing it in, all of it. The hatchback trunk was stuffed, and goods were stowed on the backseat and on the floor of the front. He quickly constructed a makeshift roof rack and put a few bags on top. My little car became noticeably lower to the ground.

Just when I thought the car was completely full and the chief and I could head off, out came a pretty young woman nursing a baby and carrying a load of clothes, towels, and diapers. I was dismayed to learn they were coming, too. I assumed she was the chief's daughter or granddaughter, but in fact she was his new wife.

Finally we all headed out for Nyanga, rattling, bouncing, and bumping along, the baby occasionally crying and the chicks cheeping in the back. About twenty kilometers east of Harare, the chief told me to stop at a gas station. "Smokings," he said. "I get smokings." I pulled into the service station; the chief was recognized immediately and surrounded by twenty or more people, crowding to shake his hand, pat him on the back, and talk. He beamed and spoke animatedly with everyone and then, eventually, returned to the car with a couple of packs of cigarettes and matches that, he told me proudly, had been gifts.

We hit the road again and I started to feel we were making good time when the car began shuddering and swerving. It was a flat tire. Exasperated, I pulled over to the side of the road to change it. When I struggled with the unfamiliar jack, the chief impatiently pushed me aside. He skillfully removed the nuts, jacked up the car, and replaced the flat tire. We stopped at the next gas station to get the flat repaired, and once again the chief was surrounded by well-wishers and supporters.

We drove for miles on the well-surfaced road until we got to the small crossroads of Rusape and began our ascent toward the Nyanga Mountains. We left the sweeping fields behind and climbed through a dramatic landscape of huge granite boulders, known in southern Africa as kopjes, and beautifully elegant flat-topped acacias. The commercial farmland, previously reserved for whites, was now behind us and we entered the "communal areas," where the country's black farmers eked out a subsistence. The two-lane paved road became two narrow strips of tarmac, like a track.

The air changed from warm to cool as we slowly climbed up into the verdant mountains, and then it began to rain. At first it was an ordinary rainstorm, then it became a dramatic thunderstorm, and soon the rain was coming down in sheets. The windshield wipers flailed erratically and ineffectually against the torrent. I wanted to stop until I could see clearly. "Go, go," insisted the chief. "I can see. I know this road." I duly continued, picking my way across the blurred countryside.

Once up in the mountains, we reentered the white farming area and continued to the luxurious Troutbeck Hotel, where we began a tortuous drive on an unpaved road, struggling up steep inclines and down, twisting and turning, the chief expertly guiding me around boulders, branches, and large patches of mud. The road led us to a roaring river. There was a bridge, but the waters were rushing over it. I said there was no way we could cross, but the chief was adamant.

He got out, adroitly picked his way across the large rocks that marked the crossing, then waved for me to follow. I gathered my courage and began to inch forward, then suddenly the chief motioned for me to stop. I was relieved, thinking he had decided we couldn't do it. No such luck. He shouted for his wife and child to get out of the car, just to be safe, and follow him on foot. My already shaky confidence was reduced still further, but the chief strenuously waved for me to drive across. Alone in the car except for the chirping chicks, I proceeded. A surge in the driving force of the river jumped the car sideways, but we steadied and eventually arrived on firm ground on the other side. I could hardly contain my relief.

Now the rain stopped, and within minutes the sky cleared to show the rosy pink of the beginning of sunset. We were almost there, the chief told me. We began driving through an orchard of apple and peach trees and Chief Tangwena became very animated. "This is my people's land, our land," he exclaimed excitedly. "The Rhodesians took it but they were wrong."

It was dusk when we arrived at the Nyafaru cooperative. The chief was swarmed with people and whisked away. I was given a hot vegetable soup and a small room, where I laid out my sleeping bag and fell into a deep sleep.

I awoke to the sounds of children outside my window. I looked out to see two small boys chasing a chicken, which they caught and swiftly beheaded. I watched with fascination as the decapitated bird took a few steps and then fell shuddering to the ground. They ran off with it to the cooking area, already plucking feathers.

In my concentration during the drive I had failed to take in the full beauty of the Nyanga Mountains. I had never seen anything like the vistas of steep peaks and sloping valleys. I had not imagined a landscape could be both mountainous and tropical. The sky was sharp blue with startling white clouds scudding across the horizon. The air was clear, fresh, and invigorating. Everything seemed new and possible.

Tinani, the manager of the cooperative, came to meet me as I stood in the garden and took me on a tour of Nyafaru. I saw the basic but functional schoolrooms and dormitories; maize fields and vegetable patches; the stream where they gathered water; and the small pond where they had dammed the flow and which they planned to stock with fish. This had all been accomplished in less than a year since the war ended.

When I was shown a scrapbook of the history of their area, I began to understand why Chief Tangwena was so revered. He had stubbornly resisted the Rhodesian government's efforts to evict his people from their traditional land. Rhodesian officials burned down his people's huts, seized their cattle, assaulted people and chased them away, but Tangwena and his community kept returning to their land.

Newspaper articles recounted how the chief had appeared in court eight times, usually conducting his own defense, and forcefully insisted that he would not leave the land of his ancestors. He had cannily written to Queen Elizabeth II, his simple words eloquently calling on her for help to solve the plight of his people. In those dark days he was one of the leading symbols of resistance to Rhodesian rule. Tinani told me how Tangwena had provided support to African nationalist fighters battling against the Rhodesians.

In 1975 Tangwena helped Robert Mugabe escape into exile by taking a path through the Nyanga Mountains to Mozambique. Under increasing pressure from Rhodesian forces, Tangwena then led his people across the border, and they stayed on the Mozambican side of the mountains until Zimbabwe gained independence. When he returned, Chief Tangwena supported the Nyafaru project to give homes to children orphaned during the war.

After our arrival from Harare, Chief Tangwena had moved on to his homestead a few kilometers away. I hiked along the pathway and found the gray-bearded old chief perched atop a hut he was building, lashing poles together to make a latticelike frame for the roof. I asked what I could do to help. "Brandy," he said. "Get brandy at bottle store." So off I went to a shop down the hill and bought a bottle of local brandy. When I got back the chief took a couple of swigs and kept up his expert work until the poles formed a steep structure, to which he would attach the thatching grass the next day. When he climbed down we drank some more as his wife tended a cooking fire. I could see why so many looked up to this lusty, headstrong leader. I asked him how he had helped Robert Mugabe escape to Mozambique. He took me by the hand and led me to a point behind his homestead. "There, we were there," he said. "Rhodesian troops coming on the road. Army trucks." Then he took me down a track and pointed toward a path into the mountains. "I show Mugabe and he goes there, into Mozambique."

That trip with Chief Tangwena was the most inspiring adventure of my first months in Zimbabwe. Over the years I kept in touch with the Nyafaru cooperative and watched with dismay as it became divided by feuding factions. When the chief died in 1984 he was declared a national hero. The Tangwena family wanted him to be buried according to tradition in his family's ancestral land, which he had so ably defended. But Zanu-PF decreed that he must be buried in Harare, at Heroes' Acre, the grandiose monument constructed to glorify those who contributed to Zimbabwe's independence. Built by North Koreans, the towering sculpture of men and women in heroic poses was much derided because the subjects look more Asian than African. It did not seem an appropriate resting place for such a son of the soil as Chief Tangwena.

Zimbabwe's teeming townships are full of life. The sheer joy of Zimbabwe's independence became tainted after Robert Mugabe's campaign against Joshua Nkomo split the nation in two. © *AP/Wide World Photos*

4

END OF THE HONEYMOON

For my first year in Zimbabwe, the events I covered were all in much the same vein. But things changed in January 1982, when Joshua Nkomo called a press conference. I headed out for his house in Highfield township, and with my windows open I could smell the wafting aroma of tobacco. The industrial area I passed through is known as "Tobacco Mile" for its concentration of tobacco-processing and -packing plants and warehouses. Most other cabinet ministers and prominent professionals had moved into the sedate white suburbs, but Nkomo kept homes in the townships of Harare and Bulawayo. Both were rambling, ranch-style houses that stood out for their size, style, and careful finish.

I enjoyed my forays into Harare's townships. Crowded, noisy, and chaotic, the townships exuded irrepressible life. After independence, the government named them "high-density suburbs," but townships they remained, flung by Rhodesian planners as far from the city center as possible with tiny plots and rudimentary services. I would often see children running along the side of a street, pushing a wheel rim with a stick; others threw balls and played in the streets and alleys. Radios blared, women hung up laundry and gossiped, others tended little corner stands selling tomatoes, onions, cooking oil, salt, soap, matches, and cigarettes. Churches and schools dotted the neighborhoods. Hot and cramped, the teeming, steaming townships are full of soul.

Nkomo's press conferences were legendary. On this occasion a choir entertained a throng of supporters outside his gates with spirited harmonies and snappy, choreographed dance moves. Inside, members of the press gathered and waited as Nkomo, like a movie star, kept us in calculated suspense. Finally he made a dramatically grand entrance and deigned to speak to us. Despite his enormous size, Nkomo was always elegantly dressed in impeccably tailored suits, well groomed, and ready for the cameras. He spoke to the press with operatic intensity, by turns imperious and imploring, excoriating and exhorting.

On this day Nkomo was angry. Robert Mugabe had appeared on state television the night before and announced that he was taking steps to establish a one-party state. "Who is this Robert Gabriel Mugabe?" shouted Nkomo at the assembled crowd of journalists. "Who does he think he is that he can call a one-party state without consulting with me? He is a little man, a sneaky man. Small men will always cheat you, just as Mugabe has tried to cheat me. Never trust a small man," said Nkomo. With a flourish he pointed at me, the shortest man in the room. I smarted at his remark and opened my mouth to challenge him but he continued.

"This time Robert Mugabe has gone too far," he said with growing vehemence. "I will never agree to form a one-party state with him. If he doesn't have the decency, the sense, to speak to me first about such an important matter, such a critical matter, then I cannot trust him and I will never form a one-party state with him. And he cannot have a one-party state without me, Joshua Nkomo, and without my party, Zapu, the party that started African nationalism in this country. We will not allow it. He cannot have it. He will never have his one-party state here. Never!"

I was startled by the fury of Nkomo's rant, yet I thought it merely a fit of pique because Mugabe had neglected to consult him. Nkomo had previously stated that he had no objections to the formation of a one-party state, as long as all parties agreed to it.

It appeared to be the African way to establish one-party states after independence. Most of Zimbabwe's neighbors—Zambia, Malawi, Mozambique, and Tanzania—were one-party states. Although they were generally modeled on the communist states of Eastern Europe, they were held up as the African form of democracy. They also copied, no doubt unwittingly, the monolithic authority of the colonial state. Experience showed that African one-party states were manifestly unresponsive, inefficient, and corrupt and denied their populations a free choice of who should run their country, but they had become the standard. Every leader wanted to have unchallenged power. Malawi's Hastings Banda went so far as to have himself declared "President for Life."

Mugabe's relentless drive to establish absolute rule dashed my hopes and those of many others that he would chart a new path for Africa by maintaining a multiparty democracy. I believed an opposition party was important to hold a government accountable, but others maintained that such opposition could flourish within the ruling party, pointing out that African political parties tended to be based on ethnic divisions and that therefore it is more beneficial to have a single party, encompassing all of a country's tribal groups.

Nkomo's spirited resistance was not against the concept of a one-party state; he was on the record as saying it was suitable for Zimbabwe. He was simply making his opening gambit in a round of bargaining for the best possible position for himself and his Zapu party in the new order.

Mugabe would have none of Nkomo's objections. The two held a brief meeting but it ended in acrimony. Mugabe soon called a press conference of his own. There was no singing or dancing at this event; instead it carried all the weighty formality of the state. It was held in a studio at the state-owned Zimbabwe Broadcasting Corporation, and as journalists arrived and, inevitably, waited, we speculated on what Mugabe was planning. He arrived displaying his usual crisp, no-nonsense, businesslike attitude, and announced that a plot by Nkomo's Zapu party to overthrow his government had been uncovered. A collective gasp of shock rose from the press corps. Mugabe explained that large arms caches had been discovered on properties owned by Zapu and therefore his government had no choice but to arrest the heads of the party's military wing, most of whom were high-ranking officers in the new Zimbabwean Army. He also sacked Joshua Nkomo and other Zapu cabinet members from their posts. Mugabe's charges were not convincing and I suspected they were just a pretext for getting Nkomo out of the way during the establishment of a one-party state.

The attack on Nkomo abruptly ended the coalition that had governed independent Zimbabwe, and within a few days Mugabe replaced it with a government almost wholly drawn from his own Zanu party. This was not just political; it had an ethnic dimension. Zimbabwe's Ndebele people, who make up about 20 percent of the population, avidly supported Nkomo and Zapu. Mugabe had purged his cabinet of Nkomo and almost all other Ndebeles. The few remaining with Mugabe were reviled by the Ndebele people as sellouts.

For a time things carried on as normal. Nkomo huffed and puffed in outrage but Zapu soon began operating as a parliamentary opposition party. Attention focused on the courts, where Nkomo's military men were on trial for their lives on treason charges. Dumiso Dabengwa, who had been the head of Nkomo's military wing, was the main accused, along with Lieutenant General Lookout Masuku and five other deputies. Dabengwa, dubbed "the Black Russian" because he had excelled at the military training he received in the Soviet Union, was widely admired for his quiet intelligence. He had headed Nkomo's military wing during the Rhodesian war but had declined to enter the new Zimbabwean Army, saying that he would advise Nkomo on security matters. Tall, with high cheekbones and an officer's bearing, Dabengwa was an imposing figure in the dock.

The treason case hinged on the weapons that Mugabe had listed, which had indeed been discovered on properties owned by Zapu. The weapons, mostly from the Soviet Union, were Zapu's supplies for the Rhodesian war, brought into the country at independence. In their defense, the Zapu officers showed official correspondence proving they had informed the army and the government about the weapons and had told them they would be stored on the farms. The officers were all acquitted of the treason charges, but they were rearrested within minutes of the court decision. Dabengwa and the others were jailed without charge for nearly five years.

I covered Mugabe's sacking of Nkomo and the treason trial of his officers for Agence France-Presse (AFP), and soon I was working for them full-time. I noted in my daily reports that a spate of armed robberies of buses was occurring in the Matabeleland area, especially on the main road between Bulawayo and Victoria Falls. In some cases the robbers shouted, "Zimbabwe is not yet free!" or "We will fight for full independence!" I heard reports that Zapu members had deserted the Zimbabwean Army in disgust at what had happened to Nkomo and Dabengwa, and taken their arms to launch opposition to the Mugabe government. The robberies looked like the beginnings of a low-level rebel resistance to Mugabe. Nkomo remained silent about them.

Although trouble was brewing in Matabeleland, the arid southern region where most of the country's Ndebele people lived, life continued as normal in Harare. But then in August 1982 an incident occurred that forced the entire country and the whole world to pay attention to the unsettled situation in Matabeleland: six foreign tourists were kidnapped by the anti-Mugabe dissidents. The young men—two Australians, two Britons, and two Americans—were part of a group traveling from Victoria Falls to Bulawayo. They were taken hostage by an armed gang, who released the females and the tour leader and gave them a note which explained that they were mounting an armed resistance to the Mugabe government because of the actions against Nkomo and his followers. Suddenly their opposition could no longer be ignored.

A massive manhunt was launched by the army across the dry expanse of Matabeleland and a dusk-to-dawn curfew was imposed over the area. The rebels had cannily deduced that an action against international tourists would capture the most headlines and attention for their cause. Suddenly the international news media were extremely interested in Zimbabwe. Correspondents, photographers, and television crews flew in from Johannesburg and London. Bulawayo was inundated by waves of journalists determined to cover the fate of the six tourists. I went down to Matabeleland to write about the kidnappings, but I also wanted to write about the rivalries between Mugabe's Zanu-PF and Nkomo's Zapu and the growing divisions between the Shona and Ndebele peoples.

The Matabeleland countryside was very different from the Mashonaland area surrounding Harare. Matabeleland is low and flat with sandy soil and dry, scrubby vegetation as befits an area that verges on the Kalahari Desert. It is much more arid than other parts of Zimbabwe, so the rural people subsist more on cattle ranching than on growing maize. Hotter, drier, harsher Matabeleland has a different feel to it from other parts of Zimbabwe. It was here that I first heard black Zimbabweans criticizing Mugabe and the government. They claimed that Mugabe was bent on suppressing them because of the rivalry between the Shona and the Ndebele, which was hard for me to accept because it destroyed my belief that Zimbabweans could transcend their tribal and racial differences.

The political situation was becoming more and more heated. When I was on a camping trip in Hwange National Park with my younger brother, John, who was visiting from the U.S., my bureau chief at AFP managed to get through to me on the park site phone. Joshua Nkomo had gone to Lupane in rural Matabeleland, apparently to try to find the tourists. Lupane was about a hundred kilometers from Hwange National Park and I was assigned to get the first interview with Nkomo about his mission. My brother and I set off immediately.

The light fell as we sped along the deserted road. We had to stop at an army roadblock but we managed to get through when I showed my press pass. What worried me most was the possibility that we would come across an unofficial roadblock manned by the rebels. I was prepared to hit the brakes and turn around if we saw any branches blocking the road, but my fears proved unfounded and we reached the tiny hamlet of Lupane at dusk. I asked a few villagers where Nkomo was and they pointed over a hill.

Nkomo was seated regally in the living room of a small house with a number of aides pouring him water, directing a fan toward him, setting up a light to his satisfaction. He told his hosts what he would like for dinner. A young woman placed a bowl of bananas on the table beside him. When I walked into the room, with my brother still in tow, Nkomo refused to do the interview, saying he wanted to speak to a more important, more senior journalist than me. He said he would only deal with the BBC and waved us away. But by now I knew how Nkomo liked to be flattered and cajoled into doing interviews. I told him the world was waiting to hear what he would say about the kidnap of the tourists. I told him that only he had the stature to speak about the situation that led up to their kidnapping and the divisions in Zimbabwe. My entreaties worked. He agreed to an interview and I began asking questions.

Speaking calmly and deliberately, Nkomo said he did not know who the bandits were who were carrying out the robberies, and he did not know who had done the kidnapping. He denied he had come out to Lupane to investigate the situation. I could see his difficulty: he did not want to admit to any knowledge of the kidnappers, as that would give the Mugabe government a chance to arrest him. I took a different tack and asked him if he would like to see the tourists freed. In response to my questions, he issued an appeal to those responsible to release the tourists and he said he would act as a mediator. He also spoke at length about the problems he faced and those of his followers in Matabeleland.

Sadly Nkomo's call had no effect. His appeal eventually appeared in local newspapers and on the state radio, but the tourists remained missing. Everyone that I spoke to, from factory workers in Bulawayo to sales clerks in Harare, agreed that the plight of the young tourists was tragic, that they were caught unfairly in a Zimbabwean political clash. But there was something deeper, a feeling I gathered, that the conflict was not just political, that it represented a more fundamental division in Zimbabwe.

More than a year later the tourists' bodies were found in shallow graves, very near the road my brother and I had traveled.

The rebels' violent raids escalated. They killed several white farmers, calculating, correctly, that the death of a white farmer would get considerable publicity both inside Zimbabwe and internationally. The rebel violence in Matabeleland became a running sore, blemishing Zimbabwe's reputation for peace and stability.

The nature of my own experience in Zimbabwe was changing. No longer was I reporting on situations where past wrongs perpetrated by the Rhodesian regime were being righted. Instead I was confronted with postindependence problems created by Mugabe. I was wrestling, in my writing, to present these complex difficulties in the proper context, which was fair and balanced and yet which told what was going on.

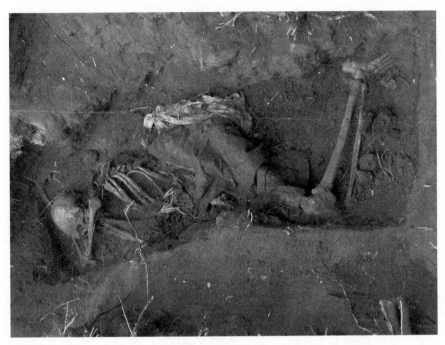

A skeleton of a victim of the Matabeleland massacres exhumed twenty years later, identified by locals as a woman who had tried to protect young girls from being raped. Thousands of graves like this are scattered across Zimbabwe's Matabeleland and Midlands provinces and are a scar on the national psyche. © *Shari Eppel*

5

MATABELELAND

"What's that?" said Dolores, waking me in the middle of the night. Bursts of *rat-a-tat-tat, rat-a-tat-tat* echoed in the darkness. "It's just some firecrackers," I reassured her as I rolled over to go back to sleep.

The next day, however, reports came through that Mugabe's residence had been fired upon by a truckload of the rebels. Our apartment was just a few blocks away and I realized with a shock that that was what Dolores had heard. I called her at work and she could tell me exactly what time the gunfire had occurred because she had checked our clock when she woke. I got right to work on the story. The truck of rebels had fired on Mugabe's residence and on the house of Enos Nkala, a former Zapu member who had stayed in Mugabe's cabinet. Ndebeles widely regarded him as a turncoat. Suddenly the Matabeleland violence had spread up to Harare, very close to home. It alarmed Mugabe so much that he ordered the street in front of his residence to be closed from dusk to dawn.

By June 1983, reports began to filter up to Harare of a huge army sweep into the Matabeleland North province, the area between Bulawayo and Victoria Falls where the tourists had been kidnapped. At first it sounded like the previous campaign for the kidnapped tourists, but then unconfirmed reports came in of the army killing rural civilians on a large scale. I went down to Bulawayo to investigate.

Bulawayo is a lovely city, with many fine old buildings and a slower, more leisurely pace than even Harare's. The joke goes that when a flight from London arrives the captain announces, "We have now arrived in Harare; please set your time back to the 1970s," but when the plane carries on to Bulawayo, he announces, "We are now in Bulawayo; please set your time back to the 1950s."

When I arrived in Bulawayo that day I could tell that things were different. Normally open and friendly people appeared tense and worried. I went with two other journalists to a contact at the Catholic cathedral in the center of the town. The usually cheerful priest looked very distressed. When we asked if there was army violence against civilians in the rural areas, he confirmed there had been. Was it an isolated incident or was it on a large scale? He said it was on a very large scale. Were there any witnesses we could speak to? Yes, there were many witnesses and they wanted to tell their stories. With that he led us into the basement, a large room filled with more than two hundred people. Many had bundles of belongings with them and were staying there; others had found refuge with family members in Bulawayo, said the priest. Some people had bandages and slings. The priest addressed the room, explaining we were journalists from overseas and we wanted to know what was happening. He then led a short prayer calling for the Lord's help for those in the room and also for those who had died, and with that a moan rose from the crowd.

We journalists decided to split up and interview as many people as we could individually. Many people spoke only Ndebele, so we found others with a good command of English to act as interpreters. An old woman stepped up and told me the army had come to her home in Nkayi a week earlier. She said they took her husband and son and shot them dead in front of the remaining family. The soldiers forced the family to sing songs praising Robert Mugabe and Zanu-PF. A young woman told me that many families in her area had been rounded up and taken to a nearby school. They thought it was a rally when they had to sing songs, but then the men were separated out and taken away. They heard shots, and then many of the women were beaten by the soldiers. An old man told me how he had heard the army trucks drive up in the night and ran into the bush. He wept as he told me how his family was beaten and then herded into a hut that was set on fire. He ran out to stop the fire but the army men beat him until he was unconscious. His swollen, bruised face was testimony to his account. A young girl described how her family had been forced to chant the praises of Zanu-PF and Robert Mugabe. Her father and brothers were pushed into their hut, the door was locked, and it was set on fire. She and the other women were ordered to keep singing.

60

The nightmarish accounts went on and on. The testimonies were jumbled and sometimes rambling, like the recounting of a wild dream, but they all ended with beatings, killings, rape, and fire. Everyone was frightened. We tried to set up a system so that we only spoke to one person from each family, to prevent repetitions of the same set of killings. After two hours my notebooks were full and the others were spent, too. Although people continued to press forward to tell their stories of terror, we had gathered enough accounts.

The priest begged us not to identify the church because he was afraid the army would raid it. He was desperately trying to find the refugees places to stay but the numbers in need were overwhelming. He said the government had refused to help and had claimed that the reports of violence were lies. He urged us to get the stories out so the international community would help stop the killing.

Stunned, we emerged from the church, blinking at the daylight. We went over our notes and began counting up deaths; soon we had more than a hundred, then two hundred. In all of our accounts the main victims were men, in their late teens to fifties. The army seemed to be clearing the area of all males of fighting age.

It was clear the violence was on a huge scale. When we got back to the hotel, the man at the reception told us that his brother, who lived in a rural area, had been killed by the army. He was afraid to go there for the funeral. People we met for dinner said their gardener's family had been beaten: some were killed and the rest fled to the city. It seemed everyone in Bulawayo had stories of the terror.

And yet in the days that followed, the local newspaper, the *Bulawayo Chronicle*, made only the vaguest reference to "some reports of troubles in the rural areas." I knew some government officials in Bulawayo and when I alerted them to the accounts they just stared at me blankly. When I asked them what they would do to stop it, they were silent. I kept searching for some explanation, at least to get the government's side of the story. I made calls to officials in the Department of Information in Harare with whom I had been friendly, but they flatly denied that any killing of civilians had occurred. People were lying, they asserted, and then demanded to know where I had got the information. They told me not to write such lies about Zimbabwe.

Other officials said the army was merely taking necessary measures to stop the violence of a few dissidents.

I could understand efforts to curb the antigovernment violence. But this was an army campaign in which hundreds, even thousands, of people were being murdered. I no longer believed that the killings were some tragic mistake, yet I still believed that if they were reported the exposure would force those in charge to stop the slaughter.

When I returned to Harare, everything seemed bizarrely normal. The weather was fine, people were friendly, and few knew anything about the Matabeleland massacres. They seemed not to want to know. Many people, from church leaders to diplomats and otherwise well-informed people, looked at me with disbelief when I recounted my stories of mass killings. They discounted my reports as far-fetched, and some suggested I had fallen prey to some apartheid conspiracy to discredit the Mugabe government. They questioned the veracity of my stories and those of other international journalists. A few accepted that some limited killings might be occurring, but they insisted that Robert Mugabe could not know about them or he would stop them. One Shona acquaintance said, "Those Ndebeles had it coming. They needed to be taught a lesson." I was chilled by her words.

When we filed reports of the massacres to our papers, the government immediately charged that the foreign press corps had fabricated the stories. Some academics at the University of Zimbabwe and in Britain alleged that we were cooking up accounts of primitive tribal animosities because of our instinctive Western bias against African democracies. I reeled from the stubborn resistance of so many to what was happening just five hundred kilometers away.

With several other journalists, I was called in to meet the government's director of the Department of Information, who was in charge of accrediting foreign journalists. We were warned that our reporting was inaccurate and we should stop immediately or face further measures, including having our accreditation revoked and being deported from the country. The government took special offence at the powerful reporting of Nick Worrall, the correspondent for the *Guardian*, and rescinded his temporary employment permit and deported him. (Ironically his father, BBC journalist John Worrall, had been deported by the Ian Smith regime years before.) Nick invited me over to his house for a farewell drink, and asked me if I would like to write for the *Guardian*. I was elated at the opportunity but at the same time awed by the responsibility, especially to keep reporting what was going on in Matabeleland.

It turned out that a specific army unit, the Fifth Brigade, had been sent into Matabeleland North to quell the rebel violence. The red-beret-wearing Fifth Brigade was a special unit that had been trained the previous year by a group of North Koreans in the Nyanga Mountains. Its commander was Brigadier Perence Shiri, and it was rumored that its soldiers were virtually all Shona. Here was the ethnic violence that I and so many others had hoped never to see in Zimbabwe. The Fifth Brigade were known as Mugabe's Praetorian Guard and its men were often seen surrounding him when he made public appearances. I was left with no doubt that Mugabe was fully aware of the killings and had almost certainly ordered them himself.

Soon reports of fresh murders in Matabeleland came in from other church and medical sources. The government, determined to suppress open reporting on the situation, decreed that no one except local residents was permitted to travel off the main Bulawayo–Victoria Falls road.

Refusing to acquiesce to such censorship, I drove with three other journalists into the Matabeleland countryside. Stopped at an army roadblock, we told the soldiers we were tourists going to Victoria Falls. When we came to a mission hospital, however, we drove off the road to visit it. The members of the medical staff were amazed to see us and were clearly nervous, as army officers had ordered them not to talk to any journalists. But after a brief meeting the hospital staff agreed to speak to us because they wanted to emphasize the gravity of the situation. The doctor in charge explained that there had been a new wave of violence in the past week. They had treated a few people who died. But, she stressed, most of those fatally injured never reached the hospital at all. She showed us wards filled with the injured, suffering from broken bones, head wounds, stabbings, and burns. Families of the wounded camped outside in the hope that they would be safe on the hospital grounds. We interviewed some of the wounded and, once again, heard accounts of frightening night attacks in which whole families were victimized. We were told of a mass grave where dozens of bodies were dumped far from the main road. We started making plans to go looking for the gravesite.

Suddenly a nurse came running into the ward to warn us that the Fifth Brigade had returned to the hospital. The doctor pushed the four of us into a closet and closed the door. After a few minutes we could hear heavy boots going down the corridor and the sound of loud voices. It sounded like the soldiers had entered the room where our cupboard was. At last the voices and steps receded. In our closet, it was so silent that I could hear the sound of our own breathing. After several minutes the doctor came back and opened the closet door. Clearly shaken by the incident, she said the officers were checking the hospital for any visitors. They had asked about our car, which had the licence plates of a rental vehicle, and the doctor had assured them it was the car of a visiting missionary inspector, who was resting. A hospital aide watched the main road and said the three army vehicles had headed west, towards Victoria Falls. So we headed east back to Bulawayo, abandoning the idea of searching for the mass graves. We had seen the injured, we had medical confirmation of deaths, we had evidence that the killings were continuing.

Mugabe had plunged the country into rounds of ethnic violence. My dream of Zimbabwe becoming an African success story was in tatters. It was a distressing time, but instead of writing off Zimbabwe and going elsewhere, I felt even more committed to reporting on the country.

In the next few months Joshua Nkomo himself came under mounting pressure. His house in Bulawayo's Pelindaba township was ransacked by the army, and then his driver was shot dead in Nkomo's Mercedes. He called me to a press conference in Bulawayo where, frantic with fear, he said he believed the government was trying to kill him, destroy his party, and subjugate the Ndebele people. The state press continued to vilify him, blaming him for any antigovernment violence and then mocking him for any reports of violence against the people of Matabeleland. Eventually Nkomo fled the country by slipping across the southern border to Botswana; he went to England, where he stayed to write his autobiography. The state press reported that Nkomo sneaked across the border dressed as an old woman.

Although Mugabe adamantly denied that the army had carried out any mass killings, pressure from the international community and church leaders forced him to commission a judicial inquiry into the conduct of the Fifth Brigade to determine if large-scale killings had indeed taken place in Matabeleland. The report was delivered to the president but never made public.

In 1984 the army's area of operations moved to the Matabeleland South province. This time there were fewer stories of mass killings. From accounts of church leaders and residents who managed to slip out of the province, it was clear that the army was taking a different approach. Soldiers sealed off the main roads to the area and prevented all food deliveries, which literally starved the population. Zimbabwe was in the grip of a three-year drought and the blockade of food deliveries reduced the population to foraging for grass seeds and wild fruits. Mission hospitals reported a huge increase in cases of malnutrition, the stunting of infants, and deaths where hunger had been a major factor.

Thousands of people identified as supporters of Zapu were also being rounded up and held in concentration camps, where they were beaten and tortured. Many came back home after weeks in the camps, but some were never seen again. The government continued to categorically deny any violence or oppression against the people of Matabeleland and accused the Western press of concocting the stories. Many people, both inside and outside Zimbabwe, chose to believe the government and discounted my stories and those of others as exaggerations. Some accused me of being manipulated by apartheid South Africa in order to discredit majority-ruled Zimbabwe. The mood of the country was deeply divided. In Harare and throughout Mashonaland many people were still praising the Mugabe government for bringing independence to the nation. They pointed to undeniable improvements in education and health as proof that the government was devoted to improving the lives of the people. Reports of atrocities in Matabeleland were angrily denounced as efforts by Joshua Nkomo to discredit Mugabe. In contrast, the mood in Bulawayo was grim and frightened. The entire city seemed to be under occupation. The police had transferred so many officers from Harare that the force in Bulawayo was predominantly Shona-speaking, while the population spoke Ndebele.

It was not fabricated stories that compelled more than ten thousand people to follow Joshua Nkomo's lead and flee from Matabeleland to Botswana. There were so many refugees that the United Nations opened a tented camp to give them shelter and food. Yet, brutal though the army's campaigns in Matabeleland undoubtedly were, they did not succeed in quelling the antigovernment violence. Attacks on government targets and on white farmers continued. In one incident a white senator was murdered.

Against this troubled background, Zimbabwe's first postindependence parliamentary elections were held in 1985. Joshua Nkomo returned from his exile to lead his party in the polls. Mugabe's Zanu-PF tried mightily to win all of the parliamentary seats, but the people of Matabeleland, bloodied and beaten, resolutely voted for Nkomo's Zapu. Throughout the rest of the country, however, Zanu-PF swept the board. The morning after the results were announced, I heard there was trouble in Harare's townships. I drove into Highfield and other areas to see women, wearing dresses adorned with portraits of Robert Mugabe, raiding the houses of Zapu supporters. They beat people, destroyed their belongings, and piled furniture into the street. I was dismayed by this open display of intolerance, but Zanu supporters I knew assured me it was just an example of "African-style democracy."

Late one night in November 1987, I was tipped off that there had been a horrific killing of sixteen people by the rebels. The white members of a charismatic Christian sect farming in the Essigodini area of Matabeleland South had been bound and axed to death one by one. A young boy managed to escape through a window and told how the adults had all prayed as they met their deaths. Yet again it appeared the rebels had cynically calculated that they would draw most attention to their cause and do the most damage to the Mugabe government by killing whites. Yet again they were right: the gruesome story grabbed headlines worldwide. The antigovernment dissidents had killed some six hundred people, but it was the deaths of seventy or so whites that garnered the most attention. Of course the killings of civilians by the army dwarfed these numbers.

The farm where the ax murders took place was set in a stunningly beautiful valley surrounded by huge granite boulders. Fresh shoots of maize, soya beans, and other crops grew blithely on next to puddles of the victims' blood.

The minister of Home Affairs, Enos Nkala, arrived and yelled at the top of his voice that the government would put an end to this violence once and for all. He waved his fists and his shouts echoed among the rocky hills, but I dismissed his rant as futile. The same massive searches, the same army repression, the same antigovernment murders: the cycle of violence seemed unending.

On December 22 there was a hastily called press conference at State House, Mugabe's official residence. Mugabe was there and, surprisingly, so was Nkomo. It was the first time I had seen Mugabe since the ax murders, and he appeared oddly upbeat and pleased with himself. When the conference began, Mugabe announced that the two leaders had agreed to merge their parties in order to end the country's ongoing violence. He said it was a victory for the entire nation, but there was an element of gloating in his announcement: given their respective levels of support in the population, this merger could only be seen as a hostile takeover. Mugabe was a cold, calculating manipulator who did not care how many lives would be lost so long as he consolidated his power.

Champagne was brought in for a toast. The ordinarily abstemious Mugabe sipped and smiled smugly while Nkomo looked decidedly glum and dejected as he drank his. It was obvious Nkomo had agreed to watch his party be swallowed up in order to save his people from continuing violence. One could only hope that he would be successful. It seemed that part of the deal was that Nkomo would be gagged by Mugabe. He no longer held press conferences or gave interviews. He was appointed one of two vice presidents but he was no longer a political heavyweight; the formidable Joshua Nkomo was now just window dressing.

An amnesty was granted and about a hundred rebels gave themselves up. I went to Lupane to see a couple of dozen men turn themselves in. They were a scraggy, underfed bunch whose skin was leatherlike from living in the bush for years, but their rags were colorful and worn with flair and lots of beaded bracelets. They looked like a cross between rock stars and spirit mediums. It was flesh-creeping to think that some of them had chopped off the heads of the Christian farmers just a few months earlier; it was also unbelievable that this small band had for years eluded the army and set in motion the massive bloodshed of the Matabeleland massacres. It became clear to me what chaos can be wreaked by a determined guerrilla group and how a large army can be so ineffective in eradicating it.

Peace returned to Matabeleland. The grieving Ndebele resumed a semblance of ordinary life, but a huge, raw wound cut across the entire region. In time the truth emerged about the horrors that had occurred. The family of an off-duty army lieutenant who had been killed by the Fifth Brigade in Lupane sued the government in a case that received considerable news coverage in Zimbabwe. Fourteen years later, a report by the Catholic Commission for Justice and Peace, entitled "Breaking the Silence," cataloged the mass killings and torture inflicted on the rural Ndebele people by the Fifth Brigade. Estimates suggest that between ten and twenty thousand people in Matabeleland were killed by the army. But even in 1998 the Catholic bishops were so frightened of Mugabe's response that they forbade the commission to release the report. After a lengthy period in limbo, it was issued by the Legal Resources Foundation, which had funded the research.

To this day the Mugabe regime has not acknowledged the murders it committed in Matabeleland, nor have those directly responsible been called to justice. The commander of the Fifth Brigade, Perence Shiri, was promoted to commander of the air force and is regarded as one of Robert Mugabe's closest supporters.

Zimbabwe's honeymoon was over. Matabeleland became an indelible stain on Mugabe's record and on Zimbabwe's postindependence history. The maturity of the country would eventually be measured by how frankly it could accept the wrongs of what had happened. The experience also matured me. I was proud that the international press had acted as the whistle-blowers on the massacres, and I believed our reporting had helped to curb at least some of the atrocities. But it was hard to reconcile the horrors committed against the people of Matabeleland with the positive developments in health and education throughout the rest of the country. I had a responsibility to report on all developments, the positive accomplishments as well as the abuses that might be perpetrated against any group, large or small. Zimbabwe's ups and downs, from the joys of independence to the atrocities of Matabeleland, made the nation's story even more compelling to me.

Joshua Nkomo greets Nelson Mandela in 1997. Mandela hailed Nkomo as the key leader of southern Africa's struggle against white minority rule, praise that greatly annoyed Robert Mugabe. © *Reuters*

6

ZIMBABWE VERSUS APARTHEID

After the tragic violence of the Matabeleland massacres, I struggled to understand what the Mugabe government had done and why. Part of me wanted to view Matabeleland as some kind of terrible aberration, but I was convinced that it had been a calculated campaign ordered by Mugabe to neutralize his chief political rival and rid Zimbabwe of its main opposition party.

Of course I was not alone in asking these questions about Matabeleland. Journalists, diplomats, and academics discussed it at length. Some were determined to believe that Mugabe's violent actions could somehow be explained or rationalized; maybe the government viewed the rebels as agents of South Africa and therefore unleashed the army's fury on the rural people among whom they were operating.

Before independence, the South African government had openly supported Ian Smith's regime by sending police and soldiers to assist the Rhodesian forces. It also helped Rhodesia break international sanctions by acting as the middleman for its exports of tobacco and chrome and imports of fuel, arms, and other necessities. Eventually, under sustained pressure from the United States, South African prime minister John Vorster reluctantly decided that the cost of propping up Rhodesia was too high and withdrew his government's assistance. That forced Ian Smith to go to the negotiating table, which led to majority rule.

But South Africa did not leave the new Zimbabwe alone. The apartheid regime recruited Rhodesian military into its army; in some cases whole units, such as the notorious Selous Scouts, defected to South Africa. The Rhodesian Central Intelligence Organization turned over, lock, stock, and barrel, the rebel group Renamo that it had created to

73

cause trouble in Mozambique. The South Africans then established a web of agents in Zimbabwe to gather information and carry out sabotage designed to destabilize the new majority-rule country that was the antithesis of its minority-rule ethos.

Not only was the new majority-ruled country a rebuke by example to South Africa's minority rule, but Zimbabwe assumed a leading role in opposing apartheid. Robert Mugabe was one of the most vociferous critics of the system, urging the international community to impose total economic sanctions on South Africa. Because of the two countries' close proximity, Zimbabwe could not offer military bases for the underground African National Congress, but the movement had high-level diplomatic offices in Harare. The South African regime's strict press regulations meant that several major news organizations based their correspondents in Harare rather than Johannesburg.

As international interest in news from Zimbabwe waned, the press moved on to covering the African perspective on developments in South Africa. I made contacts with ANC members and frequently traveled up to Lusaka, Zambia, to report on news from its headquarters there.

A neighbor in my block of flats was a young South African woman who had been a member of a radical environmental group, which was enough to get her thrown into jail. When she was eventually released on bail she illegally crossed into Botswana and then into Zimbabwe, where she was joined by her husband and small son. We became great friends and shared lots of meals, music, and lively discussions about Zimbabwean politics, South African politics, vegetarianism, Van Morrison, primary education, and so on. I met many other young South African exiles who were working as teachers, journalists, engineers, architects, and accountants. Some had been jailed in South Africa; others had led student protests and gone underground before fleeing the country.

One antiapartheid activist had escaped South Africa after being released from jail and worked as an editor in Zimbabwe while his wife was a photographer; several young men had refused to serve in the apartheid army and made their way into Zimbabwe, two taught at the Harare Polytechnic, another was a disc jockey on the radio and became a television anchorman.

Most of these exiles were members of the ANC and some were members of the South African Communist Party. They all saw Zimbabwe, despite its faults, as a viable alternative to apartheid. We enjoyed many late nights of discussions on the future of a nonracial democratic South Africa, how to get things right in Zimbabwe, how to get things right in the world.

Apartheid South Africa had made its presence felt soon after I arrived in Harare. In July 1981 Joe Gqabi, the ANC's chief representative in Zimbabwe, was assassinated at his home. I had met him at a party just a few nights before. The tightly knit community of South African exiles was badly shaken. I, too, was shocked to see apartheid's network reach into Harare. The antiapartheid struggle was not simply a compelling moral cause; it was a matter of life and death.

A month after Gqabi's murder, I was working in my office in downtown Harare when I heard the deep rumble of an explosion somewhere west of the city. There had been a huge explosion at the Inkomo armory, one of the government's largest stockpiles of weapons and ammunition. The resulting fire lasted for days. Once again, it was an act of sabotage.

The sabotage continued. In December that year a huge bomb blew the top off 88 Manica Road, an office tower well-known as the headquarters for Mugabe's Zanu-PF party. The explosion killed seven people in an adjoining bakery and injured more than 120 Christmas shoppers. Robert Mugabe had been planning to meet the entire Central Committee of his party in an upper-floor conference room but had postponed the meeting at the last moment. The bomb destroyed the floor where the conference room was located. The bloody chaos on the street sent shockwaves across the nation: it was not just South African exiles who were the targets, it was not just Mugabe and his party who were threatened; it seemed the entire nation was under siege from South Africa.

In July 1982 another series of explosions destroyed thirteen jets, representing nearly all the planes of the national air force, at the Thornhill base near the central city of Gweru. And there was more. A booby-trapped television set blew up an apartment in the Avenues, killing the Zimbabwean wife of an ANC activist. Another car bomb went off outside the home of an ANC member in Bulawayo, killing the Zimbabwean driver.

One day in 1982, an attractive young woman arrived at my office, naming a number of mutual friends as references. Olivia Forsyth had been a student activist in South Africa, where she had been temporarily jailed. After graduating from college, she was now turning her hand to journalism. She told me she had international funding to launch a feature service of correspondents across southern Africa. "Would you like to write for us?" she asked. She offered very good pay. She invited me to lunch, on her expense account.

She told me I was the best journalist in Zimbabwe, the only one with a feel for the people and the country's development. Her new anti-apartheid service needed my talents and my expertise. It certainly was an attractive offer, but I was very busy with my work for AFP and the *Guardian* and did not want to give that up. Olivia said if I was too busy then I could just do the occasional feature and direct other journalists. She would pay me as a bureau chief. We talked about our friends and the developments in South Africa and Zimbabwe. A pleasant rapport developed and she had a way of looking at me with her deep-set eyes and pressing her knee against mine. "What is there to do in Harare at night?" she asked me.

We agreed to meet again, in my office. Her charms were not lost on me, but I wanted to keep things on a strictly professional basis. When she returned from South Africa a few weeks later she said the funding was coming through. I wondered how she could be setting up such a cutting-edge antiapartheid agency while based in Johannesburg. Oh, she said, it's where all the big media are. She said her donors, who remained unnamed, wanted her to be based there. She would be commissioning articles soon, but at the moment she needed some specific information: "Where is the ANC's new office in Harare?"

Alarm bells immediately started ringing. The ANC office had recently been moved and its location was a closely guarded secret. I offered to give her their phone number, but she said she needed their address. I knew where it was, but suspicious, I played vague and did not tell her.

I reported my suspicions to an ANC friend of mine, who immediately defended Olivia. "She is completely trusted from the highest levels. She has an impeccable background from the struggle in South Africa, which is more than I can say for you. This movement does not need outsiders casting doubt on our cadres. You could get into a lot of trouble for making unfounded accusations like this."

I was stung by the reprimand but remained convinced of my first instincts. I saw Olivia at the home of one ANC heavy and then another, who confided in me that he had slept with her. And then I heard gossip that someone else had slept with her, too. She showed up at parties and at popular cafés. There was gossip about her—but then there was gossip about everybody in the hot-house environment of South African exiles.

Eventually Olivia Forsyth was exposed as an apartheid spy, but not before antiapartheid activists Jeremy and Joan Brickhill were nearly killed by a car bomb at a popular Harare café, and the ANC offices in Harare were stormed in an unprecedented raid by the South African Defence Forces, who bombed the office on the same night they hit ANC offices in Botswana and Zambia.

Olivia was taken prisoner by the ANC and jailed in Angola. She managed to escape, reportedly by sweet-talking her guards and then making a dash for the British embassy in Luanda. Eventually she made it back to South Africa where she announced that she had been serving as a lieutenant in the South African security police. Her seductive methods became so well known that young wags at the University of Cape Town wore badges with the slogan I DIDN'T SLEEP WITH OLIVIA FORSYTH.

The mix of intrigue and the romantic South African exiles committed to ending the apartheid system made my life in Zimbabwe ever more complex and fascinating. I saw the struggle to achieve democracy in South Africa as an extension of Zimbabwe's battle against white minority rule. I learned more, too, about Mozambique and Zambia and how those countries were assisting the ANC's battle against apartheid, just as they had assisted Zanu and Zapu against the Rhodesians.

Those who sought to explain the Matabeleland rebels as South African agents were swayed by numerous rumors that the South African regime was supporting a wing of the rebels called "Super Zapu." It was an interesting theory: South Africa was, at that time, supporting anti-government insurgencies by Renamo in Mozambique and by Unita in Angola. However, there was scant evidence of any large-scale South

African support of Zimbabwe's Matabeleland rebels. Some diplomats said that the United States government had warned South Africa not to support a full-scale civil war in Zimbabwe, since it was not a Marxist state like Mozambique and Angola. In contrast to the large-scale conflicts that ripped apart those two former Portuguese colonies, Zimbabwe's Matabeleland rebellion always remained relatively low-level. The Matabeleland rebels appeared to be scrambling by their wits to support their anti-Mugabe campaign and showed few signs of fresh weapons, uniforms, or supplies from South Africa.

I firmly believe that Robert Mugabe carried out the Matabeleland massacres in order to crush any opposition to his ambitions to establish a one-party state by Joshua Nkomo, Zapu, and the Ndebele people in general. Yet although he tortured Matabeleland into submission, he never succeeded in achieving his goal of a one-party state. After Zanu-PF swallowed Zapu in 1987, Mugabe ruled over a de facto single-party state, it is true, but he never succeeded in making it illegal for any other party to challenge his rule. By the time he made a formal motion, at a meeting of Zanu-PF's Central Committee in 1991, for the creation of a one-party state, it met with such surprising resistance from within the party that it was dropped. Party stalwarts pointed out that Zimbabwe would be out of step with its neighbors and donors if it imposed a one-party state.

By that time a new wave of democracy had swept over Africa. One-party states were being toppled in neighboring Zambia and Malawi. To end their long-running civil wars, the governments of Mozambique and Angola also decided to legalize opposition parties and become multiparty democracies. Zimbabwe had become increasingly reliant upon international aid, and major Western donors made it clear they wanted to help multiparty democracies, not one-party states. Mugabe was furious, but he had made his move too late.

Mavis Ngazana, our greatest friend. No photograph can do justice to this vivacious and bighearted woman who adopted us into her wonderful family. © *Michele
Mathison*

7

TWO WEDDINGS AND A FUNERAL

On November 25, 1988, Dolores and I married at the Harare Magistrates' Court. Dolores's mother and sister flew out from California for the event and we all stayed together in our small apartment. Dolores wore an ivory silk blouse and skirt that she had made in Harare; I wore a linen blazer. We drove together to the courthouse, where we were met by Alexander Joe, AFP's photographer, who served as our best man. Zimbabwe's rains usually start in mid-November, but the precipitation was late that year so the weather was unusually hot and dry.

The magistrates' court is the scene of so many weddings for basic-income Zimbabweans that a business had sprung up renting wedding dresses to allow the bride to be a queen for the day. A little trailer in the courthouse parking lot holds several white satin gowns decorated with lace and pearls and featuring stretchy, expandable backs to allow them to fit a wide range of sizes. Gloves, veils, trains, and even tiaras are available, for a small additional fee, to complete the royal effect. Several photographers also make a brisk business from taking pictures of the happy couples on the courthouse steps. We were pleased to be part of such a thoroughly Zimbabwean scene.

Within a few months my apartment had started to feel too cramped for our life together, and we moved into a thatched cottage in the Newlands area, close to the center of town. Mrs. Manomano was delighted with our decision. "Now you are married and living in a proper house," she said. "It is good." She quickly set about scouring the house and moved straight away into the small servants' quarters, leaving the rest of her family in her room in Mbare township.

We were also joined by our great friend Mavis Ngazana. We had first met Mavis on a gorgeous summer night when we went to a party thrown by a friend out in Raffingora, a small farming town 160 kilometers northwest of Harare. It was an unusual gathering that brought together the town's white tobacco farmers and its black schoolteachers and shop managers. Vivacious, outgoing, and fun, Mavis quickly adopted us, introducing us to her many friends and family, skillfully crossing all the boundaries of race, class, and gender that still divided so much of Zimbabwe. The cool night air wafted through the garden after the heat of the day, and a shimmering full moon hung over the maize field. Mavis put on some music and soon we were all dancing, even doing an impromptu conga line through the garden.

The party went on and on and Mavis and I talked about everything from music and dancing to politics and race. "Why are you so different?" I asked her.

"What do you mean?" she responded, puzzled.

"So many other Zimbabweans are closed and quiet; why are we able to talk with you so easily?"

"Well, I am different," said Mavis proudly. "I am different in two ways. I am part Zulu, because my father was Zulu and my mother is Shona, so that makes me different. And also I am barren. My husband left me because I cannot have children. Other men don't want a wife who cannot have children. So I must make the best of my life. I take care of my sister's children and I like to meet people and learn about things. It makes life fun!"

When Mavis moved from Raffingora to Harare, where she worked in a craft shop in the center of town, Dolores and I often dropped in to chat. Mavis was excellent at her job, but she was desperately looking for a better place to live. Our new house had a separate storeroom that had previously housed a family. It did not have running water, however, so whoever lived there would have to share the bathroom in our house. Neither Dolores nor I was sure the arrangement was nice enough for Mavis.

"Let me show you where I'm living," she said when I explained our reservations. So after work I drove Mavis thirty kilometers out to Chitungwiza township. We came to a small house and walked behind it to a little shed. The door could not open fully because the single bed occupied nearly the entire floor. Mavis and her sister shared the tiny room, which had no running water or windows. "This is how I'm living now," she said. "I know your place will be better." The government projects to provide affordable housing had long since broken down and I knew Mavis's chances of better accommodation were slim. Our little storeroom with two windows was much better and our house was considerably closer to her work. We offered Mavis our place at a nominal rent, and she was delighted.

With fresh, colorful paint, some old furniture purchased at auctions, and paintings by friends, we made the new house into a charming, inviting home. The property came with two dogs and soon we all fell in love with them. With Mrs. Manomano and Mavis we became a Zimbabwean-style extended family. It felt like we had lived in the thatched house for years.

Our living arrangements meant we also got to know Mavis's two nephews, eighteen-year-old Tonderai and ten-year-old Macmillan, whom she had helped her sister raise. This is not unusual in Zimbabwe, as children are often cared for by rural grandparents or aunts while the parents work in the cities. It was always fun when the boys came to visit our house. Mavis's eighty-plus-year-old mother, Milka, came occasionally after her crops were harvested, and other aunties and cousins came, too. We felt part of a large, embracing African clan.

When Nelson Mandela was released after twenty-seven years in prison in South Africa we all crowded around the television set to watch the event. Zimbabwe rejoiced at Mandela's freedom, not only for him but because it set South Africa irrevocably on the path toward majority rule. It was a victory for all of Africa. Zimbabweans' pride grew even more when, within weeks of his release, Mandela chose their country for his first trip out of South Africa.

I have witnessed the arrival at Harare Airport of many heads of state, from Margaret Thatcher to Fidel Castro and the pope, but nothing has matched the excitement generated by Mandela's visit. People lined the streets to catch a glimpse of the great African, and despite tight security, thousands crowded onto the tarmac to greet him as he got off the plane. Dancing groups performed for him, including Mrs. Manomano's Jerusalema Number One. It was an extraordinarily joyful event.

Then Mandela stepped up to the podium to speak. He said he had come immediately to thank Zimbabwe for the leadership it had given to South Africa's struggle for independence, majority rule, and basic rights. He spoke movingly of how, during his years in prison, when all seemed very bleak, he and others were inspired by the successful struggle of Zimbabweans for majority rule. "You showed us that it could be done and gave us hope," said Mandela, speaking in the slow, deliberate cadences that became his trademark. Unlike so many others, he did not read a written speech; he spoke from the heart. He thanked Mugabe, and then he gave special praise to Joshua Nkomo, who made one of his rare public appearances. Mandela praised Nkomo as *Madiba*, meaning "revered elder leader"; it was the name Mandela himself was called in South Africa. Nkomo puffed up with pride at the honor. But I saw Mugabe's face crimp to a peeved expression.

Mandela was unusually gracious and accommodating to the press, too, and mentioned how our reports had given him a window on events beyond his cell and kept him up to date with Zimbabwe's independence and the ANC's progress. Mandela's willingness, even eagerness, to answer our questions contrasted sharply with Mugabe's long-standing attitude that the press, particularly the international press, should be treated as dismissively as possible.

Zimbabweans were becoming a bit cynical about their independence, as gains in health and education slipped and unemployment grew, but Mandela's visit rekindled their pride in their independence and the assistance their nation had given to South Africa's struggle against apartheid. Mandela's trip to Zimbabwe created a moment when everyone appreciated how historic our times have been, to be part of the battle of the African people against minority rule, first in the victory of Zimbabwe over Rhodesia, and then, in South Africa, of democracy over apartheid.

In January 1992 our household went to another public event together, but this time for a very different reason. We went to pay our respects to Robert Mugabe's wife, Sally, whose body was lying in state. Mrs. Mugabe had died from the kidney failure that had plagued her health for several years. Sally was from Ghana and as a foreigner was viewed with suspicion by the closed Shona society, and this was compounded by the fact that the couple's only child had died when young and Sally had never given birth to any more. But her outgoing nature, effective work within the party, and frequent meetings with ordinary Zimbabweans had earned her the grudging respect of many. At her death scores of thousands of people lined up to view her body at Mugabe's residence. The demand was so overwhelming that she lay in state for three days and nights.

At the grounds of Mugabe's residence we filed past a group of the first lady's Ghanaian relatives, wearing their country's riotously colorful Kente cloth and traditional gold jewelry. The big room where Mrs. Mugabe lay in state was dominated by a large golden Ghanaian bed covered in white linens. At the foot of each corner sat young nuns, singing softly and playing small drums and harps. Sally was dressed in a long white gown and a white veil, like a bride, with a lot of gold jewelry. The overall effect was otherworldly. After we walked past the bed, we were surprised to find ourselves face-to-face with Robert Mugabe. It was an extraordinary gesture by a man who had always remained aloof from the crowds. His weary, bloodshot eyes flickered recognition when he saw me and in a hoarse voice he said, "Thank you for coming." It was nearly midnight and he looked exhausted.

Many Zimbabweans say that Zimbabwe's decline started at Sally's death. Mugabe had already formed a liaison with one of his secretaries, Grace Marufu, who was forty years younger than he. She was also married and had a son, but her husband was assigned a distant post in China and then the marriage was ended. By the time Sally died, Mugabe and Grace had already produced two children out of wedlock, Bona, named for Mugabe's beloved mother, and Robert Junior. Not too many eyebrows were raised by this arrangement as polygamy is still widely practiced in Zimbabwe. Mugabe stated publicly that Sally knew of the relationship and understood his need to have children.

Grace Marufu and Robert Mugabe were formally married in August 1997 in a lavish ceremony at Mugabe's birthplace in Kutama Mission in

Zvimba. The state press called it "the wedding of the century," and certainly it was the most opulent event ever witnessed in Zimbabwe. I drove out to Kutama Mission and got through the tight security with my press pass. I stood outside the small mission church and peered in through the window to see a few hundred notables packed into the pews. Mozambican president Joaquim Chissano served as best man, and other regional heads of state attended, including Nelson Mandela, who by that time was president of South Africa. Catholic archbishop Patrick Chakaipa presided over the ceremony, despite considerable disquiet among Catholics that their Church should sanctify Mugabe's adulterous relationship with a divorced woman whose baptism in the Church was questioned.

The church could not hold many people, but the reception was attended by more than twelve thousand. I walked through the marquees, taking note of the feasting and drinking, and saw the crowd applaud politely as Mugabe and his young bride took their spot at the top table. A loud cheer rang from the outer tents and rose through the crowd as Nelson Mandela walked to his table; Mugabe's smile turned into a scowl as he realized how much more enthusiastically Mandela had been welcomed than he. He seemed out of sorts for the rest of the reception.

Initially the population at large welcomed Mugabe's new marriage and children. But it soon became clear that Grace did not show any of Sally's common touch. Whenever I saw her in public, she seemed haughty and disdainful of ordinary folk, whereas Sally would have been in the crowds, holding babies and laughing with people. Grace rarely mixed with the public and did not join in many Zanu-PF activities, as Sally had always done. The new Mrs. Mugabe usually had a sullen frown on her face in newspaper photographs.

Grace built a large mansion for herself in her home town of Chivu. Then the papers reported that she was building another, much larger home in Harare's posh Borrowdale suburb. Photos appeared of the expansive, multistoried house with numerous wings and it was immediately dubbed "Gracelands." Reports claimed it was built using various government funds that were intended to help low-income Zimbabweans.

Cartoonists poked fun at her penchant for extraordinarily wide-brimmed hats and she became known for flaunting dresses, shoes, handbags, and sunglasses from top designers in London and Paris. Grace Mugabe became the symbol of the new acquisitiveness and conspicuous consumption evident in the upper echelons of Zanu-PF. The first lady personified the rapid increase in corruption among Mugabe's inner circle and their lack of concern for the plight of the common man. First Grace Mugabe became unpopular and then she was loathed.

Fiery opposition politician Margaret Dongo met with violence when she challenged Mugabe's Zanu-PF party. © *Howard Burditt/Reuters*

8

SOMETHING FOR SOMETHING
Is SOMETHING

"Nothing for nothing is nothing, but something for something IS something—corruption!" Zimbabwean music superstar Thomas Mapfumo tapped the popular mood with his song "Corruption." Although it was quickly banned from state radio, I often heard people singing it on the streets. The refrain became a popular slogan that people repeated in a jocular way whenever someone requested a favor, such as asking a supermarket employee to save them a scarce item.

Corruption had crept into daily life, with everybody experiencing requests for bribes from government functionaries to police officers to shop assistants. Everyone knew it had started at the top and then spread, inexorably, across society. With corruption came a slide in standards of living. The gains of independence were slipping away. I could feel a general disillusion growing and resentment building against those in power.

For years I could say that I had never paid a bribe, but then our phone was out of order for several weeks, which was an unmitigated disaster for my work as a home-based journalist. The state phone network had become terribly overloaded and decrepit. Every morning I went to a friend's house and called the faults department and was assured the repair crew would attend to my problem that day. But the phone crews never came. Finally I followed a PTC repair van and asked them to come to my house. They agreed, for a price.

I was also invited to pay a bribe to a building inspector who came to check new quarters we had built for Mrs. Manomano. He said the new structure was not in agreement with the building code, but if I paid him he would not report us. I refused to pay, showing him all our permits,

91

and asked for his name so I could report him. He left our property in a hurry.

It was next to impossible to get a Zimbabwean driver's license unless you paid a fee to the driving school to make sure that if you passed your test you would get the license. Otherwise, no matter how well you drove, the examiner would fail you. We saw several young people try to get their licenses legally, with no success until they paid the required fee.

These examples are not to suggest that Zimbabweans are intrinsically corrupt. Overall I found that people were honest—even very poor people confronted with considerable wealth—but the government began to operate in a way that encouraged corruption. People were hired to work in various departments such as the Passport Office, Vehicle Licensing, and Immigration on the basis of connections to the ruling party, Zanu-PF. They were poorly paid and worked in a system that encouraged "extra fees." The corruption did not start at the bottom with everyday people; it started at the top.

"This government has dishonored the principles that we fought for in the liberation struggle. They have forgotten about the people and all they are thinking about is lining their own pockets," said Margaret Dongo, Zanu-PF's most outspoken member of Parliament. "Those at the top are taking big salaries, big cars, and big kickbacks. It is time they remembered the reasons why we fought for independence. It is time they remembered who fought for them and who voted them into power." The fact that this came from Margaret Dongo, who was at the center of the ruling elite, meant it could not be ignored. People sat up and took notice. Feisty, outspoken, and charismatic, Margaret Dongo captured the imagination of the Zimbabwean public, voicing the criticisms that people were thinking but were afraid to say. In her rise to prominence and her battle against the Mugabe government, she was one of the most compelling figures I came to know in Zimbabwean politics.

When she was only fifteen years old, Margaret Dongo had run away from school and crossed the border into Mozambique, working for Robert Mugabe's forces in the guerrilla camps there. She became known for her fiery spirit and her ability to motivate and organize others. "After independence I knew I had to get an education. I had to go back to school to be able to benefit from independence," she told me. The determined young woman had qualified as a secretary, and soon she was working in Robert Mugabe's office for the Central Intelligence Organization. With her razor-sharp mind, she had learned how Zanu-PF operated and become a vital member of the party's women's league. She was a founding member of the War Veterans' Association and was voted onto the party's Central Committee. In 1990 she ran for Parliament and won the Harare South seat.

So far her story was similar to those of others who became members of Parliament or rose to prominence in Mugabe's Zanu-PF. But once she was in Parliament she refused to play by the party's rules. Margaret Dongo began questioning policies from the ruling circle, asking pointed questions of cabinet ministers, and most of all, denouncing corruption. Her actions were all the more extraordinary since at that time Parliament had only three opposition members, who were relatively inactive. The ruling party did not welcome a challenge from within its own ranks. The state news media were given orders not to publish Dongo's criticisms, and as the state controlled all the country's daily newspapers as well as all radio and television broadcasting, the public did not get to know about most of her trenchant attacks on the party fat cats. The independent weekly newspapers carried some stories quoting Dongo, but for the most part she became Parliament's silent star.

I was intrigued by this woman who broke the mold. I was impressed by her fearlessness and her barely contained outrage and went to interview her at her modest home in Sunningdale township. We sat in her small, tidy front room in which two sofas and three comfortable chairs were squeezed around a coffee table. Dongo went to get me tea and biscuits, and I caught the aroma of a hearty stew from the kitchen. The lounge had a veritable picture gallery on the walls: photos of the beaming Margaret Dongo at Parliament, with visiting Japanese politicians, and with Mugabe; photos of the entire Dongo family and of her children in their school uniforms; the children's drawings and school reports.

When she returned with refreshments, she began delivering rapid-fire answers to my questions. Several times I would have to ask her to slow down so that I could take down every colorful phrase. She was impassioned and outspoken: "We fought for a better government for all the people. But this government has forgotten that. Those at the top think they are there just to get rich. It is wrong."

She had plenty to say about education, charging that the government was allowing the schools to deteriorate and standards to slip to the level they had been at in the Rhodesian era, or even worse.

Her main issue, though, was corruption. Zimbabwe's relatively well-developed economy offered rich pickings for the politically well-connected, and the wider public was becoming increasingly bitter about being left out. After the boom years of the 1980s, when the economy grew rapidly and everyone's life improved, unemployment had grown, particularly among the newly educated youth. The government had then turned to the bastions of the West, the World Bank and the International Monetary Fund (IMF), for assistance and entered into a structural adjustment program to reduce its budget deficits and lift numerous market restrictions, including price controls. The economy started to pick up, people were getting jobs, and there was a mood of optimism.

Some analysts blame Zimbabwe's economic decline on the IMF and the World Bank. They are easy targets, but from my experience on the ground, I do not think these multilateral institutions are primarily responsible for Zimbabwe's economic woes. At the same time that Zanu-PF formally dropped socialism and the government began the structural adjustment program, a new breed of black businessmen with connections to the ruling party became prominent.

One such businessman was Leo Mugabe, the President's favorite nephew, whose uncanny resemblance to his uncle was accentuated by his similarly oversized glasses. Leo's businesses won numerous government contracts. Through his political connections he became the head of the Zimbabwe Football Association, which enjoyed a large cashflow from gate receipts at matches, and which he ran like a family business. Then Leo set his sights on an even bigger moneymaker, the new Harare Airport.

International tourism had become one of Zimbabwe's fastest-growing sectors and was creating new jobs and earning foreign currency. The charming but tiny Harare airfield was unable to cope with the proliferation of jumbo jets flown in by new airlines. After a lengthy process, the contract for the design and construction of the new airport was awarded to a French firm, Aéroports de Paris. But then Leo Mugabe convinced the cabinet that Harare should have a more distinctively African design for its airport. In the end the contract was awarded to a little-known Cyprus-based firm, Air Harbour Technologies, whose owner, Sheik Hani Yamani, had appointed as his local representative none other than Leo Mugabe.

The previous contract had included international financing from France and Japan, but the new contract from Sheik Yamani required the government to finance the construction itself. Parliament was asked to rubber-stamp the multimillion-dollar expenditure to build the new airport when Margaret Dongo stepped to the fore.

Where others quietly grumbled about the patent nepotism and the swelling cost of the airport, Margaret Dongo spoke at the top of her voice. She stood before Parliament and then took to the aisle, walking up and down in front of the assembly. Her opposition to Leo Mugabe's airport deal startled the staid chamber as if a firecracker had been thrown into it. She charged that the airport was going to cost ten times more than the previous contract and urged "any self-respecting politician" to vote against the financing bill.

"Are you all Mugabe's wives?" she asked, wagging her finger at the sheepish, overwhelmingly male members of Parliament. "Are you going to approve spending all this money that will go straight to Leo Mugabe's pockets? This is not in the interests of the people of Zimbabwe and you know it." Chastened by Mrs. Dongo's harangue, Parliament rejected the bill.

Leaders of the government were furious. The Zanu-PF whip berated the errant M.P.s and ordered them to toe the line. The bill was brought before Parliament again and this time it passed. Cabinet ministers said publicly that Margaret Dongo would be punished, and indeed, when it came time for the 1995 Parliamentary elections, Zanu-PF refused to nominate her and awarded the seat to a different candidate. Dongo refused to be sidelined and ran as an independent.

Despite a bitter campaign against her in the state media, Dongo drummed up support on a shoestring budget by going door-to-door throughout her constituency. I decided to go to one of her rallies and drove through the narrow streets of Sunningdale. The diminutive figure of Margaret Dongo stood in the center of a couple hundred people and she dominated the entire evening. She told them about what she had done in Parliament and how she would demand better schools and services. She told them stories of her time as a nationalist guerrilla in Mozambique. She sang songs, she told jokes, she talked with children. She spoke to the women in the crowd. She spoke to the men. She did everything a politician should do in a completely natural and winning way.

I was exhausted by the time the rally finished, but she wanted me to come with her as she visited some families in their homes. She went from door to door, speaking to people about the upcoming elections. She single-handedly steamrollered the entire constituency and it looked like the party candidate did not have a chance, but when the election results were announced, Margaret Dongo narrowly lost.

Of course, she did not take defeat sitting down. She took the government to court. In a landmark case, Dongo charged that the voting roll was rigged from the start, with a high proportion of false names, deceased listings, and multiple entries. She charged that the entire election process was "defective and open to manipulation particularly by a capricious and undemocratic government such as the current one." She conducted an audit of the voters' roll and proved that a whopping 41 percent of the entries were not valid. In addition, through an inspection of the ballot boxes, she proved that more votes were cast than the number of registered voters in her constituency. With such conclusive proof that the vote had been rigged, the judge had no option but to declare the results invalid.

Her court case was groundbreaking because it presented conclusive proof that Zanu-PF was manipulating the entire election process. It made their majority of 118 out of 120 seats look very questionable. The irrepressible Margaret Dongo articulated the entire country's simmering discontent and the desire for a more responsive and more accountable government.

A new election was held and Dongo trounced her Zanu-PF opponent, but sadly her political career faltered soon afterward. She started a new political party, the Zimbabwe Union of Democrats, but she made some ill-advised alliances. She misjudged the widespread support that had been built by the trade unions and the new party that sprang up from organized labor, the Movement for Democratic Change (MDC), and in the 2000 elections she lost her seat to the MDC candidate.

But Margaret Dongo remained a political trailblazer who had shown that Mugabe and Zanu-PF could be challenged. Her effective legal tactics would be the same ones used by the MDC in its court challenges of Zanu-PF victories in thirty-seven parliamentary constituencies in the 2000 elections. By highlighting corruption, by insisting on good performance by government, by legally challenging electoral practices, and by sheer force of personality, Margaret Dongo made a startling and vital contribution to the cause of democracy in Zimbabwe. She showed that loyal and patriotic Zimbabweans could fight against corruption and stand up to the stranglehold on power of Mugabe and Zanu-PF.

Chenjerai Hunzvi, head of the War Veterans' Association, who waged an intensive campaign for more benefits for veterans. Though the campaign succeeded, Mugabe's unilateral response without concern for the national budget precipitated a drastic, nearly 50 percent drop in the value of the national currency.
© *Alexander Joe*

9

THE ROAD TO BLACK FRIDAY

More than fifteen years after independence, Mavis, like many Zimbabweans, was disappointed at how she had to struggle to make ends meet. She snorted with disbelief when Mugabe gave speeches in which he listed how Zimbabweans' lives had improved. Many people who had worked to get their children educated and who had expectations that their lives and the lives of their families would improve found themselves disappointed. Their lives were not getting better.

For some time Mavis had scrimped and saved to buy things for her mother and to send her nephews to school. She also helped her brothers by buying the seeds and fertilizer they needed to get their crops in the ground—just like the majority of urban Zimbabweans helping their rural families. We all celebrated when Mavis's oldest nephew, Tonderai, got a job. "This is fantastic," said Mavis. "So many people do not have jobs. This is going to help me and the entire family."

Although disillusion was growing among the Zimbabwean public, Mugabe still enjoyed a reasonably good reputation internationally, having somehow managed to avoid blame and disgrace over Matabeleland. But he was about to lose his golden touch with the international community, overshadowed by the towering magnanimity of Nelson Mandela, whose spirit nurtured a fresh blooming of tolerance and reconciliation in South Africa. Mugabe did not respond to the new challenges by reinvigorating his government's social welfare programs or by adopting more tolerant, inclusive policies, as was happening in South Africa. Instead he reacted by staking out entirely different ground from Mandela, by attempting to dictate what is "genuine African culture." He also took steps to establish that in Zimbabwe the African nationalist movement that fought the liberation struggle, his Zanu-PF, was the only party fit to rule Zimbabwe, no matter what the democratic process said.

These issues came to a head at the Zimbabwe International Book Fair, Africa's largest literary event. The 1995 fair, with the theme "Human Rights and Justice," was the largest yet and two of Africa's Nobel winners in literature, Nadine Gordimer and Wole Soyinka, had come to participate.

Robert Mugabe was set to officially open the fair, until he heard that an organization called Gays and Lesbians of Zimbabwe, known as Galz, was to be one of the 250 exhibitors. He demanded that the Galz stand be closed, and the book fair board buckled under pressure and evicted the gay organization. This action created a huge furor, with Nadine Gordimer denouncing it as absolutely contrary to the theme of human rights.

But the controversy was not over. At the official opening, a few hundred schoolchildren were sitting on the lawn in front, and behind them stood book-fair guests and the usual party faithful. Mugabe arrived, looking very stern, and launched into a scathing attack on homosexuals. "I find it extremely outrageous and repugnant to my human conscience that immoral and repulsive organizations, like those of homosexuals, who offend against both the law of nature and the morals and religious beliefs espoused by our society, should have any advocates in our midst and even elsewhere in the world," said Mugabe, spitting the words out with venom.

The young children looked at each other, befuddled by the president's speech. I struggled to take notes as he continued the rapid-fire delivery. "If we accept homosexuality as a right, as is being argued by the association of sodomists and sexual perverts, what moral fiber shall our society ever have to deny organized drug addicts, or even those given to bestiality, the rights they might claim and allege they possess under the rubrics of "individual freedom" and "human rights," including the freedom of the press to write, publish, and publicize their literature?"

This blistering attack was not a spontaneous outburst: Mugabe delivered it from a written speech and we journalists scrambled to get a copy. The controversy over the closure of the Galz stand at the book fair had already created several news stories, but we knew this would make headlines everywhere. With a few other journalists, I ran behind the premises of the book fair to the secluded spot where Mugabe's Mercedes was parked, to ask the president about his antigay speech. Members of the presidential entourage tried to shoo us away, but we were determined to get a quote. There was a tense atmosphere as the scowling Mugabe marched to the car.

"Mr. Mugabe, are you saying that homosexuals do not have any rights?" I asked.

"That's right," he answered, grabbing my arm for emphasis. "They do not have any rights. They would like to turn the laws of nature on their head and see men try to be mothers. Impossible! They do not have any rights whatsoever." He pushed me back with such force that I crashed into the television camera behind me.

Something changed that day—a feeling compounded in the next weeks as Mugabe continued his antigay tirades. Homosexuals are "worse than pigs and dogs," he declared. He charged that homosexuality was "un-African" and was a sickness imported by decadent colonialists. It was a classic example of Mugabe trying to regain his waning popularity by attacking a minority group. In other speeches he would vilify Jews, the British, white farmers, church leaders, human rights organizations, and any group that challenged him.

The anti homosexual crusade changed the international community's perception of Mugabe. Until then he had been viewed rather favorably, despite the Matabeleland massacres. But at that point the scales tipped and from then on Mugabe was widely seen as a vicious despot, especially by the Western press. This did not worry Mugabe much, however. He was playing to different galleries. In Africa he sought support from old-school nationalists, both in Zimbabwe and across the continent; internationally he courted opinion among the anti-Western, anti colonialist set. Mugabe was doing more than attacking gays; he was attacking the growth of civic groups and the culture of inclusive community rights that was so influential in South Africa. He was stating that rights would be determined from the top, not by the community. Zimbabwean journalist Iden Wetherell told me that Mugabe was striking at what he believed was the Achilles heel of the civic groups: gay rights.

But Mugabe's anti gay campaign backfired. Of course it was popular among some conservative nationalists, but generally it was ignored by average Zimbabweans, for whom homosexuality was not an important issue. It also went against the general tolerance I had seen in Zimbabwean society. Zimbabwe's gay community, however, was galvanized by the attacks and emerged much stronger, more vocal, and more organized. Galz as an organization had been mostly white and male, but after the book fair incident it was flooded with new black members and became a mostly black organization of men and women who were determined to stake their place in society. Galz won new standing and even church groups uncomfortable with the issue of homosexuality accepted that gay people have legal rights. It was as if civil society drew a line in the sand and said, "Human rights start here."

Mugabe's vitriolic attacks on gays set off another unintended chain of events. Just weeks after his book-fair speech, Jefta Dube, a policeman on duty at a football match, went to the toilet and there was taunted by a fellow officer for being "Banana's wife." Incensed by the suggestion that he had been a sexual partner of Zimbabwe's former ceremonial head of state, Canaan Banana, Dube pulled out his gun and shot dead his tormentor.

Dube was tried for the murder and found guilty. He pleaded for his life, claiming in mitigation that he had been raped by Banana and it had ruined his life.

Dube had been one of Banana's bodyguards and had been on the president's football team. He said the president made several advances, and one evening he was ordered to the president's State House library, where the two men played cards and drank wine. He said the president played a record and tried to teach Dube how to do ballroom dancing. Dube claimed he was drugged and woke up on the carpet with his trousers at his feet. A smiling Banana said, "We helped ourselves," according to Dube, who said the president continued to molest him. He presented the court with letters he had written asking for help from the police chief, top army officers, Deputy Prime Minister Simon Muzenda, and many others. No one would intervene to stop the sexual harassment by Banana. Dube had run away from his job at State House, but army officers apprehended him and despite his pleas they turned him over to Banana.

Dube had eventually been transferred to another unit but he suffered from problems with drink, drugs, and depression before he shot his fellow policeman. He was spared the death penalty but later died in prison.

Harare was buzzing about Dube's shocking testimony. Everyone was talking about it, from diplomats to gardeners. Banana's reputation as a statesman and a church leader committed to social justice was indelibly besmirched; but people also talked about Mugabe. They said he must have known all about it and covered up for Banana. People asked why the police knew about Dube's charges and did nothing to stop it.

Dube's highly publicized revelations forced the police to investigate Banana. A dozen men, including a gardener, a cook, and other policemen, testified that Banana had forced them to have sex with him. One air-force officer said he only avoided Banana's advances by pushing the president into a swimming pool. Banana was convicted of eleven counts of sodomy and "unnatural acts" and jailed for ten years, but was released after eight months.

No one emerged unsullied from the Banana rapes. But Mugabe, the big antigay crusader, was exposed as having covered up for Banana and knowingly allowed him to abuse his bodyguards and others.

The following year I attended the book fair again. I walked among the stands in the pleasant open-air setting of Harare Gardens, behind the National Gallery of Art. There were books from Nigeria, Kenya, Ghana, and South Africa, colorful children's books, novels, and academic histories.

I watched as invigorated members of Galz succeeded in opening a stand, where they provided information about homosexuality, safe sex, and the legal rights of homosexuals under Zimbabwe's constitution. They advertised a seminar on their constitutional rights to be addressed by Edwin Cameron, an openly gay justice in South Africa's supreme court. Everything seemed peaceful until a young public prosecutor, whose father was a former cabinet minister, led a gang of young thugs to the Galz stand. They surrounded the stall, shouted abuse at Galz members, and threatened anyone who stopped at the stand. I attempted to interview the leader about his motivation, but he just shouted at me and his crew roughly pushed me away. After working themselves into a frenzy and chasing away the Galz members, the gang burned the stand down. It brought to mind a book-burning, further proof of the malicious intolerance that Mugabe was cultivating.

In this period of brewing discontent Robert Mugabe faced a direct challenge from another, and most unexpected, quarter: the war veterans. After demobilization in 1980–1, when they were given large payments, most veterans had slipped into obscurity. Numbering about forty thousand, most of them were young people who had given up their chance of education in order to fight against Rhodesian rule. After independence many, like Margaret Dongo, went back to school and got qualifications to work, but many more did not pursue education and instead languished in dead-end jobs or in the swelling ranks of the unemployed. They were left behind and could only catch glimpses of Mugabe and his inner circle enjoying a world of new Mercedes, tailored suits, and flashy wristwatches. They were treated to a day of beer and food each year when Zanu-PF celebrated Independence Day.

Things changed when an ambitious doctor called Chenjerai "Hitler" Hunzvi took over the War Veterans' Association. He took on his *chimurenga* (revolutionary) name to instill fear in his enemies. Hunzvi breathed new life into the war veterans and urged them to demand more money and jobs from the government. He led them on a series of demonstrations that became increasingly unruly. Shop windows were smashed and Mugabe and his cabinet were called numerous epithets.

I first came across these war veterans on a warm September day as I drove up to the gleaming gold Sheraton hotel and conference center to cover a meeting of African-American businessmen, led by Jesse Jackson,who had come to get in touch with their African roots in liberated Zimbabwe. My car looked decidedly shabby alongside the shiny new Mercedes, BMWs, and Toyotas in the parking lot. As I passed by a demonstration of several hundred men, one ran up to my car and shook his fist, shouting, "We want our pay. We liberated Zimbabwe and Mugabe must not forget us." I stopped and took notes about the protest. Mugabe was jeered and heckled as he stepped out of his limousine to greet Jackson and the other American leaders.

The Americans were flummoxed by the demonstration. Their image of Robert Mugabe as a great African liberator was tarnished by the spectacle of angry blacks demonstrating against him. Hunzvi had astutely calculated how best to embarrass the president.

When Mugabe agreed to speak to him, Hunzvi knew he was striking home. He upped his demands for pensions for all war veterans and gratuities for the heroic service they had rendered to the nation. The government rejected the demands as impossible: it was already coping with a ballooning deficit. The spurt of economic growth brought on by economic reforms had stalled and the government could ill afford new expenditures. But Hunzvi kept bringing the war vets to demonstrate at unexpected and inconvenient places, like meetings of the Zanu-PF Central Committee.

In November 1997 Mugabe announced that the war veterans would each get a gratuity payment of Z$50,000, at that time worth U.S.$4,500, and a pension worth Z$2,000 per month, which at that time was more than the average factory worker was earning. Mugabe said the payments were effective immediately, despite the fact that they had not been included in the budget. The financial markets, already shaky from corruption and banking scandals, were so rattled by this rash expenditure of money, without parliamentary approval, that the Zimbabwe dollar dropped drastically in value. On the day Mugabe announced the payments, the currency plummeted from Z$11:U.S.$1 to Z$21:U.S.$1. Although the Zimbabwe dollar had been slowly sliding for several years, this was the first time such a drastic plunge had occurred. The stock market took a similar plunge, further proof that the economy was directly affected by Mugabe's actions and expenditures.

As businessmen and workers alike reeled from the news, the entire country was hit by a power cut that lasted most of the night. Sitting in my office, illuminated by flickering candles, I scribbled out a story in longhand and dictated it over the phone. As I sat in the dark, I could not help but feel this was a symbol for everything happening in the country. Many others saw it as a harbinger of things to come, and of course the day became known as "Black Friday."

In October 2000, rioting breaks out in Harare. Frustrated by soaring food prices and rising unemployment, rioters blocked roads, pelted police with rocks, and set fire to vehicles. © *Paul Cadenhead/Reuters*

10

THINGS MUST GET WORSE

The lights came back on, but the despair of Black Friday continued. The government made halfhearted statements that it would turn the economy around, but suggestions of austerity were quickly contradicted by news of a large order of new Mercedes for the ever increasing number of cabinet ministers, which by now was more than forty. The growth of Mugabe's cabinet was due to his patronage system. He kept ambitious politicians onside by allotting them cabinet posts and allowing them to run their ministries as they pleased, and make as much money as they wanted. This resulted in the ministries being run as fiefdoms, with little thought being given to service and efficiency, and none to reduced spending. In the meantime, Mugabe and Grace and their entourage flew off on increasingly lengthy trips abroad, where they occupied entire wings of the most expensive hotels.

Mavis was finding it increasingly hard to make ends meet, even though she had a new and better-paying job. With rising inflation it became more and more difficult for her to buy food and provide necessities to her mother and nephews. Special treats that she used to enjoy, such as apricot jam and getting her hair done, had to be dropped. She developed an asthma problem that became an emergency. Previously she had gone to a government health clinic but its supplies had dwindled to such an extent that it could only issue simple aspirin. She went to see our private doctor, who prescribed a ventilator pump.

Mavis, like the factory workers, township dwellers, and peasant farmers, was experiencing a slow but steady drop in her living standards. Inflation was eating away at her earnings, health services were declining, and education was becoming more expensive. The improvement in

111

healthcare made in the 1980s had been eroded to the extent that many key indicators, such as the maternal and child mortality rates, had worsened to preindependence levels. Faced with the need to reduce its budget deficit according to the structural adjustment program, the government chose to reduce spending on health and education but maintained its spending on the military and the Central Intelligence Organization.

Much of the mood of Zimbabwe is determined by the maize crop. Ground white maize is boiled to make a stiff porridge called *sadza* that is the country's staple food. People eat *sadza* two and even three times a day with a sauce or relish of greens and tomatoes. If they can afford it they will have their *sadza* with *nyama* (beef) or *huku* (chicken). People eat *sadza* in volume and become used to the full feeling it gives as the maize meal swells slightly in the stomach. Most years Zimbabwe produced enough maize for domestic consumption and had a surplus for export. Questions about maize—how the crop is this year, how much the government will pay farmers for maize, how much the shops in the city charge for milled maize, how much maize a worker's salary will purchase—are issues that dominate the consciousness of all Zimbabweans. The government controls the price of maize through the Grain Marketing Board, which holds a monopoly on maize sales. It should be a sure way to make a profit, but a string of corruption scandals had left the marketing board with a huge deficit. In October 1997 the board increased the price of maize by 35 percent and then again in December by 24 percent. The increases were above the rate of inflation and certainly above workers' wage increases.

I made sure Mrs. Manomano was paid enough to buy sufficient maize meal and other provisions to eat well. In October Mavis and Mrs. Manomano would go on shopping expeditions to purchase maize seed and fertilizer for their rural families, and I would often drive them to pick up the supplies and then deliver them to their *kumushas* (rural homes) in the Seke and Murewa areas. After the buildup of heat in October, the arrival of rains in November is generally welcomed with joy by people concerned about the maize crops, but there was little celebration in 1997.

Then the government proposed a new tax to be deducted directly from workers' pay packets. Pay had already been diminished by the drought levy, which had continued to be deducted long after the 1992 drought, and the AIDS levy, which everyone knew was not helping those suffering from the disease. In December the Zimbabwe Congress of Trade Unions called an unprecedented national strike to protest the rising prices and the proposed new tax.

The unions decided not to hold any large protest marches in the streets, in order to ensure that the strike was entirely peaceful. Workers stayed home to keep out of trouble. Ordinary Zimbabweans embraced the strike as a way to demonstrate their unhappiness with the erosion of their living standards, and succeeded in shutting down virtually all industrial and commercial activity in the country.

"We've done it!" exclaimed Mavis. "We are showing the government they can't take advantage of us anymore!" This was the first time since independence that the workers had held a national strike against the government.

The usually jolly Christmas holiday period was noticeably tense. Mavis, like most other workers, found it difficult to afford the ingredients for a festive meal. Presents were scrapped as everyone knew that school fees had been increased and had to be paid at the start of the year. In January the price of other basic food items such as rice and cooking oil nearly doubled. Then the price of maize was increased yet again, this time by 21 percent. Harare exploded into angry food riots, which spread to most other major cities.

Upon hearing the news, I jumped into my car and drove into the nearly deserted city center. There I came across a gang of men setting up a barricade along Leopold Takawira Street, a major thoroughfare in downtown Harare. A young man carrying a large rock ran up to my car. "You better get out of here, *shamwari* [friend]. There's going to be trouble." I asked him what was going on. "Food is too expensive. We're protesting at the prices. We're protesting against corruption," he said before warning me again to leave the area and to hide my briefcase.

I raced back home to make phone calls to check out the rioting in other areas. Shops were looted, bakery vans were stripped of all their bread and then set alight. Angry rioters marched in their thousands towards downtown Harare, hitting every food establishment along the way. I realized how lucky I was to have encountered such a reasonable rioter. Other motorists, including fellow journalists, were attacked by frenzied mobs who smashed their cars with rocks. Just a block away from where I had been, a driver was dragged out of his vehicle and badly beaten. Factory workers and executives alike tried to avoid the chaos and get to the safety of their homes. The state radio broadcast which roads were still open and which ones were barricaded and unsafe due to rock-throwing rioters.

The rioting continued for three days, and Mugabe was forced to call out the army to quell the worst violence to rack the country since independence. Pitched battles broke out between rioters and soldiers and police on all the major thoroughfares leading to the center of Harare. The authorities issued a warning that they would use live ammunition.

I ventured out with two other journalists to Glen View township, going up a hill and on to one of the township's main access roads. Tightly packed, small houses were on our left while on our right was open land used for growing maize by the residents. It was an elevated spot with a view of the industrial factories below. Ahead was a barricade of boulders, large oil drums, and burning tires. The roadblock was manned by young men, each with a stockpile of good-sized rocks and bricks to throw. We got out of my car to speak to some of the residents, and within a couple of minutes a large army truck arrived, shooting off hissing canisters of tear gas that clouded the street. We all darted away and I ran upwind of the billows of noxious gas and behind a small house. Others sought the same refuge and I found myself surrounded by about a dozen young men, most with rocks in their hands.

Months earlier I had written that the youth who were educated thanks to Mugabe's early reforms and who were full of aspirations but remained unemployed in the stagnant economy were a time bomb waiting to go off. I wasn't certain if I should try to make a run for it.

"You're a reporter," said a large young man, gesturing aggressively at my notebook with a jagged rock. I said yes. "Why are you here?" he demanded in a threatening tone.

I said I wanted to know why people were rioting.

"Write that we can't eat because food prices are too high," he said. "We can't get jobs. We are fed up with this government. The ministers never come here in their Mercedes. They never come to the townships." He gave me his name and age.

A second man stepped forward. "Mugabe must just go. We don't want to see him anymore. Bread, bus fares, everything is too dear! We are not able to live anymore. Mugabe must go!"

Others jostled to speak to me. One young tough shouted, "We want to go to State House and kill Mugabe's children." I was startled by the bloodthirsty violence of his fury, but the others cheered in agreement.

We drove through a few partial barricades before getting back to the city center. It was hard to know who was more dangerous, the rioters or the army. Later that day I learned that three photographers had been stopped by soldiers, forced to lie down on the road, and beaten with clubs and whips.

The army sent out helicopters to determine where the rioters were active. The clattering aircraft dropped tear gas indiscriminately, affecting people who were staying peacefully in their homes. One child choked to death on the fumes. Ten people were killed in the disturbances, most of them casualties of government force.

It was not safe to go out again until the riots had ended. It was eerily quiet at home. Every now and then the silence was broken by the *pop-pop* of guns or tear gas being fired a few kilometers away. I kept track of what was going on by phoning friends in the townships, speaking to photographers covering the unfolding events, and listening to the radio. Once the violence had ebbed I drove down Simon Mazorodze Road, a major thoroughfare through the industrial area. Windows were shattered, and shops, fast-food outlets, and bakeries had all been looted. It looked like a war zone. Never had I seen ordinary Zimbabweans so angry.

The government responded by blaming white businessmen for raising prices, while the state newspapers played down the significance of the violence. A popular disc jockey, Gerry Jackson, who had broadcast calls from around the city indicating where there was violence, as a service to listeners to help them avoid trouble, was promptly fired for calling attention to the riots.

"Things must get worse before they can get better," said John Makumbe, a lecturer in political science at the University of Zimbabwe. I was interviewing him about Zimbabwe's future a few days after the riots. "The government is not going to change until the people get angry and demand better government. The people will not get angry until

115

things get worse. Then they will get angry and force change, either through elections or through violence, like the riots we just saw. When there is a democratic change, things will get better."

During the interview there were frequent knocks at his door and he dealt with students and administrators alike with efficiency and unfailing good humor. One knock was very timid and John had to call twice for the person to enter. A scruffy, impoverished young albino man shuffled into the room. John spoke to him kindly in encouraging tones and gave him some special skin cream from a box of supplies on top of a filing cabinet, then advised him on where to seek further assistance for his condition. John Makumbe is himself an albino and has had to cope with a lifetime of prejudice. Albinos suffer acute sensitivity to sunlight, ever present in Zimbabwe, so they need to use sunblock creams. They also have congenitally bad eyesight and require special glasses and sunglasses. They have to overcome countless insults in society. "Many people don't want to shake my hand or stand in a buffet line after me because they think I taint the food. People don't let pregnant women look at me, as if I will give them a curse. These things happen all the time," John told me. In addition to their special needs, most albinos need the same things that all Zimbabweans need—education, skills, and employment.

"I have been very fortunate and I want to help my fellow albinos battle this prejudice," said John, who founded an organization to help others overcome the health and social obstacles before them. He is also a pugnacious battler on many other fronts. He is fighting corruption as the founder of the Zimbabwe chapter of Transparency International; and as a founder of the Crisis in Zimbabwe Coalition he has been a key leader of the coalition of more than 250 civic organizations working to restore democracy and the rule of law.

It is hard to believe that such a vital force as John Makumbe was nearly strangled at birth. "The midwife started to throttle me when she saw my condition. But my mother was still alert and told her to stop," he told me. "My parents are educated and worked at a mission school and were not superstitious. I was raised in a supportive environment like any normal child. The other important thing was that my parents could see that my eyesight was not good so they took me to a doctor to get glasses.

116

That was crucial because it permitted me to do well in school. It was not until I went away to school that I encountered discrimination."

By then, John says, his character had been formed, and he was not going to accept second-class treatment from anybody. I think his wonderful sense of humor developed as a way to deflate those who insulted him. His winning personality helped him earn the affection of a young woman, but her parents objected because he was an albino. John was dejected but he picked himself up and went back out into the world, finding a new girlfriend who impressed him as being intelligent and serious. She accepted his proposal of marriage but once again her parents objected, the mother saying she would kill herself if her daughter married the albino. But this time John and his intended, Virginia, were persistent and after a year of effort they persuaded the parents to give their approval to the marriage. "Before my mother-in-law died, she said she was glad that she changed her mind, because I have been such a good member of the family," Makumbe says proudly.

It is not just from rural Zimbabweans that John faces discrimination. Two American television teams have balked at using footage of Makumbe, on the basis that he was too unattractive to appear onscreen. "Can't you find somebody else who says the same things but who is not so, uh, visually challenging for our viewers?" one correspondent asked me. I was appalled by so blunt an admission that appearance was more important than substance.

John's experience at overcoming prejudice has given him great insight into racism in Zimbabwe. "The racism of whites toward blacks is easy to spot and to deal with," he told me. "The racism of the Mugabe government toward whites used to be subtle but now it is becoming more open, as Mugabe looks for scapegoats to blame for the failures of his government. And there is more racism here. Between the Shona and the Ndebele. Between the different Shona subgroups. Those ethnic prejudices are types of racism, too. And we must battle them all."

When John told me that the situation in Zimbabwe must get worse before it would get better, I asked him, "How much worse?"

"Look around in Africa. Look at the roads in the countries you visit. Zimbabwe's roads are still in good condition. Look at how people live. People in Zimbabwe still live relatively well. I think things must get much worse before people insist that things improve. And let's be clear about one thing: this government is now only concerned with its own power and it is not listening to the people."

After the food riots, things settled down to a semblance of normality, but it was a changed, charged, more uneasy atmosphere. The government was jittery. The state newspapers and broadcasters began to allege conspiracies, led by Britain and whites, to topple the government. Police began to erect roadblocks around the capital to check vehicles for weapons. At the same time, the government continued to allow the economy to deteriorate, stubbornly refusing to accept that economic decline was the core reason for its growing unpopularity.

Mugabe then worsened the situation by announcing in August 1998 that he was sending Zimbabwean troops to the Democratic Republic of Congo (formerly Zaire) to prop up Laurent Kabila, who was under attack from rebels supported by neighboring Uganda and Rwanda. I read the startling news in the state *Herald* newspaper and immediately began working on a story.

"Congo? What are we going to do in Congo?" asked Mavis incredulously when she saw the news on television that night. "Congo never helped us in the liberation struggle. Congo hasn't been involved in any of our affairs. And it is a mess there, everybody knows that. Why does Mugabe want us to get involved up there? Don't we have enough problems here at home?"

In the 1980s Zimbabwe had sent troops to neighboring Mozambique to defend the oil pipeline that pumped the landlocked country's fuel supplies from the port of Beira. But then, Zimbabwe had been defending a strategic interest to secure its fuel supplies and also helping a country that had given Mugabe and his guerrilla fighters bases during the war against Rhodesia. But Zimbabwe had no history of involvement with Congo. The country was widely regarded as the most chaotic and corrupt in Africa and few could understand why Mugabe, with considerable problems at home, would want to incur such expense by sending the military there.

But Mugabe had laid the groundwork for the intervention. A year earlier he had warmly welcomed Kabila to Harare just months after the guerrilla leader toppled the regime of Mobutu Sese Seko. He then pressed the Southern African Development Community to give membership to Kabila's new Democratic Republic of Congo, despite the fact that no elections had been held and that Congo had few links with the rest of the southern African members.

When Mugabe announced that Zimbabwean troops would go to Congo, he also attempted, as the chairman of SADC's Security and Defence Committee, to get other SADC countries to send troops as well. Most member countries refused; they also made sure that Mugabe vacated that sensitive committee as soon as his term expired. In the end only two other SADC countries, out of fifteen members, agreed to send troops: Angola, which shared its sensitive northern border with Congo, and Namibia, whose leader, Sam Nujoma, had become a kind of mini-Mugabe, copying his attacks on homosexuals, building a lavish palace and altering the constitution so that he could prolong his stay in power.

In response to public complaints that Zimbabwe could not afford such a military adventure, Defence Minister Moven Mahachi responded that it would not cost much, because the government already had to pay the army's salaries in Zimbabwe and the Congo government had agreed to pay for their food and other provisions in Congo. Military experts scoffed at the explanation as obviously deceptive; the Zimbabwean public did not accept it either.

Iden Wetherell, who was now editor of the weekly *Zimbabwe Independent*, was scathing about Mugabe's intervention in the Congo war. "Mugabe wants to teach the pesky South Africans a lesson. He is resentful of the acclaim for Mandela's diplomacy and wants to reclaim his mantle as the region's preeminent statesman. He doesn't care about the economic cost, he thinks Zanu-PF won the country in the liberation war and now he can do what he likes with it. Mugabe says he's sending our troops to bring order to the Congo, but I think it will have the opposite effect: it will make Zimbabwe more like the Congo; more corrupt, more bankrupt and more chaotic."

It was the kind of pithy, incisive assessment I had come to value from Iden. His cutting analysis and biting wit make him a stimulating friend and the *Zimbabwe Independent* a compulsory weekly read. Although Iden became the government's most trenchant critic, they found it hard to dismiss him as a reactionary white. He was well known as a student activist in the 1970s and had been kicked out of Rhodesia by Ian Smith. He was a member of Joshua Nkomo's Zapu and knew many leaders of Zanu-PF because they had addressed rallies in Britain together. Nor could the *Zimbabwe Independent* be dismissed as a mouthpiece for white interests, since its publisher is a black Zimbabwean, Trevor Ncube, and the reporters are all black. I often visited the newsroom. They were a wonderful team with whom to discuss the latest issues, controversies, and scandals.

Iden and I fell into the habit of having lunch together every Friday, the day his paper was published and he could relax a little. Friday became the high point of our professional week as we recounted quotes, dissected personalities, and analyzed events. By the late nineties we were joined at our lunches by Mercedes Sayagues, who came to Harare as a press liaison officer for the United Nations World Food Program. It was a measure of Zimbabwe's reputation as the place with the best infrastructure, where things worked properly, that the WFP set up its regional headquarters in Zimbabwe.

Brimming with brio and panache, Mercedes hit Harare like a meteor. An attractive thirty-something who was well-read, articulate, outspoken, and often outrageous, Mercedes shook up the dowdy capital city.

At first Mercedes did not take to Zimbabwe. "What is it about this country that people love so much?" she asked me. "People here live like chickens: they get up with the sun and they go to bed when it is dark. Restaurants close here at nine P.M.!" I explained that the pleasure of Zimbabwe was not its nightlife; it would take time for her to appreciate the country's more subtle attractions such as climate, pace of life, and the stimulating atmosphere of a new democracy.

It wasn't long before Mercedes admitted I was right. She had begun to enjoy Harare, probably because she was raising a young daughter on her own and found that the slower pace of the city made it easier to juggle the demands of work with her parental responsibilities. When the WFP wanted to bring her back to their Rome headquarters, Mercedes declined and decided to stay on in Zimbabwe as a freelance journalist.

Writing for South Africa's *Mail & Guardian,* she won a cult following for her racy columns on southern Africa's sexual mores as well as for her zesty analysis of the region's politics. She wrote about her own ex-

periences with the female condom and *vuka vuka,* traditional herbal aph-
rodisiacs. She traveled throughout Mozambique and Angola and consistently highlighted the point of view of the man in the street, skewering
the pretensions of those in power.

She certainly added glamor to our lunches. At first we dubbed her
"Contessa" for her imperious manner and elegant Italian wardrobe. Then
she became "La Passionaria" for her heated, heartfelt opinions on landmines, the need for better sex education in Africa, human rights, and
many other topics.

Mercedes, Iden, and I all agreed that the war was a disaster for
Zimbabwe. It soon became clear that Mugabe, his generals, and others
of his ruling clique were making money in Congo. In return for Zimbabwean troops, the Kabila regime signed over control of huge interests in
mining and timber. Mugabe's elite made fortunes while the struggling
taxpayer footed the bill for the twelve thousand Zimbabwean troops. A
United Nations investigation found that Zimbabwe was one of the major
plunderers of Congo's resources. Mugabe's right-hand man, Speaker of
the House Emmerson Mnangagwa, was named as running a large-scale
traffic in illegal diamonds.

For the ordinary Zimbabwean, however, the Congo war caused
everyday life to deteriorate rapidly. Severe fuel shortages disrupted
everyone's lives; some food items became scarce because they were being
sent to Congo. Inflation increased as the government printed money to
pay for the war. Families grieved for sons whose bodies were returned
from Congo, while the government refused to say how many troops were
in Congo or what the casualties were.

Then the press came under fire. One Sunday in January 1999, the
Standard reported that junior-level army officers were so opposed to the
war that some were talking about a coup against the Mugabe government.
The army furiously denounced the story, and within days the *Standard*'s
editor, Mark Chavunduka, was arrested. A few days later the reporter who
had written the story, Ray Choto, was also taken. The paper's lawyers could
not locate the two men because the police had turned them over to the
army. They obtained court orders demanding that the two journalists be
produced, but the minister of defense, Moven Mahachi, was conveniently
out of town. The top civil servant in the Defence Ministry, permanent

secretary Job Whabira, dismissed the judge's ruling contemptuously, saying, "We don't take orders from courts."

As days went by with the two still missing, I felt visceral anguish. I had known Mark for years when he had been editor of *Parade* magazine, Zimbabwe's most popular monthly. And Ray and I had worked together on a couple of stories; he was a good, aggressive reporter. I attended vigils for the journalists in front of Parliament and at the central Africa Unity Square, but the government refused to release any information.

It came as an incredible relief when I heard the two men would appear in court after ten days. I dashed to the magistrates' court where they were to be charged. Ray came up to me as he left the courtroom and I grabbed his hand to shake it, but he recoiled. When I looked at his hand I saw it was swollen and misshapen from beatings and repeated electric shocks. We hugged instead.

Mark and Ray immediately held a press conference describing their days of torture in gut-wrenching detail. They had been warned not to tell of their mistreatment on pain of death but they decided it was imperative to let the public know. They described being held in a blood-stained basement where they were told their blood would soon be on the walls, too. They were beaten with clubs, subjected to electric shocks on their hands, toes, ears, and genitals. Their heads were repeatedly held underwater for long periods. Their army and CIO interrogators wanted to know the army sources for their story. Examinations by doctors confirmed injuries consistent with their accounts. Minister of Defence Mahachi dismissed their charges of torture by saying, "They must have injured themselves."

The proof of torture was bad enough, but it was also illegal for the police to have handed the journalists over to the army. The police and Ministry of Defence had blatantly refused to obey court orders to produce the journalists in court. Despite the fact that the two men identified several officers who had tortured them, and the courts ordered the police to investigate the allegations of torture, no one was ever arrested or charged.

Leading lawyers told me that they were alarmed by the government's blatant disregard for the law. All the judges of the supreme and high courts joined together to issue an unprecedented letter to Mugabe urging him to pledge that his government would uphold the rule of law and obey court orders. They also released the letter to the press.

But Mugabe gave no such assurance. Instead he turned on the judges. In a televised address to the nation he was formal and stiff as usual, but he displayed a new angry, belligerent air. Far from promising the nation that he and his government would follow the rule of law, Mugabe suggested that journalists who dared to write critical stories of the army should be prepared for torture. He similarly warned judges that if they were to make any demands on him they would be dismissed.

I kept thinking of John Makumbe's words: things must get worse before they can get better. Living standards were plummeting, the army was in a distant war, corruption was enriching a few, the rule of law was breaking down, officials were torturing journalists. How much worse did things have to get?

Opposition leader Morgan Tsvangirai in Harare market. The young man is apologizing for his Zanu-PF T-shirt, saying it is the only shirt he has. This photograph was taken in February 2003, when Tsvangirai was about to be tried for treason. © *Michele Mathison*

11

RESURGENCE OF HOPE

Despite Zimbabwe's growing problems, I was struck by the determined optimism I encountered everywhere, from executive offices to corner newsstands. Zimbabweans refused to sink into despair about the fate of their country, and they were infused with a new surge of enthusiasm and hope when both a promising new political party was formed and a separate campaign was launched to persuade the government to create a new constitution.

It was no mistake that the new party, the Movement for Democratic Change, was launched in Chitungwiza. Harare's largest township has nearly a million people crammed into row after row after row of small houses, and it had been badly hit by the food riots—first by the rioters, who looted the area's large shopping center, and then by the army and riot police, who bludgeoned anyone they found on the streets. Many peaceful residents were tear-gassed in their homes. The new party reflected the hopes and aspirations of the working people of the townships, a key constituency which had been taken for granted by the Mugabe government.

The new party grew out of the Zimbabwe Congress of Trade Unions, which had called the national strikes to protest against Mugabe's economic policies. Many people I knew, academics, lawyers, human rights leaders, and university students, were attracted to the new party. In the weeks before it was launched, people I interviewed would tell me excitedly about the MDC and how it was going to change the face of Zimbabwean politics.

The new party also attracted many white Zimbabweans. Since 1980 most whites had stayed out of politics, not wanting to be seen as die-hard Rhodesians, but nearly twenty years later there was a small but dedicated band of whites who were involved in community groups work-ing with the black majority. Many of these people were drawn to the new party and their talents were welcomed.

The party was led by Morgan Tsvangirai, the popular leader of the Congress of Trade Unions. I had interviewed Tsvangirai many times. At first I found his English halting and rough, but he expressed an intelligent analysis of the problems facing Zimbabwe's working class. Tsvangirai grew up in rural Zimbabwe in the 1950s and 1960s. He had to give up his hopes of education when his father died and he went to work to support his seven brothers and sisters. He got his education in the trade union movement, where he became a local official of the mineworkers' union and then moved up through the umbrella group, the Congress of Trade Unions. As the leader of the congress from 1989, Tsvangirai transformed it from a sleepy adjunct to Mugabe's ruling party into the country's most potent challenge to the government.

In December 1997 a gang went to Tsvangirai's office, where he was beaten unconscious and nearly thrown out of the tenth-floor window. Luckily his secretary walked into the room and startled the attackers. Despite some of the attackers being identified, no one was ever tried for the crime. The physical attack and the government's regular vilifi-cation of him in the state media seemed to forge Tsvangirai into a stron-ger and more determined leader. His English improved considerably, so that he displayed a firm command of the language, even in a difficult interview. Most noticeable was the fact that all those who worked closely with him spoke highly of him, from the trade union movement to new associates in the formation of the MDC.

Mercedes and I drove out to Chitungwiza township to witness the launch of the new party, but there was trouble. Riot police ringed the hall and tried to refuse us entry. Tear gas was fired and young party sup-porters and journalists were chased away. The government was already making it clear it was not in favor of the creation of a new political party. We drove around the hall and could see many people inside, then saw a gate open and quickly drove in. The large hall was filled with thousands of cheering people. We had missed the opening speeches but we watched as Morgan Tsvangirai addressed the crowd and introduced the provisional shadow cabinet.

No one in the new party seemed fazed by the police's actions. I was impressed by the joyful, jubilant atmosphere of the gathering. Such exuberance had been missing from public meetings, particularly Zanu-PF's rallies, for years.

Tsvangirai announced that the MDC would contest all 120 seats in the parliamentary elections due just months away in 2000. He called for the immediate withdrawal of Zimbabwean troops from the Democratic Republic of Congo, accountable economic policies, and respect for the rights of all Zimbabweans. He showed off the party's symbol, an openhanded wave that was a sharp contrast to the threatening clenched fist of Mugabe's Zanu-PF. The crowd gave a rousing cheer to Tsvangirai, shouting the party's slogan, *"Chinja maitiro,"* which means "Change the way things are."

There had been a few opposition parties in the 1990 and 1995 elections that attempted to break Zanu-PF's stranglehold on the country's politics, but they had quickly faltered. The Zimbabwe Unity Movement created by the mercurial former Zanu-PF stalwart Edgar Tekere, the Forum Party led by retired Chief Justice Enoch Dumbutshena, and Margaret Dongo's Zimbabwe Union of Democrats had all succumbed to bitter infighting, widely suspected to be the work of undercover agents from Mugabe's nefarious Central Intelligence Organization. It was clear from the start that the MDC had the potential to break out of the limitations that had restricted previous opposition parties. From the trade unions it had a mass base of support, and from the professionals it had sophisticated strategists. It looked like a party to be reckoned with.

While the MDC was being created, the increasingly assertive civic organizations were taking a different course. They, too, were determined to get a government that was more responsive to the people's needs, but they chose to press Mugabe from a different angle, pushing for reform of the root cause of Zimbabwe's problems: the constitution. Church groups, women's organizations, human rights groups, trade unions, and professional bodies came together to form the National Constitutional Assembly. They held numerous public meetings, which initially attracted just twenty or forty people, but as word spread hundreds started to attend.

They had a good point. The constitution that brought Zimbabwe to independence was an agreement cobbled together by lengthy negotiations in London between the Rhodesians, Mugabe's Zanu-PF, and Nkomo's Zapu. British foreign secretary Lord Carrington presided over the Lancaster House talks. The constitution had served its purpose of bringing the country to independence but it was so riddled with special guarantees—"sunset clauses"—for the Rhodesian white minority that it was not a framework of sound democratic principles to guide the nation. In particular the constitution said that for ten years whites would have twenty seats in Parliament, far out of proportion to their numbers in the population, and would be protected from government seizure of their properties, specifically farms. Such compromises were probably necessary to bring the country to majority rule but did not result in a document that would stand the test of time.

The constitution had been further weakened by a string of amendments powered through by Zanu-PF's domination of Parliament. Carried out in the name of "Africanizing" the constitution, they concentrated power in the executive, doing away with the post of prime minister and merging the head of state and the head of government into one executive president who wielded sweeping powers. The president controlled the administration of elections, and had considerable influence over the judiciary, the police, the economy, and the press. Most importantly there were no limits to the number of terms the president or members of Parliament could serve. In short, the constitution was remodeled to be suitable for a one-party state. The architect of these far-reaching modifications was Eddison Zvobgo, a clever Harvard-trained lawyer and Zanu-PF baron who made no bones about his ambition to succeed Mugabe one day.

In recent years Zimbabweans had watched as South Africa created a new constitution through a thoroughly democratic process in which the entire nation was involved from the grass roots up. The resulting document won international praise for protecting the rights of all citizens, and South Africans of all colors spoke of their new constitution with pride. Zimbabweans wanted something equally good for their country.

When church leaders presented Mugabe with a petition calling for a new constitution, the president said coolly that he would consider their request. A few weeks later Mugabe surprised nearly everyone by agreeing to form a commission to draw up a new constitution. There were

130

celebrations at the offices of the NCA, and the public snapped up newspapers to read the amazing news that the government had accepted change.

"Don't celebrate yet," warned John Makumbe, who had been a leader of the constitutional assembly. "Mugabe is a very crafty politician. He won't give anything away easily, certainly not his control."

Makumbe was soon proved correct. Mugabe invited representatives of the constitutional assembly and many other critical groups to be part of his commission, but he also announced that all 120 members of Parliament would be members of the commission, too. In other words Zanu-PF would be a majority on the commission.

The commission got off to a popular start by holding dozens of public hearings across the country where citizens could stand up and say what they wanted to see in a new constitution. Critics and supporters alike were astounded by the large turnouts for these meetings, and more had to be scheduled. At the hearings I attended, ordinary people, many speaking in Shona and Ndebele, stood up to declare what they wanted to see in a new constitution and often what they wanted their country to be like.

"I want the constitution to give us a new president," said one older man who was somewhat confused about what a constitution can do. But his sentiment in favor of change was echoed by many in the church hall in Harare's Mbare township. (More than three hundred had gathered on a weeknight in response to an advertisement in the *Herald*.) Others called for a president to be limited to two terms in office, for the president to be prevented from traveling all over the world, for the president to be stopped from having a huge motorcade with armed guards. A man in glasses called for the constitution to require a balanced budget. Other public hearings were held throughout Harare, in all the major cities, and in some selected rural areas.

These meetings were covered extensively in the press and people read avidly about the changes the participants called for. From the press accounts it was obvious that the overwhelming desire of the people was to reduce the powers of the president.

But it was a different story once the Constitutional Commission began to discuss the reforms. In classic Zanu-PF fashion, squabbles and

131

infighting slowed down the drafting of each section to a snail's pace. Then suddenly a completed draft was presented to the commission, supposedly from its leaders. The draft document had all the language of democracy and key phrases like "individual rights," "separation of powers," and "independence of the judiciary," but a reading of the full constitution showed that it did not reduce the power of the executive at all. In fact it consolidated and in many respects actually increased the presidential powers.

There were howls of protest from representatives of civic organizations on the commission, who asserted that the draft was a repudiation of what the public had called for so strongly. But when it came to the crunch, the Zanu-PF members of Parliament and other party faithful, many of whom had barely attended the sessions, voted in a solid block to accept the president's draft.

A well-funded, extraordinarily slick media campaign heralded the new constitution as a triumph for the new Zimbabwe. The February 2000 constitutional referendum was promoted as the people's chance to take Zimbabwe's democracy into the new millennium. A Zimbabwean version of the song "We Are the World" was released, in which a star-studded array of the country's top musicians urged everyone to join together to support the new constitution for the good of the nation. State radio and television gave the song saturation coverage. Colorful T-shirts supporting the constitution also appeared and boosted many people's increasingly threadbare wardrobes. Zimbabwe had never experienced such a well-orchestrated publicity campaign. No expense had been spared.

This ultrasmooth campaign was the brainchild of Jonathan Moyo, whom I had known for years. I interviewed him often when he was a lecturer in political science at the University of Zimbabwe and an arch-critic of the Mugabe government. I even commissioned an article by him which ran in the *Guardian*, denouncing Mugabe's lack of respect for democracy. Moyo had written that Mugabe had to be "dragged kicking and screaming" away from his goal of a one-party state. "You are doing great work," Moyo once told me. "Zimbabwe needs good journalists like you." He had moved to Kenya to work for the Ford Foundation, but left under a cloud and was later sued for allegedly embezzling considerable funds. Moyo then went to South Africa to work for

Witwatersrand University and bought a grand house in the swanky Johannesburg suburb of Saxonwold. Soon the university complained of breach of contract, and that is when Moyo reappeared in Zimbabwe, to run what critics called "Mugabe's constitutional circus."

Moyo's campaign had a huge budget, which was never made public. The National Constitutional Assembly, on the other hand, could only muster a few advertisements in the privately owned newspapers denouncing the president's draft. State television and radio refused to run the civic coalition's calls to vote against the proposed constitution. Such limited opposition was no match for Moyo's media steamroller.

I viewed it all with a jaundiced eye. Mugabe had astutely created an atmosphere of change and progress with the nationwide public hearings and had promoted the draft constitution in ringing words of democracy that were contradicted only in the document's fine print. The state's newspapers and radio and TV stations had kicked into full gear, promising a better future for all. I found myself humming the maddeningly catchy proconstitution song.

I thought the sophisticated campaign would succeed in getting Mugabe's constitution endorsed by a majority in the referendum, but I had underestimated the canny and frustrated public. I joined that public a few days before the referendum when I went to get my national registration papers, which all citizens and long-term residents are required to carry. The once efficient system of issuing birth and death certificates, passports, and national registration papers had become cumbersome, time-consuming, and corrupt. It was run by the registrar-general, Tobaiwa Mudede, who had been appointed by Mugabe in 1980 and who displayed an open disdain for the public, stating on several occasions that holding a passport was a privilege to be bestowed by the government, not a right of all citizens.

Following the advice of others who had gone through the tedious process of registering, I got to the office early, at 6:30 A.M. The line already snaked around the entrance. The gates remained closed until 8 A.M., when the hundreds of people filed through and formed another line. And then we waited and waited and waited. By eleven o'clock we were still standing, sitting, leaning against the wall or lying on the ground in the same spots where we had been at eight. There were about five hundred of us, a cross section of the country. There were young professionals carrying briefcases and using cell phones, young mothers with their babies, and people from the rural areas. By far the largest number of people came from the townships. As time wore on, the crowd became restless and started grumbling, but officials came out and said we would be attended to in due course and those who created any disturbance would be evicted by the police who stood at the door. There were several stages to the process and after each we would be ordered to return to the line and wait for our number to be called.

A thunderstorm broke out and most of us huddled under a leaky veranda. It wasn't difficult to pick up the mood of seething anger among those waiting. An old woman in a shabby dress and worn-out shoes began arguing and then shouting. The officials had refused to issue her national registration because they said her identity papers were too frayed. They had told her to go and have the document copied and certified and then return and start the process again from scratch. "You know I have come here all the way from Mutoko [a distant rural area]. You know I don't have money to pay you a bribe," she said in Shona, her anger visibly rising. "You are causing trouble for an old grandmother. I am not going to vote for you again. I won't ever vote for Zanu-PF again." The waiting crowd broke into spontaneous cheers and applause. Two police grabbed her arms and took her away and warned the rest of us to be quiet or we would be kicked out, too.

A little later a flurry of activity rippled through the line. Leaflets were being passed out. I took one entitled "15 Reasons to Vote No in the Referendum." It was in English, Shona, and Ndebele. "1. It will increase Mugabe's powers. 2. It will weaken Zimbabwe's democracy . . ." People studied them carefully.

My number was called and as I went into an office a guard challenged me about the pamphlet and accused me of distributing them. As I waited in yet another line, I watched the surly woman who stamped our papers take one of the pamphlets and put it in her handbag.

I eventually succeeded in getting my national registration papers, but much more important, I picked up the mood of the people. My day at the registration office told me that average people were not inclined to endorse the constitution in any way. I also felt the sparks of this current of antigovernment feeling in other places, in the bank, and at the supermarket. I bumped into an old friend, a news executive at the Zimbabwe Broadcasting Corporation. "Mugabe and his crowd are out of touch. They shout at anyone who tells them that people are against the constitution. They call them traitors. They think they can tell people what to believe. They don't realize that the people have rejected them. They are going to get a rude surprise." I was surprised because I had thought he was just a government flunky, but he supported my hunch about the impending referendum and also my belief that, clever as Mugabe was at manipulating public opinion, he was not listening to the feelings of the people.

On the day of the referendum, the voters resoundingly rejected Mugabe's draft constitution. I was at the counting station at Allan Wilson School in central Harare and watched as officials announced the results with disbelief. I had already filed a story and quickly called to update it with the news that Zimbabwe's voters had delivered an unprecedented rejection of Mugabe just four months before the crucial parliamentary elections.

Jubilation broke out across Harare. People left their apartments and danced in the streets, singing and cheering. At the headquarters of the National Constitutional Assembly it was like New Year's Eve: people of all races and backgrounds were hugging and kissing and jumping up and down. Young men started shouting that Mugabe had been given a yellow card, like in a football match, and that in the parliamentary elections he would be given a red card and sent off the field altogether. For days afterward people were smiling, believing that they had won a great victory that was going to make things better in the country. They had seen democracy bring change in South Africa, Zambia, and Malawi. Now, they said, it was Zimbabwe's turn to vote in a new government.

Mugabe did not appear on state television for a few days. When he did make an address to the nation, he appeared unusually tense, tight, and terse. He said he accepted the people's decision, but he did not say he planned to take a different approach to governing the country. He vowed to carry on.

In March 2000, a farm invader renames a farm after Josiah Tongogara, the leader of Mugabe's guerrilla forces that fought against Rhodesian rule. © *Howard Burditt/Reuters*

12

MUGABE STRIKES BACK

It was clear that Mugabe and other members of his cabinet were shocked and angered by the vote of no confidence. As a seasoned observer of Mugabe, I felt that he had merely put up a facade of acceptance, while working on a strategy for reversing the referendum defeat. A Zanu-PF member of Parliament told me privately, "The president is furious and refuses to believe that the defeat reflects the will of the people. He blames the party for not campaigning hard enough for the constitution."

The opposition MDC and civic groups that had campaigned against the referendum were still rejoicing and the mood among people was jubilant. "We'll give Mugabe the red card, give him the red card!" said a young university student I knew, brazenly handing out the red plastic cards that spread throughout Harare.

The challenge to Mugabe's rule spread even within Zanu-PF where, a week after the referendum defeat, members of the Central Committee pressed him on when he intended to retire. Mugabe insisted it was not yet time for a discussion about his retirement. Within two weeks of the rejection of his constitution, he had come up with a new strategy that would crush his opponents, quell the stirring of unrest within his party, and reinvigorate his image as the most radical African leader: the land invasions.

One evening at the end of February 2000, the lead headline on the nightly news was "Zimbabwean people reclaim the land that is their heritage." I sat up and paid closer attention. The report showed a parade of dancing, flag-waving people marching down a country lane and onto a white-owned farm. When the camera zoomed in, I saw that the people were carrying clubs and *pangas* (machetes). They smashed down a gate and spilled into a farm homestead shouting, *"Hondo! Hondo!"* ("War! War!")

Since the official ZBC news only filmed what they were ordered to film by cabinet ministers, I could see that this "spontaneous eruption of the people's will" had been carefully staged to allow the ponderously slow ZBC crews to capture the event. The glowing way in which the first land invasions were described made it clear that they had the full backing of the government. I smiled grimly to myself: So this is how Mugabe is responding to the defeat of his constitution.

White-owned farms in every province were occupied by a motley crew of war veterans, Zanu-PF loyalists, and unemployed youths. Within a few days the number of farms occupied grew from a handful to a few dozen and then a few hundred. Brandishing clubs wrapped with barbed wire, axes, and iron bars, the war veterans threatened the farmers and forced many of them to flee their properties. They slaughtered cattle and sheep for feasts and set up shanty camps on the properties; they disrupted planting and harvesting; they also beat the farmworkers and chased many of them away, too. The white farmers called the police to help them respond to the trespassers, but the police refused to intervene.

Government trucks and buses were ferrying people to the farms, using stocks of chronically scarce fuel. Army officers and agents of the Central Intelligence Organization were seen at many of the farms, speaking on cell phones and organizing the logistics of the invasions. An enterprising reporter for the *Zimbabwe Independent* got one of the CIO cell phone numbers and called it. He was urged by the CIO agent to show up at the Zanu-PF headquarters in Harare so he could be transported to a plot of land that would become his own.

A press conference was held by Dumiso Dabengwa, minister of Home Affairs in charge of the police. He appeared perplexed by events and uncertain of what his position should be. Dabengwa said the invasions were a legitimate demonstration of the people's anger at the control of so much land by whites, that the struggle against Rhodesia had been fought to win back the people's land. He said he would, however, send police to bring order to the situation, and try to keep the veterans' demonstrations peaceful and lawful. I mused on the irony of Dabengwa, the once proud military leader of Joshua Nkomo's Zapu who was impressively unbowed despite being jailed by Mugabe for seven years without charges, now defending the unlawful actions of Mugabe's supporters. He looked distinctly uncomfortable and refused to answer many of our questions. I could understand why many people from Matabeleland said they had lost respect for Dabengwa. He no longer looked like a leader; he looked like a lackey.

Dabengwa was right to be uneasy. Within a day he was contradicted by a statement from Mugabe, who said that no action could be taken against the war veterans because they were only demonstrating for their right to the land. From then on police refused to offer any protection to the farmers or their workers, saying the problem was a political matter and they could not intervene.

Mugabe, shocked by the no-vote of the constitutional referendum, gave up on Harare, Bulawayo, and the country's other cities as lost to an educated and dissatisfied population who were wise to his rhetoric and other tricks. But he felt he could still win support from the rural areas, where an estimated 70 percent of the population lived. And he felt he could win support by promising them land. It was his trump card.

State television reported that white farmers had bused their workers to polling stations to vote against the referendum en masse. They played over and over again footage of white farmers writing checks out to the new opposition party, the MDC. The state news conveniently omitted the fact that the referendum was defeated by the overwhelming votes against it in the cities, not from the votes in the rural areas.

Of course the land situation had been a festering problem for years. The Rhodesians had systematically stripped the country's blacks of all the best land since 1890. By the time of independence in 1980, nearly half of the commercial farmland reserved for white ownership had been taken from Africans after World War II, when British soldiers had the option to take up choice farms as a reward. Many black Zimbabweans bitterly remember when their families were forcibly removed from their ancestral land and dumped in more arid, rocky land on the edges of the central plateau. Chief Tangwena was battling the Smith regime to retain his people's land in the 1970s.

This had created a bitter resentment among rural Zimbabweans that brought them to support the guerrilla war against Rhodesian minority rule. Robert Mugabe's Zanu-PF fighters promised rural blacks that they would get their land back, and the land issue was the toughest part of the deliberations at the Lancaster House talks in London. It was agreed that redistribution would be achieved through purchase of the white-owned farms on a willing seller–willing buyer basis at market prices. The British government confirmed it would fund a large-scale resettlement program. American observers at the talks also gave verbal assurances that they would grant large sums of money to land reform.

In the first years of independence the land redistribution was impressive. In the first ten years more than fifty thousand families were resettled on 6.5 million acres purchased from whites. The numbers were notable, but the results were mediocre. Most of the projects failed to become productive; the resettled black farmers remained among Zimbabwe's poorest and required continued government assistance years later. The main reason for this was that the government allocated plots on the resettlement project to the most impoverished farmers and the party faithful. Many of these people did not have an aptitude for farming or the burning desire to develop new land. The resettlement would have been more effective if those selected had been farmers who had already succeeded in developing their plots in the marginal communal land where they had been confined by the Rhodesians. These farmers who had a proven track record would be the ones who could make the most of the new land. Another reason for the mixed result of the initial resettlement was that much of the land offered for sale by the white farmers was the more marginal farmland. A further reason was that the resettled farmers did not own the new property but merely held a permit to farm it for five years. Some of the resettlement programs were structured as cooperatives, where many families were to work together on one large farm. These programs were virtually all failures and eventually the government abandoned them altogether. The British government had funded the first round of resettlement and promised more money if the government came up with a more effective approach, but by the end of the 1980s, land redistribution had stalled and there were no new initiatives from government, donors, or white farmers to advance land reform.

The failure to reshape land ownership was hidden by the dramatic success of the agricultural sector. With the arrival of peace and with encouragement from the government, the peasant sector flourished on its old lands. In the Rhodesian era the black farmers were expected to scratch out a meager subsistence and nothing else. They faced difficulties getting seeds and fertilizer and even greater hardships in taking their crops to market. After independence the seeds and fertilizers were readily available and they could even buy on credit. And selling their surplus maize and other crops became much easier thanks to the Grain Marketing Board, which in the early years of independence built up an impressive network of silos across the country.

One morning I had gone out into the "communal areas" with an agricultural adviser from the government's Agritex Department. The government fielded hundreds of Agritex advisers in all areas of the country. We rode on a small motorcycle into the most remote areas, visiting several families. The government adviser explained to them how to prepare their fields, when to plant certain crops, at what time they should do weeding, and what pests to be on the lookout for. He was warmly welcomed by each family, as he visited them a few times each year. Some farmers showed him their first attempt at growing cotton, others their new peanut crop that he had encouraged. He was pleased to see that a young woman had taken his advice to rotate her maize crop to a different field. One older couple was incredibly productive with large, well-tended fields; other farms were more haphazard, but all the farmers were hardworking. I was impressed with what could be produced on crowded, inhospitable land with a bit of training, seeds, and a lot of hard work. I could also see the overcrowding of the communal areas, the land where blacks had been confined by the Rhodesians and where most remained after independence.

The government's help caused production from the peasant sector to skyrocket. From being a negligible contributor to the national maize crop, the small holders regularly contributed up to 60 percent of the national maize harvest. But the output of the peasant sector was entirely dependent upon rainfall. As Zimbabwe is prone to droughts every three or four years, there were often seasons when the harvests of the black farmers were very small and in many areas the crops were a total write-off. In the drought years the commercial farming sector, run by the whites, kicked in and produced enough maize, under irrigation, to feed the entire country and often to have a bit for export, too. The commercial farmers also grew nearly the entire wheat crop and the lion's share of the tobacco.

"Zimbabwe doesn't need more subsistence farmers, we need more productive farmers," I was told by a specialist in agricultural development in the mid-1980s. "Land reform is not just a question of redistributing the land. To be successful there must be considerable training and support to the newly resettled farmers. Agritex has a team of advisers that are the envy of Africa. If we boost the work of Agritex in the process of redistributing land, if we also redevelop the communal areas, the entire country will benefit. And young blacks should be trained to manage large commercial farms. No one wants to stay a peasant farmer, or at least to see their children stay peasant farmers. They want to better their lives."

But instead of continuing and improving upon the good start it had made in land reform, the Mugabe government neglected the situation. It simply left the farmers to carry on. Throughout the 1990s the government largely ignored land redistribution and rural development, and also slowly starved Agritex of funds so that its fleet of motorcycles became grounded for lack of fuel and its skilled advisers sought work elsewhere.

The white farmers meanwhile had enjoyed unparalleled prosperity since 1980. With peace and stability they were able to increase their production and build impressive dams for irrigation. Their wealth could be seen in spanking new four-wheel-drives and Mercedes. It was easy to view these commercial farmers as hangovers from colonialism, profiting from an unjust system, but my visits to commercial farms made me think differently. I saw farmers improving the housing, pay, healthcare, and schooling of their workers. Much more important than the altruistic impulses of some farmers was the sheer economic importance of their output. They employed five hundred thousand workers, the largest source of employment in the country. Tobacco was the country's biggest export, earning the most foreign currency year after year. The maize grown by commercial farmers ensured that the country was self-sufficient in its staple grain in drought years as well as good years. There was no question that substantial land redistribution was needed, but it was crucial that the land reform be carried out in a way that would maintain agricultural productivity.

Whenever Mugabe spoke of land it was with fiery rhetoric at election times. There were halfhearted stabs at forcibly purchasing a handful of farms, but there was no effort to produce a large-scale plan sufficient to address a simmering national problem.

In February 1998 trouble erupted in the central Wedza area, where several thousand peasant farmers streamed onto some prosperous white-owned farms. I drove out there with Mercedes Sayagues and found a group of several hundred people camped out on a rocky hillside. It was a hot, sunny day and most people had found shelter under the trees. They could look across a field where cattle were grazing to the farmer's rambling house and swimming pool, surrounded by a lush garden watered by sprinklers.

There was a carnival atmosphere; several women were boiling water to make *sadza;* others showed us the makeshift shelters they had built and the open areas where others slept. "This is our land now," said a young woman, pointing to the wooden sticks they had used to mark out their various plots. "We will be very happy here. The farmer can stay in his house, we will just grow mealies [maize] here."

They had been organized by Zanu-PF officials from Harare, who transported them to the commercial farms and told them to move onto the fields. "They told us we could have this land and it is very much better than our old land back in Svosve," said our guide.

As we drove along the farm road we saw another stream of people, many barefoot, walking along with bundles of belongings on their heads. We watched them help each other step through a barbed-wire fence and walk into a new field.

The white owners had complained to the police and didn't want to speak to the press. "You can see what the problem is," said the wife. "We are not being aggressive or threatening or trying to chase them away.

We are even providing them with water so there is not a health problem. We are waiting for the police to sort out this problem."

But the local police didn't know what to do. They said they were waiting for instructions from the Mashonaland East provincial governor or from police headquarters in Harare.

The Svosve people stayed on the farms for nearly two months and their claims to the new land received considerable coverage in the state media. Finally they were carted back to their old land, but only after Mugabe promised them they would get new land in time for the next growing season in October.

It all smacked of a stage-managed demonstration to dramatize the need for land reform. Sure enough, a few months later, in September 1998, the government held an international donors' conference for land redistribution. Top officials from Britain, the U.S., the European Union, the United Nations, aid organizations, and many other potential donors flew into Harare to attend the conference. Having become used to an easy ride from the donor community, the government simply made an appeal for more than a billion dollars for land resettlement. Notably absent were any new plans detailing how the new land redistribution would be carried out.

At the conference I spoke to many donors who were unhappy with their recent experiences with the Mugabe government. The British government, for one, conclusively dismissed allegations that they had reneged on their independence pledge to fund land redistribution. They showed that they had donated more than £40 million to Zimbabwe's land redistribution and pointed out that some of that amount had still not been spent. Other donors who had given generously to Zimbabwe in the past told me tales of misallocation of funds, lack of transparency, and the failure of projects. They were also unimpressed with the plan for land redistribution, which was little different from the initial resettlement of 1980, which even the Zimbabwe government accepted had largely failed.

All the donors were also aware of the revelations a year before that three hundred farms compulsorily purchased by the government had not been used for the resettlement of poor black farmers but instead had been doled out to cabinet ministers, army officers, and other party bigwigs.

I sat in the lavish gold and purple conference center, built with state funds, when the government opened the pledging session, where donors were expected to announce grants of millions. There was a pledge of some Chinese tractors but little else. Cabinet ministers attending the meeting were flabbergasted and some even showed anger, warning that the failure of the international community to cough up money would result in violence.

The donors were in no mood to be blackmailed. They responded with a plan drawn up by the United Nations Development Programme for gradual land resettlement based on compensation for white farmers, reduction of poverty of those resettled, and considerable training program. Donors pledged funds for the first stage of nearly four hundred thousand acres and said that, after implementation and monitoring of this stage, they would fund further stages. It was a carefully designed plan that could turn Zimbabwe into one of the world's success stories in the difficult arena of land reform.

But a gradual, tightly monitored, transparent plan was not what the Mugabe government had in mind. A committee meeting of donors and the government, supervised by the UNDP, was to be held within six weeks. The donors met but Mugabe's representatives never showed up. The ambitious UNDP plan never got off the ground because it was not what the truculent Mugabe wanted.

There is more than enough blame to go around all sides in Zimbabwe's land controversy. White farmers refused to accept that large-scale redistribution was needed. Donors who were aware of the simmering problem did not take an early lead in persuading the government to revise and continue with their plans. But the largest share of the blame must be apportioned to the government for losing interest in effective land reform. It only returned to the issue when it thought it could make money or political capital out of it.

When the farm invasions began again in 2000, I viewed them as Mugabe's retribution for his defeat on the constitution and an attempt to drum up rural support in the upcoming elections. I managed to go to a few occupied farms and interview some of the "war veterans." Most were much too young to have fought in the war. They were not poor peasants at all but unemployed youths from the cities, many of whom said they were paid to camp out on the farms. Some told me they did not want land at all; it was jobs they wanted. I never saw them actually doing the hard work of ploughing, planting, and weeding that is farming.

Soon the invasions took an ugly turn. In the Macheke area, about a hundred kilometers east of Harare, a white farmer, David Stevens, and his black farm manager, Julius Angoche, were dragged from their farm and driven away by a group of war veterans. Four white farmers tried to help the men and followed the abductors' truck. When they were fired upon, they went to the nearby police station for safety and to report the kidnapping, but armed war veterans stormed into the police station and hauled them out as police stood by and watched.

The next day all six farmers were still missing. Police said they were looking for them but appeared to be doing very little. Other white farmers meanwhile were mounting a search. After hours of tension, two of the missing farmers were found, bloodied and swollen with bruises, and taken to the local hospital. Although still in shock they insisted on speaking to the press from their hospital beds. They told us that they had been beaten through the night until they were unconscious and left for dead. When they regained consciousness they had managed to untie their bonds and hike through the bush.

Later two more of the farmers were found, and they had an even grimmer story to tell. They, too, had been subjected to vicious beatings for hours. They confirmed that David Stevens and Julius Angoche had been murdered.

Stevens was no ordinary white farmer. He was an idealistic man who believed that independent, majority-ruled Zimbabwe could succeed. He treated his workers well and provided good accommodation and schools for their children. He had been an active member of the MDC because he felt the new party offered all Zimbabweans a better chance. Although the identities of the killers of Stevens and Angoche were well known to the police, no one ever stood trial for the crimes.

On April 18, 2000, the twentieth anniversary of Zimbabwean independence, I was phoned by a farmer in the Nyamandlovu area of Matabeleland North. He told me his neighbor, Martin Olds, was under siege at his farmhouse. Like David Stevens, Olds was not a run-of-the-mill white farmer. He supported a school for orphaned children and worked on other community development projects. He paid and housed his workers well.

Olds had phoned his neighbors to say he was under fire from nearly a hundred "war veterans," but when the neighbors had gone to help, police stopped them at a freshly erected roadblock only a kilometer away from Olds' house. Olds had also called for medical assistance, saying he had been shot in the leg, but when the ambulance arrived the police refused to let it pass.

The farmer who had called me was on his cell phone at the police blockade as a gun battle raged at the Olds' homestead. I alerted other journalists and then called my friend at the police barrier. Normally even-tempered and affable, he was distraught and choking back tears. As the neighboring farmers were held back by police, the invaders had set fire to Olds' house, and when he emerged they had shot him dead. My friend had watched, stunned, as the police permitted the killers, in a convoy of thirteen vehicles, to pass through their barricade and proceed back toward Bulawayo, merely waving at the armed men going by. My friend was threatened with arrest when he shouted at the police to apprehend the men.

This young farmer, like Olds, supported the MDC and had transported his staff to MDC rallies. "These guys are really behind the MDC," he had recently told me about his employees. "They want to go out and attack the war veterans and chase them away, but we have had to restrain them, to avoid violence. I tell you, there is so much support for the MDC they have got to win the elections. People see things clearly. This country will come right soon and then we can all live together." Now, shaken by what amounted to the state-sanctioned killing of his neighbor, he was not confident of anything. "I don't know if we will be able to stay on our farm. I don't know what the future is for Zimbabwe."

Speaking on state television that Independence Day, Mugabe effectively declared war on the white farmers. "Our present state of mind is that you are now our enemies because you really have behaved as enemies of Zimbabwe," said Mugabe. "We are now full of anger. Our entire community is angry and that is why we now have the war veterans seizing land."

In early May another white farmer was killed, in the Beatrice area near Harare. Alan Dunn was watching television with his wife and three teenage daughters when there was a knock at the door. He was dragged a few feet away to the garage, where he was bludgeoned to death by assailants who fled without taking any property. Dunn had been warned of threats against him and had left the property two weeks earlier. He had returned that weekend to pay his workers and to allow his daughters to pack their belongings for the new school term.

At the farm the next day I viewed the blood-spattered walls of the garage, then spoke to his workforce. They were devoted to him because of his fair employment practices and because he had helped nearby communal area farmers by ploughing their fields with his tractor. He was so well respected by the community that they had asked him to run for a seat on the rural council. With solid support from the black community, he won the seat hands-down over the unpopular Zanu-PF candidate. Dunn was also known as a supporter of the MDC.

One of his employees told me, "There were some strangers who came and asked questions. They found out that Mr. Dunn came back to the farm to pay us. I had fear in my heart so I went to Mr. Dunn and I told him to leave. He told me not to worry and now he is dead. I loved Mr. Dunn."

The worker said he had no doubt who killed his employer. "He was killed by Zanu-PF supporters because they knew he backed the MDC. He was a very good man and a very good employer . . . if we had any problems, he helped us. He even helped people on the [government] resettlement scheme by giving them fertilizer and transporting their crops to the market. Now who will give people free transport? The government? I don't think so."

I phoned MDC leader Morgan Tsvangirai for a comment. "It is part of a terror campaign that has been going on for three months," he said. "White farmers who support the MDC are seen as a challenge to Zanu-PF and they are made to pay—some with their lives." I also phoned the war veterans' leader, "Hitler" Hunzvi, who had spear-headed the farm invasions. He was unmoved by Dunn's death. "There is nothing to say. He is dead," he told me. On the day Dunn was mur-dered, Hunzvi made a speech, publicized in the state media, in which he told British passport holders to leave Zimbabwe. "This is not Zimbabwe-Britain. This is Zimbabwe on its own. We are now going to search for those people with British passports and tell them to leave our country. They are not Zimbabweans and they are the ones causing lots of problems."

The government claimed that Dunn's death and the murders of twelve white farmers and thirty black farmworkers were the result of unruly elements that had sprung up from land hunger. But the pattern of these and other murders gave a message with chilling clarity: white farmers who supported the opposition or who challenged Zanu-PF in any way would not just lose their farms, they could lose their lives. By May well over 1,200 white-owned farms had been occupied by Mugabe's supporters.

The white farmers were not the only targets of Mugabe's wrath. On April 15, the day that David Stevens and Julius Angoche were killed in Macheke, two MDC supporters were killed in the Buhera area of eastern Zimbabwe. Talent Mabika and Tichaona Chiminya had been making preparations for a rally at which Morgan Tsvangirai would speak. (Buhera is Tsvangirai's birthplace, and although he could have picked a safe seat in Harare, he decided to run for Parliament in Zanu-PF's rural heartland.) As the two MDC officials were driving with a third person, a vehicle marked ZANU-PF MANICALAND PROVINCE drove up and forced them off the road. Their car was firebombed and Mabika and Chiminya were burned while the third person in the car managed to escape.

Before she died a few hours later in agonizing pain, Ms. Mabika iden-tified her killers. The survivor of the incident confirmed Ms. Mabika's identification, saying that the petrol bombs had been thrown into the car by Joseph Mwale, an agent of the CIO, and Kainos Zimunya, a Zanu-PF official in Buhera. Nearly a year later, as the result of a lawsuit pressed by the MDC, the two accused were summoned to appear in court. Although they were frequently seen in Zimbabwe, they never stood trial.

By mid-May nineteen people—the majority of them black—had been killed in incidents across Zimbabwe and more than a thousand people had been tortured, according to well-documented reports by the Human Rights NGO Forum.

Mugabe's campaign for the June 2000 parliamentary elections was under way.

The contrasting images of these two posters sum up the choice offered to voters in the presidential election in March 2002.
© *Howard Burditt/Reuters*

13

GIVE PEACE A CHANCE

It was an incredible and inspiring time to be in Zimbabwe. With the defeat of Mugabe's constitution and then his backlash with the start of the land invasions, I could observe the forces vying for the country's future. As threats to the independent media increased and violent state repression against the opposition party grew, members of various civic groups decided it was time to make a public stand. A broad coalition of organizations roughly the same as the NCA planned a peace march through central Harare on April 1, 2000.

By the time I arrived that clear, sunny Saturday morning at the Causeway Post Office, just a few blocks from the city center, hundreds of people were tentatively gathering at the corners and in parking lots. They were worried that the highly visible police would arrest them the moment they assembled in the street. At first the police did indeed chase away the marchers, but they regrouped and about a thousand people began moving down Central Avenue.

Banners calling for peace were held aloft. Young people in tie-dyed shirts and peace signs joined the group. Police stopped the group again and arrested about ten people at the front. Those arrested peacefully resisted the police by sitting down in the street, so the police picked them up and carried them to a waiting van as photographers snapped the scene.

The others did not run; they pressed forward. There was a tense standoff for several minutes as the marchers faced a line of police with batons and tear gas canisters at the ready. The riot police appeared to be unnerved by the hundreds of people holding out their open palms and saying, "Peace, peace." Surprisingly, they gave way and the march proceeded toward the center of Harare. At first the procession was very tentative, as the participants expected to be arrested or engulfed by tear gas at any moment. But as the march gathered pace, more and more people joined in from parked cars and street corners. Quickly the march swelled to more than a thousand people and then to more than two thousand. The confidence of the marchers grew and then soared. Saturday morning shoppers cheered them on, as did busloads of travelers.

I walked alongside the march, scribbling down the slogans on the banners and interviewing people as I went. I saw Saturday shoppers stop, puzzled by what was happening, then brightening as they read the banners: GIVE PEACE A CHANCE; TOLERANCE; TRUTH; JUSTICE AND RECONCILIATION. A nun carried a placard reading CRY, MY BELOVED COUNTRY. The peace march grew even larger. I could see gay rights groups carrying rainbow-colored banners; a church group carried a large banner with A SPIRIT OF PEACE. A group of journalists held aloft posters with the faces of Mark Chavunduka and Ray Choto, captioned NO TO TORTURE, YES TO PRESS FREEDOM. As the group marched down the main thoroughfare of Jason Moyo Avenue a group of construction workers building a high-rise office tower shouted their support and waved their hard hats. The oppressive atmosphere that had been building in Zimbabwe seemed to evaporate. A growing elation and confidence that democratic freedoms could be restored to Zimbabwe by public demonstrations like this one swept through the march and the entire city center.

The event was to culminate by marching down First Street, the pleasant pedestrian mall running through the center of the city. By that time the parade had grown to somewhere between four thousand and five thousand people and was marked by a joyful, carnival atmosphere. But the jubilant mood was suddenly shattered. "War vets!" someone shouted. "There are the war veterans." I looked to my right and saw a group of about a hundred people running up Union Avenue toward the peace march.

This was a meeting of the two opposing sides in Zimbabwe: the large, celebrating cross section of society in the peace march and the small, angry, armed band of Mugabe's supporters. The war veterans held a placard that said ZANLA AND ZIPRA—WE ARE BACK! referring to the guerrilla forces of Mugabe and Nkomo in the war against Rhodesia. Many in the group brandished poles, clubs, and iron bars. I was taking notes nearby, and a policeman stood beside me.

All of a sudden I found myself lying on the ground, clutching my head. A large rock of concrete was beside me and I realized it had knocked me down. Stunned, I looked up at the buildings to if see it had fallen from there. As I got unsteadily to my feet there was pandemonium all around me. Rocks were flying and people were screaming. The men with clubs were thumping whomever they could. People who fell to the ground were beaten more severely and blood was spattering on the pavement. The police were nowhere to be seen.

I staggered a few feet and saw a man lying on the ground. I tried to help him up but he was shaking uncontrollably and I realized he was in convulsions. I ran into a nearby shop and asked somebody to call an ambulance. Back on the street others tried to give first aid to the man. People were milling about, many with bloodied faces and hands. I interviewed a few people about what had happened but everyone seemed as confused as I was. I realized my face was bloody, too, from where the rock had hit me. There was still no sign of the police.

"Come here," shouted a young black man, taking my arm. "The war vets are coming back here and they want to kill you." He led me to a parking lot and hid me behind some cars. "Don't let them see you, keep your head down. They are going after whites."

Sure enough, I heard the war veterans shouting, *"Hondo! Hondo!"* ("War! War!") and more pandemonium. Crouched behind the car, I could see their feet running by. In those terrifying minutes I wondered what had happened to the Zimbabwe that had promised freedom and liberation. As if to counterbalance my despair over the destruction of Zimbabwe's multiracial democracy, the young man came back to give me further assistance. "I've got my car, I can get you out of here," he said. As he drove me back to my own car, I found out that he was a computer programer who worked for a big firm in town. "I was just shopping in town and then I was enjoying the march when I saw the war veterans come. They were attacking all the whites. I saw they were coming back so that is why I helped you. We have all got to fight this. It is no good."

Back at home I was immensely relieved to find Dolores already there. She had been in a different part of town and had hidden in the entrance to a big shop when the war vets came by. I filed a story about the ill-fated peace march to the *Observer*. And then my phone began ringing. CNN, Sky News, BBC, Radio France International, Radio New Zealand all wanted to interview me about the violence at the peace march.

"Why are you giving so many interviews? Haven't you done enough?" asked Dolores. I realized that I still had blood on my face. But I wanted the world to know exactly what had happened. If anyone called me, I wanted to tell them what had taken place.

Dozens of people were injured that day, many with broken bones and requiring hospitalization. The man I had seen convulsing in the road was in a coma for three days but eventually recovered. Other journalists had followed the war veterans back to the headquarters of Mugabe's Zanu-PF party; earlier some had filmed the gang arming themselves with the bars, poles, and rocks before attacking the march. Despite photographs in the privately owned press that clearly identified many of the perpetrators, no one was ever arrested.

A week after the peace march, with bruises and scabs still on my face from the attack, I went to the war veterans' headquarters to interview their leader, "Hitler" Hunzvi, to record his justification for the violence. In the waiting room, a newspaper photograph showed the war veterans brandishing iron bars and poles on their way to attack the peace march. "Don't go to any demonstrations like that again or you will be killed," said Hunzvi with a sinister snigger. "We will kill you. You look like a white farmer and they are our enemy."

He told me the war veterans would stamp out any opposition to Mugabe. They would seize all the white-owned farms in the country and they would not be afraid to use violence against anyone who dared to protest against Mugabe. "All this opposition, it is just coming from the whites. They are paying money to make this opposition, so we will stamp it out. They have no place in Zimbabwe."

It was a rambling interview, with Hunzvi going off the point of my questions to give his twisted version of history, mostly blaming whites for every problem facing the country. This burning resentment against whites seemed to be his driving force, despite the fact that he had been married to a white Polish woman with whom he produced two sons. (She complained that he beat her frequently and she eventually fled Zimbabwe.)

Hunzvi veered from talking softly in a high-pitched, almost childish voice to shouting fiercely. He was polite but with a sarcastic tone that suggested he despised me. As we parted, he wagged his finger at me and said, "Don't forget what I told you. Be careful where you go or we will get you."

It was hard to believe that this volatile, dangerous man, seething with anger and malevolence, was one of the most powerful men in Zimbabwe. I looked around the streets milling with black Zimbabweans and wondered if many of them shared Hunzvi's bitterness. From their smiles and greetings to me, it did not seem so. And I remembered the assistance given to me by the young black man after I had been attacked at the peace march. I could only conclude that Mugabe, Hunzvi, and their supporters were trying to stoke the fires of antiwhite sentiment among the population. I could not believe they would succeed.

Reporters for the *Zimbabwe Independent* protest against the bombing of the *Daily News* in February 2000. The peaceful gathering was dispersed by some two hundred riot police with tear gas and truncheons. © *Howard Burditt/Reuters*

14

AN ACCEPTABLE LEVEL
OF VIOLENCE

"Mataga is the place to go," Mercedes said to me with characteristic determination. "There's a lot of violence there, a lot of intimidation, and yet the opposition is putting up a spirited stand. That is the place to go to cover the election."

The government was not in a strong position as it went into the June 2000 parliamentary elections. The economy had faltered and unemployment was growing. Inflation was up and previously comfortable families had cut back considerably. Many working families could afford to have meat only once a week; the land invasions had not created the outpouring of enthusiasm that the government had hoped for; the Congo war was unpopular. Worst of all, there was a serious fuel shortage, forcing motorists of all colors, shapes, and sizes to wait in lines for hours at service stations. Everyone knew it was because the government was sending all the fuel to Congo and had not paid its oil bills to Libya and Kuwait over the past year. The violence throughout Zimbabwe, far from intimidating people, only seemed to increase their outrage. They were still excited about the defeat handed to Mugabe in the constitutional referendum and were confident Zanu-PF could be beaten in the elections.

Mataga's location in the center of the Mberengwa East constituency is extremely remote: it would take seven hours just to get to Zvishavane, the nearest big town, and from there the drive was on dirt roads. Worse, for a journalist filing for a daily paper, it was out of cell phone range. But Mercedes had a point. The stories coming out of Mataga were strong.

The MDC candidate there, Sekai Holland, was outspoken and indomitable. I had known her for many years as the leader of the Association

163

of Women's Clubs, a network of organizations in rural areas that Holland had forged into a vocal pressure group. The government had tried to mute its criticisms by using new legislation to take over the association's board. Holland had taken the government to court, and after a long, drawn-out legal battle, the supreme court had ruled that the Association of Women's Clubs had the right to continue as an independent organization. It also struck down the clause in the legislation which gave the government the power to take over the boards of charitable organizations, an important legal victory not only for Holland's organization but for all civic groups critical of the government. She was also a founding member of the MDC. Now she was running for Parliament in her home area, where she had spearheaded a great deal of community development work.

Violence was a major part of the Zanu-PF campaign against her. She was chased out of the area three times, but she kept returning. A refuge she had built for victims of violence was attacked and burned down by the Zanu-PF youth militia, yet Holland kept coming back and drawing large crowds of support in the area.

There were no white-owned farms around Mataga, which meant I would be able to write about the contest between Zanu-PF and the MDC without it being dominated by the issue of the farm invasions. Although I had written about the controversial land issue, I was more concerned with the government's efforts to strangle the new opposition party. Mugabe wanted the world to read the conflict in Zimbabwe as one between white farmers and blacks. He wanted to appear on the world stage as the great African radical who rid Zimbabwe of the last vestige of white colonial rule. I hoped that a firsthand account of what was happening in Mataga would expose the government's vicious campaign of violence and torture against the opposition.

We met Sekai Holland in Harare the night before we left to visit her constituency. Big, brash, and indomitable, she regaled us with stories of how she had been threatened and how her supporters had been beaten. The stories spilled out in a jumble, each one told as if it were a thrilling adventure rather than evidence of state violence and intimidation. "Zanu-PF knew that people support me so they nominated my uncle, Rugare Gumbo, to stand against me! They are trying to start a family feud! But they won't stop me!"

Mercedes and I and Victor Mallet of the *Financial Times* set out for Mataga early the next morning. The drive was very long indeed. We pulled into the old mining town of Zvishavane at 6 P.M. and found rooms at the Hotel Nilton, whose bright yellow and white paint highlighted the building's stylish art deco design. The faded hotel was enjoying a miniboom when we arrived, having become the base for many international officials who were observing the election process.

The news we picked up over beers in the bar was not good. There was such heavy intimidation in Mataga, the observers told us, that they did not feel safe to travel there. They said they would not travel to Mataga until they had a satellite phone to ensure communications at all times. The road was bad and only four-wheel-drive vehicles could make it, but we were in a small passenger car. "We *must* go there," said Mercedes. We headed out for Mataga at the crack of dawn.

The dirt road was very rough and again and again our small car had to slow down to a snail's pace as we picked our way around boulders and maneuvered over parts of the road that had washed away. At one point we came to a complete stop. It appeared that the road had ended, but we pushed our way through what looked like a narrow footpath and found it again. As we traveled, we saw spray-painted signs for the MDC and several posters for Zanu-PF tied to trees.

Eventually we pulled into Mataga, which at first glance appeared to be a pleasant settlement of small shops and a post office. A closer look indicated that things were not right. There was very little activity in what should have been a busy marketplace. Several of the shops were burned-out shells, with doors torn off their hinges and shattered windows. Two had smoke drifting up from them, indicating they had been attacked very recently.

We went to the post office to ask where we could find a particular church leader who had been recommended to us. Before we could get to the counter, we were surrounded by a gang of young hoods who demanded to know what we were doing in Mataga. We explained that we were journalists observing the election campaign. They did not like the sound of that. Despite our protestations they moved closer to us and started to push us.

We jumped back into our car and drove up to some of the vandalized shops, which had been thoroughly looted, with everything stripped from the shelves. We asked two young women sitting on the ground outside what had happened. Their faces full of fear, they just looked at us and shook their heads. A truck roared by with some of the young men from the post office. One pulled a machete dramatically across his neck and then pointed it at us. The truck circled around and came closer, and again the machete-wielding man made his threatening gesture. When they drove by a third time the young women ran away.

A man whose butchery had been destroyed began to explain what had happened in the past few days, but then the truck of toughs came by and threatened him. We realized that anyone who spoke to us would be at risk.

We drove over to the police station, on top of the hill behind the shops, to see if we could get an official explanation of the terror in the town and to find out what they were trying to do to control it. As we went in to see the officer in charge, one of the young men who had threatened us came out, chatting amiably with a policeman. The officer in charge laughed when we described what had happened. "This is election time and those young boys are just campaigning. They can be a bit rough," he said.

We asked if there had been any trouble or violence in the town and he said no. When we pointed out the burned and looted shops within sight of his office, he dismissed it as just some electioneering, but not a serious problem. We asked if anyone had been injured or killed. "No, no, nothing like that. Everything is peaceful." When we insisted there were reports of people being beaten and tortured, he became stern in his denials. He said we should be careful because many people in Mataga would be angered by our questions. There was a malevolent air at the police station.

"You are the police, you should be guaranteeing our safety to work here," said Mercedes. The officer became more threatening and said we should leave town immediately.

Our suspicions would prove to be well founded. Some time later I interviewed a police officer who had fled Mataga because he could not stomach what was going on. He told me that a young man caught wearing an MDC T-shirt had been beaten to death by police in that very station just a few days before our visit, and many others had been tortured there. He gave me a detailed description of how the police had been infiltrated by agents of the CIO. The police station was the base from which the Zanu-PF youth militia launched attacks throughout the constituency.

It was obvious that the town was under siege and that no free campaigning was possible. We could find no sign of any MDC supporters, or even people who would talk freely about the situation in the town. We decided to leave right away, but as we headed out of town we were confronted by a roadblock. There were no uniformed officers, just a rough gang. A young man with bloodshot eyes leaned in the driver's window and demanded to know what we were doing. He shouted at us to get out and reached in to grab the keys. Victor replied coolly, "You have no authority to give us orders." He pushed the guy out of the window and hit the gas. We charged through the roadblock as rocks were thrown at us from all sides. It was a relief to see Mataga recede behind us in a cloud of dust.

The yellow Hotel Nilton was a cheering sight when we got back to Zvishavane, but there was little chance to catch our breath. Almost immediately we were approached by a young man who had heard we were journalists and wanted to tell us about MDC polling agents being attacked by war veterans. He gave us directions to a house that he said was full of MDC refugees from Mataga and other places in the constituency.

At the house we found clusters of ten and twenty people huddled around fires at the back. Inside, the kitchen was full of people and the living room held yet more. We could see from bundles of clothes and possessions that these people were staying in the house, which was so full that some had to sleep outside. These were the owners of the burned-out shops we had seen in Mataga and leaders of community groups who had been attacked as opposition supporters. The situation was desperate. More than sixty people were crammed onto the property. Although everyone was valiantly trying to keep their spirits up, it was clear they were under threat and very frightened.

One very articulate young man who had just completed a course to be a polling agent for Sekai Holland told me: "I was traveling back to Mataga with other agents on the bus, but then the bus stopped and a group of Zanu-PF youth militia got on the bus. They grabbed us and dragged us off the bus. They took us to Texas Ranch and beat us. Some were taken away and even today I don't know where they are." A large wound cut across his forehead and his hand was bandaged. (According to several accounts, Texas Ranch was a center for the local war veterans, where they tortured people suspected of supporting the opposition. It was a farm abandoned several years before which had now been taken over by a veteran named Biggie Chitoro.)

"I managed to run away into the bush and made my way back here. I want to help make these elections to be good, but there is so much violence," he said. "We do not even feel safe here in Zvishavane. Some of us have been attacked when walking from town to this house. Zanu-PF youths have come and shouted at this house. We have all lost our homes and we don't know where to go."

Next we interviewed nurses who had worked at the district hospital. They had been beaten by Biggie Chitoro for giving medical treatment to some of his victims and fled the hospital when police refused to protect them. We were told one of the victims of Chitoro's torture was at the Zvishavane hospital.

The following morning we went to the hospital and applied to see the tortured patient. The medical staff were worried that their hospital would be attacked. In Mataga and other hospitals that treated victims of state violence, wards were raided by war veterans and youth militia. Victims had been dragged from their beds and beaten yet again.

The Zvishavane hospital was like many others I had visited in the provinces. It was spotlessly clean and smelled of disinfectant; the nurses' uniforms were clean but very worn. The large wards were cheerful, with lots of windows giving plenty of light, but full to bursting with rows of beds holding patients with complaints ranging from broken arms and legs and head wounds to malaria and other fevers. On closer inspection we learned that drugs were in such short supply that even basic painkillers and antibiotics were restricted to the most desperate cases. Most others had to simply lie in their beds and hope for recuperation.

Eventually we were taken to see James Zhou. We were met by the horrific sight of the severely injured man lying facedown on the bed. His injuries were among the most appalling I have ever seen. His backless hospital gown revealed two gaping bloody craters where his buttocks should have been. He had burns, cuts, and bruises everywhere on his body, but his backside had been completely flayed off.

In a whisper he told us how his brother, Finos, had been nominated the MDC candidate for the Mberengwa West constituency. James and Finos had been abducted by Biggie Chitoro and taken to Texas Ranch. They were stripped and beaten for two nights. He was beaten repeatedly on his buttocks and burned by flaming plastic bags dripped onto his body. He was beaten with an iron bar over and over again. He told us in excruciating detail how his brother had been tortured and then died. Somehow James managed to crawl through the bush to safety. "Politics is a dirty business," he said in a quivering voice.

I asked if I could photograph his injuries and he agreed. My photos were so shocking that they were never used by the *Guardian* or the *Observer*, but I was able to give them to lawyers for use in the trial of Zhou's torturers.

Two men arrived at the bed and James burst into tears. They were his surviving brothers. "Please write the story of what has happened here to our brothers," said the oldest. "We want the world to know what is going on here."

We left the hospital and began the long drive back to Harare. The atmosphere in our car was one of shock and disbelief. Our experience of the violent oppression against the opposition party was even more sobering than we had expected. To see people struggling to uphold the basic standards needed for democratic elections in the face of omnipresent state violence was humbling. To chronicle what we had witnessed was not just a good story; it was our duty.

We arrived back in Harare to find Don McKinnon, the new secretary-general of the Commonwealth and former foreign minister of New

Zealand, in town as part of a tour of African members of the Common-wealth. Both local and foreign reporters gathered at State House for a press conference with McKinnon and Zimbabwe's foreign minister, Stan Mudenge.

McKinnon is a big, bluff ex–rugby player with a hearty, hail-fellow-well-met demeanor. He was selected for the Commonwealth's top executive position because of his friendly relations with virtually all member nations from his days as New Zealand's foreign minister and his support for the antiapartheid movement. He came to Zim-babwe, within weeks of taking office, to pave the way for a Common-wealth observer mission to attend the controversial parliamentary elections. He did not come prepared for a confrontation with Mugabe.

Mugabe kept McKinnon waiting for their meeting until the last minute, and beyond. McKinnon was forced to wait at State House past the time his flight was scheduled to leave Harare. I had seen Mugabe force other officials to cool their heels for him when he anticipated that he would not like their message, notably United States secretary of state Madeleine Albright, who also had to wait when her flight was scheduled to leave. McKinnon was forced to wait for more than an hour before Mugabe finally arrived.

The press corps waited, too, on the wide veranda of State House. In front of us were the carefully manicured rose gardens and lush lawns that looked much as they must have in the colonial era. Two stuffed lions flanked the red carpet leading to the front entrance; they were im-pressive in size but very moth-eaten and had clearly seen better days, even as trophies. The atmosphere of a bygone time continued in the gracious building's expansive front room, where the press conference would be held. The oriental carpets, the porcelain in display cabinets, and the brocade curtains created a thoroughly European atmosphere, with only the ubiquitous framed photograph of Robert Mugabe in the center to remind us that we were in Africa.

There was an air of expectancy amongst the journalists. As well as the state violence in Mataga, two MDC suppoters had been murdered in Kariba and scores brutally tortured. These atrocities had been well docu-mented. A report by the local Human Rights Forum confirmed nineteen killings. We knew that McKinnon had been briefed on all this by human rights organizations and by the MDC. As he was the chief executive of the Commonwealth, the organization of fifty-four former British colonies which promotes democracy among its members, we felt he was bound to denounce the election violence and pressure Mugabe to stop it.

But McKinnon and Mudenge emerged all smiles, arm in arm. McKinnon announced that Mugabe had agreed that the Commonwealth could send a team to observe the elections. After the short statement the questions came fast and furious.

"Mr. McKinnon, there are numerous reports of state violence against the opposition. Several people have been killed. Is this acceptable in democratic elections in a Commonwealth member?" asked Victor Mallet.

"There is no state violence, none at all. That is not true," interjected Mudenge before McKinnon could answer.

Then, attempting to calm the situation, McKinnon said, "President Mugabe told me that he would like to see the violence decrease. He assured me that violence will be kept to an acceptable level for the rest of the campaign."

David Blair of the *Telegraph* asked, "Mr. McKinnon, with so many reports of violence, do you believe free and fair elections are possible in Zimbabwe?"

"I believe it is possible to have free and fair elections. That is why I came here," said McKinnon. "There are obviously some concerns and we need to see the violence reduced."

Mudenge interrupted again, saying, "There are countries where more than nineteen people have been killed, such as South Africa, and they have held free elections."

Grant Ferrett of the BBC asked, "Mr. Mudenge, when will the Zimbabwe government restore the rule of law in Zimbabwe?"

Mudenge responded with a look of mock astonishment. "We have always observed the rule of law in Zimbabwe. There has been no breakdown in the rule of law in this country whatsoever," he said.

The press corps erupted in spontaneous laughter at the outrageous assertion and Mudenge's ham acting.

Mercedes stepped up. "Mr. Mudenge, I have just returned from Mataga where I interviewed several victims of torture and saw their injuries. They name the perpetrators of this violence, yet no action is being taken to arrest them or to protect the victims. What action is being taken by your government to stop this violence?"

"I am not aware of any charges of torture," said Mudenge. "These are fictitious stories. Tell any so-called victims to report their allegations to the police."

At that Mercedes, incandescent with outrage, retorted, "The police stations are exactly where people say they were tortured!"

"Nonsense! Rubbish!" shouted Mudenge, and stomped angrily away from the press conference, taking a visibly flummoxed McKinnon with him.

I had been planning to ask McKinnon: "What is the acceptable number of killings in a democratic election?" but the press conference ended so abruptly that I did not get my chance.

This was a key point when the international community could have put public pressure on the Mugabe government to stop political violence and to hold the elections under free and fair conditions. But the crucial moment had been lost.

The violence did not abate during the election campaign. It only increased. Virtually every constituency reported beatings, torture, and murders by Zanu-PF war veterans, youth brigades, CIO agents, and police. Teachers were targeted because they were community leaders and, as educated people, were suspected of supporting the opposition. One schoolteacher caught reading a copy of the independent *Daily News* was beaten to death.

I was amazed by the resilience of so many of the people that I interviewed, and how many people firmly believed that a change for the better was within their reach and were willing to risk attack to bring that about. Despite the horrors there was a feeling that it was the government that was desperate, that it was lashing out because it was afraid of losing. There was a courageous optimism that the will of the people would triumph. To me, this was the best of Zimbabwe. It was the determined struggle for democracy that had initially attracted me to the country, and now I saw the people's will in action. It was inspiring.

The MDC valiantly continued campaigning in every constituency, even though many candidates and officials had to go into hiding. "We can do it, we can vote for change," said Mavis after attending an MDC rally. "*Chinja maitiro!* We will succeed. They can't stop us!"

I myself went to several rallies, in Harare and in outlying areas. The Zanu-PF rallies were depressing affairs, with Mugabe and cabinet ministers waving fists and shouting angry, hateful speeches to listless crowds that had been forced to attend. Grace Mugabe sat with her husband at one, playing with her gold sunglasses and not even attempting to disguise the contemptuous look on her face. I watched cabinet ministers whom I had previously respected, men and women with masters and doctorates from prestigious institutions in Britain and the United States, incite violence against opposition supporters.

The MDC rallies were a dramatic contrast. People walked for miles despite the constant threat of attacks by war veterans. The singing and dancing was spontaneous and full of joy. A popular speaker was young Tawanda Spicer, the teenage son of our friends Newton and Edwina Spicer. He was fluent in Shona and spoke with the fervent conviction of youth. Another man imitated a well-known sports announcer and recounted the election campaign as if it were a horse race. His voice grew higher and louder as he got to the end: "It's very close," he would say in Shona. "Zanu-PF has all the advantages. They are trying to push down the MDC. But the MDC is still running, it is pulling even, and now getting ahead. The MDC wins!" And everyone would laugh and cheer. These rallies were overwhelmingly black, both speakers and audience, but the whites who attended spoke Shona and interacted well with everyone. Zimbabwe had come a long way from the days of the bitter white Rhodesians. The air of celebration at the MDC rallies never failed to lift my spirits.

Mercedes and I persuaded some other journalists to return to Mataga with us. Although I did not relish the prospect of being threatened again, it was vital for us to see how voting was conducted in Mataga. It would be a good indication of how fair the elections were.

Once again we drove for hours up and down the twisting, turning, hilly roads to reach the friendly sight of the Hotel Nilton. We fell into our beds, and at first light we headed off for Mataga. Once again there was very little activity in the market town, but at a community hall we found a line of a few hundred voters waiting to cast their ballots. As fully accredited journalists we had the right to go in and watch the polling and speak to election officials and polling agents, who said everything had been going peacefully. Yet we saw that many people were visibly nervous and afraid to speak to us.

Back outside we interviewed the Zanu-PF candidate for the area, Rugare Gumbo. "No, no, there has not been any violence here, this has been a peaceful campaign," he said in response to our questions, as smooth as any politician anywhere.

We confronted him with the burned-out stores and the dozens of people who had fled Mataga with injuries. We told him about the killing of Finos Zhou and the gruesome torture of his brother. We asked him why his supporters had repeatedly prevented his opponent, Sekai Holland, from campaigning in the area.

"Well, maybe a few of my young supporters have been over-enthusiastic in their campaigning," said Gumbo suavely. "I try to restrain them. But some of these stories you have, they have been told by trouble-makers who just want to discredit me and the ruling party."

When we told him we had evidence of the violence, he just smiled and walked away.

In the polling station, young men in the green military-style uniforms of Mugabe's youth militia were following voters behind the screen where they would mark and cast their ballots. Officials were situated so they could see behind the screens and have a clear view of those voting.

We noticed a group of men standing by the entrance. One big man wore a black cowboy hat, a black leather waistcoat, jeans, and black cowboy boots. He looked like a bad guy ready for a shoot-out at the O.K. Corral, except that sheathed daggers instead of pistols in holsters dangled from his studded belt. As he swaggered in and out of the polling station we could see officials and voters cowering.

Mercedes immediately marched over to an official to point out that the man was illegally loitering near the voting booths. "Why is this man loitering here?" she demanded. "He is not a polling official and has no business here. He should not be here."

The obviously frightened official took Mercedes over to the man in black and left it to her to lodge the complaint. The man said he was helping an elderly person vote, which was one of the specified reasons that a person could go into a polling station. Mercedes wanted to see who he was assisting. He said she could not tell him what to do. She responded that she was a journalist accredited by the government to see if all was proper at the polling stations. She said she would report him to the observers if he did not leave.

I asked someone nearby who the big man was. "That is Chitoro," he whispered nervously. "Biggie Chitoro." Here was the man who had led the terror campaign in the area, the man identified as having killed Finos Zhou and torturing his brother James so horrifically. It was he who had taken over the Texas Ranch and turned it into a center for beatings and torture. My blood ran cold.

I called Mercedes over and warned her the man she was haranguing was the notorious Biggie Chitoro. Chitoro then left the polling station and slowly sauntered past the line of voters, giving each one a threatening look and pointing at some. The intimidation was palpable. He climbed into a flashy yellow pickup truck with ZANU-PF emblazoned in big letters on the side. A posse of young men jumped in the back.

We ran up to the truck and began asking him questions about Texas Ranch, about the violence in Mataga, about the Zhou brothers. He laughed and denied everything. He said it was actually the MDC who had inflicted violence on the ruling party. He told us we did not understand elections in Africa and drove off in a cloud of dust.

We followed Chitoro and his gang and watched as he went to another polling station at a school. He told us to go away, and we said the same to him. Chitoro then went to a nearby hospital, and took us to a man with a big stitched cut across his head. He claimed the man had been attacked by the MDC, but when we interviewed him he gave a vague story that contradicted Chitoro's version.

Chitoro drove off in the Zanu-PF truck. We stayed behind and were told by hospital staff that they had treated many people with injuries inflicted by Zanu-PF, but none who had been beaten by the MDC. They explained how frightened they were of Chitoro as he had beaten up doctors and nurses at another hospital for treating MDC supporters. The black-hatted cowboy had terrorized the area.

We drove back to Harare with firsthand evidence that Zanu-PF officials were interfering with voting and that people identified as committing torture and murder were not even being questioned by police. Other journalists and international observers reported similar incidents in other constituencies. Whatever the results, the elections could not be considered free and fair.

When it came to the finish line, the results were very close. Of the 120 elected seats, Mugabe's Zanu-PF won 62 and the MDC 57. Another opposition party won one seat. Despite all the intimidation, violence, and murder, Mugabe's party came within a hair's breadth of losing a majority of the elected seats. Mugabe, however, was bolstered by the fact that he could personally appoint thirty members of Parliament, which then gave his party a larger majority: 92 of the total 150 seats.

In Harare, MDC candidates won landslide victories, with majorities of nearly 80 percent. In Bulawayo and the Matabeleland countryside people also voted overwhelmingly for the MDC. Zanu-PF won, by much smaller margins, in rural Shona constituencies. The MDC had proved itself to be a truly national party, winning in almost all urban areas and many rural ones. The MDC had support from both Shona and Ndebele populations as well as from whites. In contrast, Zanu-PF was exposed as a party with support limited to rural Shona constituencies.

Zimbabweans of all walks of life were dejected. They could not believe that Zanu-PF had managed to stay in power. So many people had faith that Mugabe would be voted out, just as the referendum had been defeated a few months earlier. A bitterness and depression that I had not felt during the campaign settled over Harare.

The Commonwealth observer mission, led by former Nigerian leader General Abdusalami Abubakar, had watched the elections in all parts of the country. Forty of its representatives from African, Asian, and Caribbean states regrouped in Harare to report on their findings. They judged that the elections had been "disfigured" by widespread state violence. The European Union delegation categorically rejected the elections as "not free and fair." But neighboring South Africa, which also sent an observer mission, found that the elections had been fair, a judgment that overlooked so many obvious problems that it was clearly dictated from Pretoria. President Thabo Mbeki's government was unwilling to criticize Mugabe, a fellow leader of a liberation struggle to end white minority rule.

The MDC was despondent, but slowly, in the weeks that followed, the party made the best of the situation. Against all odds, the nine-month-old party had done very well to win fifty-seven parliamentary seats. Previously there had only been two opposition seats in Parliament, so the new presence of such a large opposition would change the whole tenor of the assembly. Some new MDC M.P.s told me they hoped that some Zanu-PF M.P.s would cross the floor to vote with them. Committed to peaceful, democratic change, MDC leaders said they would press for their legal rights through the court system. They were still confident they could compel the system to respond fairly.

"We will take Zanu-PF to the courts to challenge their victories in more than thirty constituencies," Morgan Tsvangirai told me a few days after the election results came out. "We have documented evidence of violence, of manipulation of the voters' roll, and of irregularities during voting and counting. We are confident the courts will overturn many of the Zanu-PF victories and through that we can gain a majority in Parliament. Until then our M.P.s will challenge the government in Parliament and hold it accountable for its actions."

Tsvangirai had lost his seat in Buhera; the grisly evidence of the murders of Talent Mabika and Tichaona Chiminya would form part of his court challenge. "We are disappointed, yes," said Tsvangirai. "But we have not given up, not at all. We are determined to use the legal system to stand up for our rights and for the democratic rights of all Zimbabweans."

Public opinion generally matched the opposition party's reaction. "We can't believe that the MDC lost. We know that Zanu-PF cheated. The beatings and the torture and the murder was terrible and everybody knows it," said Mavis one evening. She also reported what people were saying on the commuter vans. "People are upset that the MDC did not get a majority in Parliament because they really hoped that we would give Mugabe the red card and send him away," said Mavis. "But some people are saying that with good M.P.s, maybe that will make things better. Zanu-PF won't be able to continue running this country however they want." People still had faith that things would improve.

Journalistic colleague and great friend Mercedes Sayagues watches her nine-year-old daughter, Esmeralda, bid farewell to their nanny, Christine Chinake, who had helped raise her since she was a baby. Mercedes was expelled from Zimbabwe in February 2002. © *Howard Burditt/Reuters*

15

TARGETING THE PRESS

As Mavis predicted, Zimbabwean public opinion bounced back. Not cowed by the barrage of state violence, a wide cross section of the people responded with a defiant determination to resist Mugabe and Zanu-PF and demand democracy and good government.

I was surprised and encouraged by this response, which I witnessed throughout Zimbabwe, from my local grocery store to a rural homestead. Once I was stopped at a roadblock and a policeman noticed some MDC literature that I had picked up at a rally. He nodded and said, "We will win in the end."

When the new Parliament opened, several thousand MDC supporters gathered in front of the House of Assembly in Africa Unity Square to welcome their new M.P.s. The large turnout caught the police and Zanu-PF by surprise. Mugabe and his wife, arriving in a vintage open-topped Rolls-Royce, at first waved to the crowds, until they realized they were being greeted by jeers and hoots of derision. A bunch of young people began singing a lusty song which alleged that Grace's children were fathered by a local businessman, Peter Pamire. Mugabe looked straight ahead with a stony expression on his face; he had never endured such public humiliation.

Inside Parliament the fifty-seven MDC M.P.s wore black armbands in mourning for all those who had died during the election campaign. The night before, they had boycotted the reception Mugabe traditionally held for the newly elected Parliament.

By the time Mavis returned from work that day she had already heard about the insults hurled at Mugabe at the opening of Parliament, even about the ribald song questioning Mugabe's paternity. "It's a rumor

181

that's been spreading around Harare for some time, but I don't think it's true," she told me. The businessman in question later died in a suspicious accident in which investigators found that the brakes of his new car had been tampered with.

Mavis's reports from the commuter vans were always a great help to me in assessing the public mood. "Guess what people said today about Muzenda?" she asked one day, referring to Mugabe's senior vice president, Simon Muzenda, who was known for his halting speech and simple views. "They poke such fun at him, saying he is rough and thick. It's cruel but it's funny. One joke is that Muzenda is with his girlfriend when his wife phones him on his cell phone. He is very surprised and blurts out, "How did you know I was here?" Oh, everyone on the taxi laughed and laughed at that one."

Sometimes, when I was working on a story, I would ask Mavis to sound out opinion on the vans about specific issues like land or the economy. She excelled at these assignments and would come back with a range of colorful, pithy opinions. She could also give me insights into what people were thinking in the rural areas because she often visited her mother, Milka, who was now well over eighty-five and still working her maizefields with a *badza* (hoe). We sent her packages of sugar, biscuits, and other treats, and Mavis made sure she always had good supplies of seeds and fertilizer. We called her "Ambuya" (Grandmother). She came to visit us during seasonal breaks but she never stayed long, because she always wanted to get back to her fields. Once when we were enjoying one of Mavis's special chicken and *sadza* meals together there was a light shower of rain. Ambuya Milka became very agitated, jumped up from the table and paced the room. She said she could smell what the precipitation was doing to the earth and she wanted to be ready to weed her fields. She left before dawn the next morning.

Although Mugabe posed as the champion of Zimbabwe's black subsistence farmers by seizing white farms, his rhetoric rang very hollow with the actual farmers, like Milka. At the same time as the government was grabbing land, it was neglecting the peasant farming sector. There were inadequate supplies of seeds, and fertilizer became virtually unavailable. I heard how farmers who sold their surplus maize to the state giant, the Grain Marketing Board, which was by now badly in debt and racked by numerous corruption scandals, were not paid for months. Previously the board had paid farmers promptly, but in 2000 many farmers did not get paid until November, when the seasonal rains had already begun—much too late to purchase the seeds needed to get a crop in the field. The Agritex advisers, who had assisted scores of thousands of peasant farmers, had virtually ceased their visits because their department was starved of funding. An agricultural network that was the pride of Africa slid into disuse.

By neglecting the subsistence agricultural sector and at the same time violently dismantling the white-owned commercial sector, the Mugabe government ensured that Zimbabwe would suffer widespread shortages of staple foods. Patchy rains were another negative, but not decisive, factor.

Ambuya Milka worked hard, but like most other farmers in 2000, she did not harvest enough maize for her needs. She went to a local meeting where the government was distributing food aid. She had to sit all morning at this meeting singing Zanu-PF songs and listening to long speeches about Robert Mugabe. At midday she stood up and said she wanted her maize so she could go home and continue her work. The Zanu-PF official said she must stay and praise Robert Mugabe for the maize. Ambuya Milka dismissed him, saying, "It is not a gift from Robert Mugabe. He did not pay for it. It comes from the taxes that my sons and daughters who work in the city are paying. That is where this maize comes from." She took a bag of maize and marched off.

When Mavis told me this story, I expressed concern for her mother's safety. "Don't worry," she said. "My mother has always been this way. Everyone knows her. She is respected."

Because of what I heard from Mavis, Milka, and other grass roots contacts, I was not surprised when a national opinion poll revealed the divisions in the country. The poll, expertly conducted by the Helen Suzman Foundation of South Africa, interviewed a wide cross section of Zimbabweans from both the urban and rural areas, from Harare and Bulawayo and Matabeleland. Nearly 70 percent of those polled said they wanted to see change in the country. Mugabe and Zanu-PF had the support of about 30 percent, but these people represented the least educated, least skilled, and poorest segment of the population. The majority thought corruption and inflation were the biggest problems in Zimbabwe. They did not rate white ownership of farms, or whites themselves, as significant problems.

The poll also suggested that the parliamentary elections had been rigged. In most areas the poll results corresponded with the election results, but in some constituencies the poll findings were dramatically divergent from the voting results, which made the votes for Zanu-PF suspect.

The poll findings were widely covered in the independent press, particularly the *Daily News*, which had gone from strength to strength in Harare. In a few years it had reached a circulation of more than a hundred thousand, while the state-owned *Herald* watched its readership inexorably dwindle. This infuriated public relations supremo Jonathan Moyo, who, despite stage-managing the losing constitutional referendum, had won Robert Mugabe's ear. He had also run the publicity for the parliamentary elections and been made minister of Information.

I made an appointment to interview my old friend, but after waiting in his office for an hour and a half I was informed that our appointment would be the next day. I returned and waited again, but I was told it had been postponed. When I called for another appointment I was told he did not have time to speak to me. It was exasperating, but not unusual behavior for a cabinet minister. Mugabe's government had become increasingly inaccessible to the press as it had become unresponsive to the people's needs. I had hoped speaking to Moyo, in his new position as government spokesperson, would give me insight to the thoughts of Mugabe and his inner circle, but I now realized that Moyo was worried I would confront him about his outspoken criticism of Mugabe just a few years earlier.

Insisting that he be addressed as "professor" and clearly enjoying his almost daily appearances on television, Moyo became a figure of public ridicule. Cartoons lampooned his receding hairline and egg-shaped head as well as his empty rhetoric. He also became known for flying into fits of rage over relatively minor incidents. One time when I phoned him for a comment, he harangued me for twenty minutes before hanging up. After that he stopped answering my calls. Moyo was often seen on state television fulminating at remarks by the opposition or the British government or the latest statistics on economic decline. To watch his angry tirades was to get an insight into the thinking of Zanu-PF and Robert Mugabe.

In January 2001, infuriated by a story in the *Daily News*, Moyo declared in the *Herald*: "It is now only a matter of time until Zimbabweans put a final stop to this madness [i.e. criticism of the government] in defence of their cultural interest and national security." He vented a similar threat on state television.

Two days later, friends phoned me early in the morning to say that a huge explosion had rocked their house: the *Daily News* printing plant had been bombed. It was not the first violence against the paper. A hand grenade had been thrown into their offices in April 2000; reporters and photographers had been repeatedly arrested and beaten; even street vendors hawking the newspaper had been beaten by Mugabe's youth militia. Editor Geoff Nyarota made a well publicized show of support for the vendors by going out on the streets with them to sell the *Daily News*. Death threats phoned to Nyarota were traced back to the headquarters of Mugabe's Zanu-PF party. In another incident a man confessed to being hired by the Central Intelligence Organization to assassinate Nyarota, but he decided not to go through with it because Nyarota was friendly to him in the elevator.

I drove out to Harare's industrial area and was stunned when I arrived to see the roof blown off the large three-story structure and the walls buckled. Inside, the destruction was worse, the huge presses mangled beyond any repair. The police had been called in the early hours of the morning, but had still not arrived. Independent forensic experts determined that the explosives had been three antitank landmines, probably of Eastern European origin, detonated with dynamite sticks. The type of explosives used would only be available in Zimbabwe's military. Few people had the expertise to plant and set off such explosives to achieve maximum damage without getting blown up themselves. To the surprise of no one the police conducted an unenthusiastic investigation and nobody was ever arrested for that bomb.

It is a measure of the high level of professionalism and determination of the owners and staff of the *Daily News* that the paper managed to publish again the next day, using the presses of fellow privately owned newspapers.

Jonathan Moyo became known as "Mugabe's Goebbels" for his heavy-handed control of state newspapers and television and radio networks. His control of broadcasting was especially troubling, because the state continued to hold a monopoly on all television and radio stations, a stranglehold inherited from the Rhodesian regime, and because radio is the main source of news for Zimbabwe's rural population.

Moyo stepped up his attacks on the foreign press, too, calling me and other correspondents "terrorists," "liars," "merchants of violence," and "agents of imperialism." I knew Moyo had jumped ship from being one of Mugabe's stiffest critics to becoming his right-hand man, but I was amazed by how vehement he had become in his attacks on anyone perceived to be critical of the government. With bitter disillusion I watched how power twisted his character. I thought I had become inured to Moyo's insults, but when my name started to feature in front-page headlines and articles, I realized that I had to lodge a protest against Moyo's libellous charges. To leave them unchallenged would allow Moyo to claim his allegations were true.

In January 2001 I annoyed Moyo again. The MDC M.P. for Bikita in southern Zimbabwe had died (of natural causes), and fresh elections were being held to choose a successor. Determined to wrest back this rural seat, Zanu-PF threw its full weight into the campaign by sending in "Hitler" Hunzvi and a band of war vets and youth militia.

I drove down to Bikita with Mercedes, BBC correspondent Grant Ferrett, and David Blair of the *Daily Telegraph* as passengers. We found Bikita plunged into cycles of violence and chaos that bore more resemblance to a civil war than a parliamentary election campaign. We saw settlements that were deserted because the inhabitants had fled to the hills to avoid violence from Hunzvi and his gang; we attended an MDC rally and saw two Zanu-PF vehicles drive up and threaten the small crowd; we interviewed bloodied youths who had been beaten with iron bars by Zanu-PF youth militia as Hunzvi stood by.

As we drove toward one rally, a truck sped up from behind and tailed us very closely, then pulled up alongside. "It's Hunzvi!" said Grant. "It's Hunzvi and his militia! They're waving for us to pull over!" Looking to my side, I caught a glimpse of a wild-eyed Hunzvi hanging out of the passenger window of his speeding truck and gesturing insistently for me to stop. The vehicle was packed with the youth militia in green uniforms waving their fists threateningly.

I resolved to concentrate on the road in front, not the frightening spectacle beside us. I was not going to stop and allow Hunzvi and his lawless bunch to threaten us. I scanned the countryside for some public place where witnesses might provide some safety from this crazed vehicle, but there was nothing but rolling hills. Hunzvi's truck pulled ahead of us; another Zanu-PF truck was coming up behind us. Hunzvi went over a steep hill and out of view. As we came over the hill I could see his truck had gone far ahead and was braking, so I slowed down, pulled over onto the verge and made a quick U-turn. As I sped away from Hunzvi, the second Zanu-PF vehicle drove toward us and swerved, as if to hit my car. I accelerated to get away as quickly as possible from those vehicles and the threat of assault by Hunzvi and the militia. We all laughed wildly at our escape.

This was my first brush with the youth militia. The gangs of violent young Zanu-PF youths in green military-style uniforms had begun roaming the countryside and cities in 2001. Cabinet Minister for Youth Border Gezi had set up five camps where youths were supposed to do "national service" and learn job skills. But the young men and women were deployed to enforce Zanu-PF rule and to intimidate anyone viewed as an enemy of the ruling party. The Zimbabwean public quickly dubbed them "Green Bombers" for their uniforms and their violent tactics. I had interviewed several former youth militia and they told of being taught to beat people on the soles of their feet and on their buttocks. The gangs spread out across Zimbabwe and became enforcers of the party's rule.

Hunzvi did not get us that day, but his intimidation succeeded in winning Bikita for Zanu-PF. Moyo was infuriated by our reports about the blanket of violence that Zanu-PF threw over the area. He denounced us by name or as "agents of British imperialism posing as journalists" in the *Herald* and on television. His Ministry of Information was steadily increasing its repression of the press and tightening its control of the state news media. We responded with increased determination to continue doing our work as we saw fit.

The *Herald* had never been a great newspaper or even a good one, but it was a compulsory read for a journalist: as the government became more inaccessible, the state mouthpiece became the best way of learning of its intentions, reasoning, and policies. One morning I read with a jolt that Mercedes Sayagues's employment permit had been canceled and she was ordered to leave Zimbabwe within twenty-four hours. Mercedes was in South Africa to meet with her editor at the *Mail & Guardian,* and that morning she called me from Johannesburg.

"A funny thing just happened and I don't know what to think about it," she said in her usual melodic Latin accent. "I was meeting with my editor when he got a phone call from Harare. It was a reporter from the *Herald* asking if he could be their correspondent from Zimbabwe because I had been deported! Can you believe that? Isn't that funny?"

I broke the news that the *Herald* had reported that she had been given twenty-four hours to leave the country.

"I see," she said. "Then this *is* serious. Oh my God, what about Esmeralda?" Mercedes had left her nine-year-old daughter with friends for her short trip. If she was refused entry into Zimbabwe, she would not be able to pick her up. We agreed that she would return to Harare in the morning and the press would be at the airport to put pressure on Immigration to allow her to reenter the country to collect her daughter.

The small band of journalists writing for the foreign press met that afternoon. We agreed to form an organization, the Foreign Correspondents Association of Zimbabwe, and to issue a statement protesting the treatment of Mercedes. Somehow we believed that this problem could be sorted out, that we would be able to carry on doing our jobs and living our lives as normal. Clear-headed and open-eyed in our approach to just about any event or development, we could not see that our lives as journalists in Zimbabwe were about to change.

Just then BBC journalist Joseph Winter got a call on his cell phone from his Senegalese wife, Ann Marie. "What?" said Jo. "Immigration? To our house?" The room fell silent. Ending his call, Jo told us immigration officers had come to his home and said that he had to leave the country.

The next morning Mercedes flew into Harare Airport. I was waiting with the other journalists in the arrivals hall when I got a message that Mercedes had asked for me. I went to find her at the immigration desk. Immigration officials refused to allow her to enter Zimbabwe, despite the fact that she held a valid temporary resident's permit. We explained that she needed to get her daughter, and the officials phoned the head office. They gave her twenty-four hours to pick up her daughter, pack her things, and leave the country.

That day Mercedes and Jo both got in touch with lawyers, who pressed an emergency court hearing and won a stay in their expulsions, granting them five days to pack and settle their affairs and to launch a legal appeal against their deportations. The situation appeared to have calmed, for the moment at least. But that night I was woken by my phone at 2 A.M. It was Jo Winter and I could hear crashing in the background. "Andy, the war vets are tearing down our door. They say they want to kill us! Please come!"

I rolled out of bed, threw on some clothes, and drove through the dark streets to Jo's townhouse. I could make out a group of about six men bashing at Jo's front door with what looked like a log. Reuters photographer Howard Burditt had just arrived, followed by his bureau chief, Cris Chinaka. Then up roared a big silver 4x4 and out stepped a petite woman. This was Jo's lawyer, Beatrice Mtetwa. The four of us approached the gang and Howard set off his flash at high speed. This seemed to frighten them and they ran to a nearby car and drove off.

Jo emerged from the house with his terrified wife and baby daughter. A British high commission official arrived and whisked them away.

Suddenly I thought about Mercedes. I dashed over to her house a few blocks away to see if she was getting the same treatment, but she had been left alone. We later found out that the thugs had gone to Mercedes' previous home and mistakenly threatened the new tenants.

They had a busy night, as they also went to the home of the lawyer who negotiated for Jo and Mercedes to have five days' grace.

Returning to the Winters' house, I noted how quiet the street was now that the thugs had left. "Oh, they'll be back as soon as we leave," said Beatrice matter-of-factly. I was incredibly impressed to see a lawyer out at that hour of the morning in such a threatening situation. Then and there I asked Beatrice if she would represent me if I ever got into any trouble. It was the best snap decision I've ever made.

True to Beatrice's prediction, shortly after we left, the gang of toughs came back. They broke down the door, ransacked the house, and stayed there to give trouble to Jo or anyone else who might go to gather their belongings. The Winters left the next day for London.

Mercedes knew she was at risk of the same rough treatment, but she was determined to stand up for her legal rights. Beatrice supported her in this, and Mercedes and her daughter left their home to stay at a safe place. For the next few days she proceeded with the legal application against the revocation of her employment permit, but when Justice Minister Patrick Chinamasa declared in Parliament that Mercedes was a spy for the Angolan rebel movement, Unita, she decided it was too dangerous to stay on and resolved to leave.

The next morning Mercedes strode decisively into the airport, looking characteristically stylish and dramatic in leopard-print trousers. Esmeralda held a Zimbabwean flag. She told the assembled press, "As a journalist I have been reporting on human rights abuses and the general breakdown of the rule of law in Zimbabwe. The action taken against me is small compared to those Zimbabweans who have been murdered, tortured, and beaten. I look forward to coming back to a Zimbabwe where human rights are respected."

There was considerable worry that government agents would try to arrest Mercedes before she could get on the plane, so she did not want to linger in the highly visible departures hall. She hugged her employee, Christine, who had helped to care for Esmeralda for nine years. The three sobbed as they held each other in a tight embrace. Photos of that touching scene were used across the world.

Government officials were indeed waiting for Mercedes. As she went through Immigration she was served with papers declaring her a "prohibited immigrant" forbidden from returning to Zimbabwe. It was an old legal action used by Ian Smith's Rhodesian regime to get rid of critical journalists and activists. "There goes freedom," said a well-known legal expert at the airport. "Freedom of the press and all our other freedoms. I was here in Rhodesia and saw journalists get thrown out by Ian Smith then. This is exactly the same."

Losing Mercedes was a terrible blow. I could always count on her to have an outraged or outrageous opinion about everything from Mugabe's antihomosexual rants and Jonathan Moyo's attacks on the press to sexual practices in rural Shona society. Moreover she was always so well read and well informed that her provocative views were backed up with facts and figures.

Jonathan Moyo justified the action against Jo Winter by claiming he had renewed his work permit by bribing a government official. It was an outrageous lie. Jo is honest to the point of being viewed by more cynical hacks as a bit of a Boy Scout. As for Mercedes, she was certainly glamorous and seductive enough to fit the profile of a Mata Hari espionage agent, but Moyo's charge that she was a spy was patently false.

As I wrote up the story of the expulsion of the two journalists, I asked John Makumbe for a comment. "Mugabe is carrying out a coup against democracy," he said. "He is not going to stop with the press and the judiciary. He will attack any other democratic forces, including the MDC and civic organizations. He will attack anything that might get in the way of his winning the 2002 presidential elections. Mugabe is trying to claw back the political space he lost in 2000 with the defeat of his constitution and the near defeat of his party in the parliamentary elections."

The loss of Jo and Mercedes left our band of foreign correspondents decidedly diminished. It shrank still further when Jonathan Moyo refused to renew the work permit of David Blair, correspondent for the *Daily Telegraph,* a few months later in June. Blair's departure, amid a barrage of threatening headlines in the state press, left me the last foreign correspondent in Zimbabwe. (Several other journalists wrote for international publications but they were all Zimbabwean citizens.) I was safe so far because I had managed to get a permanent residence permit

in 1997, when there had been a thaw in relations between the government and the press, before Jonathan Moyo had reappeared as the scourge
of the independent press. The permanent residence permit gives one
the right to reside and work in Zimbabwe without any time limits. Without it I would have certainly been ejected like Mercedes, Jo, and David.
The permit meant that Moyo could not expel me so easily. But it also
made me a target.

As things became more difficult in Zimbabwe, Mrs. Manomano remained a reassuring daily presence in our life. Here she is (right) with Mavis (left) and a visitor from the United States, AIDS expert Dr. David Katzenstein. © *Andrew Meldrum*

16

MATTERS OF LIFE AND DEATH

Immersed as I was in the turmoil surging through Zimbabwe, home became a haven where I found solace in our daily routines. I spent more time in the garden, which we had transformed into a verdant African savanna of acacias, palms, and other indigenous trees. Pulling weeds, pruning shrubs, watching new leaves shoot was a soothing way to slough off the tensions and worries from the troubling stories I was working on.

Mrs. Manomano's presence was also reassuring. She and Dolores kept the house in great order, except for my office, which had become a chaotic conglomeration of stacks of newspapers, magazines, notebooks, and other journalistic flotsam. Our relationship with Mrs. Manomano grew into a comfortable familiarity. Her sons and daughters-in-law and her grandchildren all came and spent time with us.

But then Zimbabwe's growing troubles invaded our family life. During the past months we had seen one of Mrs. Manomano's sons, Wanda, grow progressively thinner and weaker, and he was often racked by a terrible cough. Eventually he went to Harare's Parirenyatwa Hospital, previously a whites-only facility, now open to all. The hospital's name had been changed to honor Tichafa Samuel Parirenyatwa, the country's first black doctor, who was active in the African nationalist movement. By the time Wanda went to hospital Dolores and I suspected he was suffering from AIDS, which had killed another of Mrs. Manomano's sons, Takemore, a year earlier.

Mrs. Manomano was constantly at the hospital, so I knew the situation was serious. When I went to visit Wanda I found the entire Manomano family around his bed: more than a dozen people were in the

195

small room, the women sitting on pieces of cloth on the floor and the men sitting in chairs by Wanda's side.

Wanda looked even thinner than he had just a week before. He was skeletal and he had lost most of his hair. Yet when he smiled, wanly, I could see the same face as before. He resembled his mother very closely. Wanda thanked me for coming and said he was embarrassed for me to see him in such a terrible state. I told him there was nothing to be ashamed of, that AIDS is a disease like many others. He looked at me blankly, as if he did not know what I was talking about. Mrs. Manomano and other family members told me heatedly that AIDS was not the cause of Wanda's problems, that witchcraft and an evil curse were making Wanda ill. They said they were getting some *mushonga* (strong traditional medicine) to counteract it. I did not want to contradict them, so we moved on to small talk about the weather and the Harare Dynamos, Wanda's favorite football team. I could see everyone in the family was making a great effort to pretend that things were normal and that Wanda would get better. As I left, Wanda and I agreed that when I saw him again we would discuss how the Dynamos played in their next match.

Afterward, as I walked through the wards and saw room after room of similar family gatherings around beds—wakes for the dying—I realized that in the minds of these people the sufferers were not dying of AIDS but of witchcraft, diabetes, tuberculosis, or high blood pressure. Anything but AIDS or an AIDS-related illness.

Wanda died a few days after my visit. Mrs. Manomano was stoic about it and took a week off to bury him in their *kumusha* (rural home) in Murewa. She and other members of the family bought large quantities of meat, cooking oil, and other ingredients to feed the mourners. Family members gathered at our house and played drums the night before they left for Murewa.

But at a certain level, people did know what was causing so many deaths. Shortly after Wanda died, his ex-wife came to visit. Big, hearty, healthy Rhoda said, "I am glad I divorced him. He was playing around with other women and if I had stayed married to him then I would be dying now, too." Despite all the family's denials, she knew it was AIDS.

AIDS had become an inescapable part of Zimbabwean life. We noticed from television broadcasts and public appearances that the war veterans' leader "Hitler" Hunzvi, now an M.P., was also getting very thin. His once round face had become sunken and gaunt; the collars of his shirts were now much too big for his scrawny neck. Then he collapsed when making a speech in Bulawayo and was admitted to the hospital, reportedly for malaria. He was transferred to Harare and uniformed youth militia stood on guard around his bed. But they could not dispel the rumors that Hunzvi was dying of AIDS. Zimbabweans knew when people had AIDS, just as long as it was not a family member. Ever the showman, Hunzvi invited the Zimbabwe Broadcasting Corporation to film him at his hospital bed. He sat up in bed on the nightly news, denying that he had AIDS. His cadaverous figure was hardly recognizable, but he told the camera that he simply had a bad case of malaria and was improving. He rambled on about people trying to attack him and to poison President Mugabe. He talked deliriously about his childhood and snakes and yet the camera kept rolling. Within days he died.

Hunzvi was a medical doctor. If only he could have brought himself to face up to his disease, he could have issued a public health warning to others.

In the early 1980s, when Zimbabwe's health services were widely hailed as the success of Africa and a model for Third World nations, the country had quickly established procedures for testing donated blood for HIV and AIDS. The government's Blood Transfusion Service had screened all blood, making Zimbabwe one of the first countries in the world to do so.

Tragically, neither the rest of the government medical services nor society at large responded so rapidly or effectively to the deadly challenge of HIV and AIDS. What started out as a limited problem grew exponentially. Surveys of pregnant women at antenatal clinics showed HIV infection rates of 25 percent and then a year later of 27 percent. These "sentinel surveys" warned people what the national rate was heading toward, and it did, indeed, climb to those frightening heights.

By 2000 Zimbabwe was tied with Botswana for the unenviable record of the world's highest HIV infection rate, at 35 percent of the adult population. The rate for the total population, including children, was estimated at 25 percent, one in four people. One of the reasons it became so widespread was that many men have multiple sexual partners, including their wives, girlfriends, and prostitutes.

Although Robert Mugabe would occasionally make a brief reference to the need to battle the scourge of AIDS, his government did very little to actually try to reduce the levels of infection. Public education about HIV and AIDS remained basic and ineffective. What was needed was a continual blitz on the population that would reach men and women in both cities and rural areas. What was especially needed was an effective educational campaign to reach teenagers and children before they reached puberty and became sexually active. Education would have helped to slow the rate of increase in infection, but with millions of people already infected, the country also desperately needed adequate treatment for the ill. And on that level the government also failed the country. As the numbers of the sick and dying grew, the once vaunted healthcare system was disintegrating as a result of successive budget cuts.

As cabinet ministers, soccer stars, musicians, and army generals succumbed to the disease, no mention was made of AIDS. It was as if everyone was conspiring to maintain the silence. Shrouded in ignorance and superstition, it was no wonder that infection rates climbed so high.

When antiretroviral drugs began to be available, allowing people with AIDS to return to normal lives, the inequalities in Mugabe's Zimbabwe became yet more evident. Only the most wealthy, such as top army officers, businessmen connected to Zanu-PF, and leading party officials, could afford the drugs; others continued to die. The denial persisted.

The government imposed an AIDS levy on all wage earners, requiring employers to deduct 1 percent from all paychecks and put the money into a state AIDS fund. A National AIDS Council was appointed to allocate the money, but it was dogged by complaints that it was not dispersing the funds to bona fide community groups, distributing them instead to fronts set up by Zanu-PF supporters. The government sacked the council members three times and appointed new boards, but the funds from the AIDS levy remained ineffective in helping those suffering from the disease.

Although so many Zimbabweans continued to deny the facts of AIDS, a few stood up and battled the ignorance. I had known Lynde

Francis since I first arrived in Zimbabwe in 1980, when she was the vivacious director of Pamberi College, which specialized in educating former nationalist guerrillas who had missed out on schooling. An earthmother type with flowing hair and caftans, she had taken me under her wing and introduced me to her wide range of friends, from former guerrillas to journalists, artists, and musicians. Now as Zimbabwe's AIDS epidemic took hold, Lynde took the brave step of announcing publicly that she was HIV-positive. She spoke out at public meetings, on radio, and television, describing how she was leading an active life and holding off progression of the disease by reducing stress, eating healthy foods, and taking a positive attitude. She was inundated by requests for support, and opened her home as a drop-in counseling service. It became known as The Centre and everyone there, from the counselors to the receptionist to the security guards, was HIV-positive. When antiretroviral drugs were introduced, international donors made some available to The Centre, which gave them to its clients.

At that point Lynde herself was not taking the antiretrovirals, and although she appeared healthy and radiated optimism, her once ample figure was thin. "We don't have enough drugs for everyone, so it's terribly difficult," she told me over dinner one night. "We decide who will get the drugs by looking at whose life is absolutely threatened by AIDS and we also look at who has changed their lifestyles in response to being HIV-positive."

Mavis, too, responded to the crisis with her uncommon good sense and forthright honesty. She took a course offered by a nongovernmental organization, the Zimbabwe AIDS Prevention Programme, to become a peer counselor. She proudly wore anti-AIDS T-shirts and spoke frankly about AIDS at her workplace, a well-known Harare pottery. People in the factory called her *Tete* (Auntie), and came to her office to seek advice. She displayed a photo of her beloved brother, Phillimon, who had died of AIDS a few years earlier. She told her colleagues how he had to go back to the rural areas and die in a hut, cared for by his aging mother. "If you don't want to die from AIDS, then you must protect yourself," she would tell her workmates. She kept a bowl of condoms by the door, so people could discreetly take them as they left her office. Mavis's superb ability to communicate with people helped her become one of

Zapp's most effective peer counselors, with one of their highest rates of people referred for counseling and testing.

After watching the obdurate refusal of so many Zimbabweans to face up to the problem of AIDS, going to Uganda to write about that country's success in lowering its HIV infection rates was like a breath of fresh air. On arrival I saw large public education posters at Entebbe Airport and on billboards on the road to Kampala. My taxi driver was quite open about the threat of AIDS. "We must be vigilant about AIDS," he said. "If we don't want to get sick then we must use condoms."

I soon realized just how differently the Ugandan government and people were approaching the crisis. Here ministers provided leadership by being open about the disease and encouraging public education. President Yoweri Museveni spoke frequently about AIDS and met with HIV-positive people and groups representing families affected by AIDS. The government encouraged private groups to work in any area they could. The result was that Ugandans from all walks of life talked freely about AIDS. After reaching a peak HIV infection rate of 27 percent of its population in 1988, Uganda's infection level declined to below 10 percent in 2003. Although the level is still high and there are many people still contracting the disease and many more suffering from it, the Ugandan example represents a great step forward and a sharp contrast to the head-in-the-sand approach all too common in Zimbabwe.

Although Kampala is a dilapidated city in comparison to Harare, the capital exuded a much more positive atmosphere. Uganda has experienced decades of war, ethnic violence, mass killings, and economic collapse, but now it is on the way up. The open attitude displayed by Ugandans in discussing AIDS carried over into their discussions about African politics, especially Zimbabwe. My conversation with Robert Kabushenga, who has a radio talk show, was typical of many I had in Uganda.

"What is going on in Zimbabwe?" Kabushenga asked me over a beer at a café overlooking a bustling Kampala street. As I drew a breath to begin, he answerd his own question: "Can't they see that it is just like what we went through in Uganda? By seizing the white farms Mugabe is cutting off his nose to spite his face. It is just like what Idi Amin did to our Asians. In the end it did not really help us Africans. Our economy plummeted and still twenty years later we are not as well off as we were then. Can't the Zimbabweans see that?"

When I returned to Harare I was forced to concentrate on matters closer to home. Dolores asked me if I had noticed that Mrs. Manomano was looking thin and weak. She told me that Mrs. Manomano had missed work. The government health clinic had broken down to such an extent that we took her to our own doctor who, after some tests, diagnosed inoperable stomach cancer. We were devastated. We found out that Mrs. Manomano had suffered diarrhea for some time but had not told us about it. Dolores called the local hospice, whose nurses assessed Mrs. Manomano's situation, provided painkillers, and gave her counseling about life and death. They were superb.

At first she felt better, because of the painkillers, and she wanted to continue working, but she was much too weak. Instead, Rhoda, her daughter-in-law, came to our house and Mrs. Manomano would sit and watch and talk with Rhoda. She got thinner and the hospice people began giving her morphine. One evening, seeing her light still on when I finished work, I went to visit. We talked a bit but mostly I just sat in her room. Two days later she died.

There was a flurry of activity as Dolores, Mavis, and her family members took her body to a funeral parlor. Mrs. Manomano belonged to two burial societies, which are a Zimbabwean phenomenon. People group together and make monthly payments and when they die the society assures them of a proper burial. We used to joke with Mrs. Manomano and ask her why she belonged to two burial societies when she could only be buried once, but she steadfastly kept up her membership with both.

Mrs. Manomano's rural home was in Murewa, due north of Harare. On the day of her burial we piled into the car and drove for about ninety minutes on the main road. After another fifteen minutes on a dirt road, we arrived at her homestead. It was such an easy drive and so accessible to our home in Harare, yet like virtually all of rural Zimbabwe, it was a world apart. Mrs. Manomano had a modern rectangular house with paned glass windows and a corrugated iron roof, and next to the house was the pen where she kept her cattle. She had told me a great deal about the cattle over the years. Nearby were the homes of other family members who had looked after her cattle and maize field. All around was an expanse of flat, dry land stretching out to the distant hills on the horizon. A few large granite boulders jutted out. It was June, Zimbabwe's winter, and the maize had been harvested. It was a bright day and the sun had warmed the sharp, chilly air. The setting was austerely beautiful, yet I knew it was grindingly hard work to scratch out a living on this land.

Many people had gathered from surrounding villages and members of the Jerusalema Number One dance troupe came from Harare. We filed into the little house and saw Mrs. Manomano, looking impossibly small in the coffin, paid our respects, and filed out. As we all stood outside the house, some men began drumming and others began dancing and singing and wailing. The coffin, now closed, was carried out to a spot with views over the sweeping landscape. The graves of her sons and other family members were nearby. The coffin was lowered into the grave, and then a minister from the Salvation Army spoke. Members of the family talked about Mrs. Manomano; then I spoke about how she had been an excellent employee for more than twenty years, how she had been a star dancer, and how she had performed at our wedding.

It was a simple ceremony yet very moving. I was touched by the impromptu elegies and how they caught the heart of Mrs. Manomano's stubborn, traditional, conservative nature. I knew the family had its share of rivalries and feuds, but they were set aside for the burial.

A hymn was sung and then rocks were put on top of the coffin until they covered it. Then we took turns shoveling the earth into the hole. Once it was full more rocks were put on top and then some women did a complicated sweeping of the earth, which was necessary to indicate if any witches came to tamper with the grave.

People stayed on for a meal of *sadza* and meat, which by that time was very scarce. As the light fell, the cold started to bite. Mavis, Dolores, and I were quiet in the car as we drove back, moved by the simplicity and dignity of the burial.

In Shona custom a memorial is held for the deceased a year after their death. We helped to provide supplies for the service and the meal and were planning to go to Murewa to attend the memorial, but by June 2002, things had changed so much in Zimbabwe that I was warned by her family not to come for the ceremony. They said Mugabe's war veterans and youth militia were nearby and it would not be safe for us to go there. They worried that we, as whites, would be attacked and that the family would be victimized later for associating with us.

Waiting for democracy. Residents of Harare's Glen View township line up to vote on the first day of the presidential election in March 2002. © *Howard Burditt/ Reuters*

17

WE WANT TO VOTE

When the MDC so narrowly lost the parliamentary elections in June 2000, the next chance for the opposition to challenge Mugabe at the polls had appeared very distant, nearly two years away. But in politics two years is not very long at all. Before we knew it the time had come for the presidential election where Mugabe, at seventy-eight, would stand for reelection to a six-year term against MDC candidate Morgan Tsvangirai, who was forty-nine.

The MDC had been very active in Parliament, leading many spirited debates and asking pointed questions of government ministers. But everyone was painfully aware that they simply did not have enough votes to challenge Zanu-PF's rubber-stamp majority. Especially worrying was the fact that the government was rushing two highly repressive bills through Parliament, the Public Order and Security Act and the Access to Information and Protection of Privacy Act.

The public order bill granted police even stronger powers of arrest and dispersal of public gatherings than similar legislation used by the Rhodesian regime. It made it illegal to have public gatherings of more than three people without the prior approval of the police, and made it a crime to publicly criticize the president and the police.

The press bill, drafted by Minister of Information Jonathan Moyo and his personal lawyer, gave the government the ability to close down newspapers and stop individual journalists from working. There was considerable opposition, even from within Zanu-PF. The parliamentary legal committee declared the press bill unconstitutional. Defending his legislation, Moyo delivered a scathing attack on the press in Parliament. He repeated the allegations that Mercedes had been a spy, claimed that

Iden Wetherell of the *Zimbabwe Independent* had been an agent of the Rhodesian government, and named me as a conspirator in a plot against the government. There was heated debate but the Zanu-PF machine forced the bills through Parliament. Together the two new laws substantially restricted the basic freedoms that Zimbabweans had enjoyed since independence.

Stymied by their lack of a majority in Parliament, the opposition party had pursued their legal challenges to Zanu-PF's election victories in thirty-seven constituencies, but only a handful of the cases had actually been heard and the results were mixed. In some cases the MDC succeeded in getting the Zanu-PF victories nullified; in others the judges ruled that the elections were valid. Zanu-PF had appealed against some of the verdicts and got them overturned. When by-elections were held to replace those seats that remained empty, Zanu-PF had used its full panoply of tactics to ensure victory: faulty voter registration, violence by the war veterans and the youth militia, and partisan administration of voting and counting. Many of the by-elections were in remote rural areas where it was difficult to monitor the situation properly. The MDC's remaining challenges to the Zanu-PF victories had become lost in the labyrinth of court scheduling. As a result the MDC had made few gains and could not challenge Zanu-PF's parliamentary majority.

The Mugabe government was also finding the courts an obstacle in its land occupations and determination to rule by force, but if it did not like a court ruling, then it would not enforce it. The courts repeatedly found the land seizures illegal according to Zimbabwean law and ordered the invaders to be evicted, but the police did not carry out the orders. The courts ordered investigations into several murders, but few were held. The government's attitude toward the rule of law was summed up by the then attorney general, soon to be justice minister, Patrick Chinamasa:

"I belong to a generation which brought fundamental revolutionary changes not through the law or the legal process but through the barrel of a gun. The law is only a political concept. It can be used as a tool from any political angle."

In November 2000, when it was hearing a case about the land invasions, the supreme court was invaded by an unruly band of war veterans who shouted, "Kill the judges!" and chased away the bench. The chief justice of the supreme court, Anthony Gubbay, took early retirement after being threatened by Mugabe's minister of Justice. "If you stay on, the government will not be able to guarantee your safety," Patrick Chinamasa warned him. Gubbay stepped down in March 2001 after numerous attacks in the press and threats by war veterans. Mugabe then decreed that the supreme court would be enlarged from five to eight judges, appointing three new judges with close ties to Zanu-PF. Two of the new judges had received large farms from the government; the new chief justice, Godfrey Chidyausiku, was a former deputy minister in Mugabe's government and his first act was to reverse rulings that declared the farm invasions illegal.

Under similar pressures, other judges from the supreme and high courts resigned, whereupon they were replaced with Mugabe's adherents. Faith in getting a fair hearing in the courts was rapidly disintegrating.

At the same time the government was politicizing the police force. War veterans and youth militia were installed in senior positions at stations across the country. Police stopped dealing with the general public in an evenhanded way and instead made trouble for anyone suspected of supporting the opposition.

I experienced this infiltration of the police firsthand. I had enjoyed friendly relations with our local station as a member of the Neighborhood Watch, had got to know many of the officers, and often had friendly chats with them when we ran into each other at the supermarket or the bank. But now things changed dramatically. A new, young officer in charge had been appointed and some different constables came in. The atmosphere at the station became hostile. I was shouted at when I went in to pay a fine for speeding. Later, some of the officers I knew came to my house to tell me they had been accused of supporting the opposition. They were warned not to be friendly to whites and threatened with beatings or being sacked.

"These Zanu-PF people are being promoted without having taken any exams and without any qualifications," one sergeant told me. "The force is no longer being run professionally. It is being run politically." Another showed the wounds from a vicious beating he received after he assisted someone known to be an MDC supporter.

Yet, despite the new laws designed to suppress public demonstrations and critical press coverage, despite the behind-the-scenes inroads that Mugabe and Zanu-PF were making to control the courts and police, a buoyant feeling rose throughout the country as the presidential election approached. Again people seemed to feel that change was just around the corner.

Morgan Tsvangirai shrugged off numerous death threats to make appearances throughout the country to large, enthusiastic crowds. Just holding the rallies was a victory, as often they were canceled at the last minute, after pressure from the government. Tsvangirai was threatened and detained by police, then released, while the people who attended the rallies knew they risked beatings and harassment afterward. But still they came in their thousands.

I drove to a rally in the eastern border city of Mutare. It is Zimbabwe's prettiest city, with the surrounding green mountains visible from every corner of the bustling main street. Whenever I go there I am impressed by its beauty afresh. But getting to the rally proved difficult. The police had thrown up several roadblocks; they were allowing cars to get through, but only at a snail's pace. At the stadium I watched as people streamed in on foot. Once inside, most people took off their jackets and shirts to reveal MDC T-shirts. Some put on MDC caps; others brought out banners for Tsvangirai. As the crowd swelled, a carnival atmosphere enlivened the dusty township football field. Drums were played, people danced, choirs sang. I interviewed a cross section of people, young men, old women, mothers with babies on their backs. They all told me how the police and militia had gone door to door in Mutare's Sakubva township the night before, threatening residents with violence if they attended Tsvangirai's rally, and some showed me wounds and bruises where they had been beaten by Mugabe's youth militia. Others were eager to tell me why they were supporting Tsvangirai: they wanted a better economy and an end to corruption, and they wanted a return to freedom and security. They wanted change. The various groups gelled into a cheering whole when Tsvangirai and other MDC leaders arrived. Tsvangirai got onto the podium and thanked people for being so brave as to attend, and advised them to stick together when leaving so it would be more difficult for gangs of Zanu-PF thugs to attack them. Tsvangirai denounced the political acts the police were carrying out against him and his party, but he cautioned the crowd that not all the police were bad. Many officers supported the MDC but were afraid for their jobs. Tsvangirai spoke out against the war in Congo, where so many Zimbabwean soldiers were losing their lives, and attacked Mugabe's corruption. He also talked about how the country could be returned to peace, stability, and prosperity. The crowd laughed at his jokes and cheered his exhortations.

As soon as the rally came to an end the crowd filed out. No one wanted to get caught after dark. I left with a group of journalists, all of whom were impressed by Tsvangirai's positive tone, but even more impressed by the commitment in the face of danger shown by so many ordinary Zimbabweans. This proved to be typical of Tsvangirai's rallies.

Mugabe's rallies were a dismal contrast. Even with the government bringing in busloads of schoolchildren and rural people, the crowds were small and dispirited. Security was heavy and threatening. Most noticeable of all, Robert Mugabe's speeches were bitter diatribes against Tsvangirai, whom he called a "tea boy" serving the interests of the British and other whites. He incited violence against the opposition and offered no new policies to help Zimbabwe out of its crisis. The speeches were largely met with stony-faced, sullen silence, and there were no spontaneous displays of support. At a rally I attended in Glen View township the only cheering was for the announcement that the staple maize meal, which was in scarce supply, would be sold at low prices to those at the rally. Throughout the proceedings, Grace Mugabe pointedly looked down her nose, through a pair of gold Gucci sunglasses, at the assembled masses.

Mugabe turned to the usual suspects to drum up support or, more correctly, to bludgeon the opposition. I was shocked to find out that Biggie Chitoro was back on the campaign trail in the Mataga area, leaving a wake of bloodied, beaten, and tortured residents. Press reports on the murder of Finos Zhou and the torture of his brother James had forced the police to take some action against him, so in an unusual effort to appear to be maintaining the rule of law, they arrested Chitoro and charged him with murder. He was imprisoned awaiting trial, but shortly before the presidential elections, Mugabe issued an amnesty in which virtually all those accused of political violence were released. Chitoro was back with a vengeance.

Chitoro was unusual for having been jailed at all. CIO agent Joseph Mwale, identified as having firebombed the car in which two MDC activists died in Buhera, never faced any charges, despite a court order for him to be arrested. During the presidential election campaign, he ran CIO operations in the eastern mountain town of Chimanimani where there were numerous reports of vicious beatings and torture.

As the voting days drew closer, it was evident that the state's roll of registered voters was being seriously skewed. Zimbabweans wanting to register in the cities found the process unnecessarily difficult. After registration closed, the government declared it was carrying out further registration in undisclosed rural areas. A few weeks later it announced that 400,000 new voters had been added to the roll. The registrar-general, Tobaiwa Mudede, who had been cited in court cases as blatantly partisan, refused to make the roll of all registered voters available to the MDC for scrutiny.

The large observer mission from the European Union was determined to watch the presidential poll carefully, having judged the June 2000 parliamentary elections to be illegitimate. The Mugabe government refused to allow British observers to be part of the EU mission, charging that Britain was actively seeking to overthrow Mugabe and therefore could not objectively observe the polls. The EU did not accept this charge, but gave way in the interest of getting its observers deployed across the country. But as the mission demanded to see the voters' roll, the Mugabe government balked. At a hastily called press conference, the head of the EU mission, former Swedish cabinet minister Pierre Schori, revealed that he had been ordered to leave Zimbabwe immediately and the entire observer mission of nearly two hundred was to follow him out of the country.

Since the presence of EU observers discouraged the most blatant violence, it was clear that the presidential election campaign would continue to be violent and the voting process itself opaque. Mugabe must have calculated that the EU would certainly declare the election not free and not fair, and reasoned he might as well expel them from the beginning.

Other observer missions also experienced problems. Several of the South African observers were attacked by Mugabe's war veterans and youth militia when they attempted to visit the MDC offices in the Midlands province. Two of their vehicles were damaged and their driver was injured.

A week before the March 9 elections, Tsvangirai was arrested and charged with treason for allegedly plotting the assassination of Mugabe. Tsvangirai had been tricked into attending a secretly filmed meeting in Montreal with a dodgy Canadian lobbyist, Ari Ben Menashe, who made several references to "eliminating Mugabe." Tsvangirai made no such comments, but talked instead about a democratic process of unseating Mugabe and the transition that would be needed.

A few days before the election, I interviewed Tsvangirai in the garden of his Harare home. MDC security guards carefully watched all comings and goings, but I never saw any guns, and I found Tsvangirai to be determined, committed, and relatively relaxed in spite of all he had been through. His descriptions of the positive changes he intended to bring to the country were articulate and persuasive.

I asked what he would do about Zimbabwe's land issue if he were to become president. Would he return all the land seized from white farmers? It was a tricky, thorny question that could lead to him being labeled a stooge of the whites, on the one hand, and a supporter of Mugabe's most controversial policy on the other. Tsvangirai replied that the crucial problem facing Zimbabwe was maintaining its agricultural production while reforming land ownership so that it was more equitable. The first thing he would do, he explained, would be to have a land audit, where experts would look at the state of Zimbabwe's land and determine how many large-scale farms would be appropriate, how many small-scale, what crops would be best to grow and what measures were needed to make Zimbabwe both self-sufficient in food and able to export. On the basis of that, he said, he would form a policy for boosting agricultural production while transforming land ownership to an equitable balance of white and black ownership and small-scale and large-scale farms. It was a good answer, diplomatic and well thought out. Tsvangirai was careful not to fall into the pitfalls of either side, yet he did not dodge the issues.

As happens so often in interviews, the best part came after I had asked all my questions and closed my notebook. We were speculating about what was driving Mugabe and Zanu-PF to inflict so much violence and suffering. "What you've got to understand," said Tsvangirai, leaning closer to me for emphasis, "is that a liberation movement that has fought a war to gain power only values its own power. It does not respect laws because it had to break laws to win power. It does not respect international opinion because it had to operate without that approval. It does not respect democracy because that is not how it came to power. They only value their own power. That is why we see Mugabe dismantling everything else just to keep his power."

Tsvangirai was undoubtedly popular, and his campaign was helped by the myriad difficulties that that the average Zimbabwean was facing, which were likely to increase the already substantial vote that the MDC had received in the parliamentary elections.

The fuel shortage had lasted for nearly two years and had caused massive disruptions in the economy. After waiting in lengthy lines for eight hours, getting a tank of petrol, or even half a tank, had become a victory worth celebrating. "Zimbabwe has come to the point where filling up your car is better than having sex," Mercedes had quipped in typically provocative fashion before she was expelled from the country. Multiply the problems faced by the ordinary motorist by the problems facing industries needing to make deliveries by trucks and commuter vans, which take the majority of Zimbabweans to work, and it is easy to see how even the simplest tasks became fraught with difficulty and tension.

Once again the country was lifted by a groundswell of infectious optimism. The support for Tsvangirai was so overwhelming, especially in the cities, that people believed no amount of fiddling or intimidation could prevent his victory. The mood was as tangible as during the constitutional referendum two years earlier.

But Mugabe still had a few tricks up his sleeve. As voting got under way it became immediately clear that there were serious problems. In the rural areas polling agents for Tsvangirai were attacked and prevented from monitoring the voting and counting: some were abducted; others were chased away by gun-toting mobs. The result was that a very high percentage of rural polling stations were completely controlled by government officials who could do whatever they liked.

A different tactic was used in the cities, where voting was deliberately slowed down. Throughout Harare, from townships to wealthy suburbs, voters lined up from dawn. I was moved, as I drove around, to see so many Zimbabweans determined to exercise their democratic right. But when I drove around again at midday I could see that the lines had barely moved. With my journalist's credentials I went into polling stations and watched as just a few voters could cast their ballots per hour, while thousands waited in the lines outside. I had witnessed many voting days and I knew that ordinarily there was a steady stream of voters going in and out. But now, in one polling station after another, I saw just one or two voters casting their ballots every few minutes.

The government's intention was obvious. The support for Tsvangirai was strongest in the cities, where the MDC had won previous elections by margins of 80 percent, so the fewer people who were able to vote, the fewer votes for the MDC. The numbers of polling stations in Harare and other cities had also been reduced.

Determination turned into frustration, which in the hot sun built up into anger. At one township polling station, a rough count showed there were nearly five thousand people waiting in line. Tensions were high, and I was quickly surrounded by twenty people. "Why can't we vote?" asked a young woman with a toddler clinging to her skirt. "We came before breakfast and now it's nearly dark. This is not right!" An older woman said, "They are cheating us. You must stop them from cheating!" I tried to explain that I had no power to change the speed of voting but could only write about it for an overseas newspaper.

"Then tell the world," said a tall man. "Tell them these elections are crooked. Tell them that we are not being allowed to vote!"

Mavis, her nephew Macmillan, and several friends had gone out early to vote at Highlands Primary School. As evening fell they were still stuck in the line. Officials shouted that voting had ended for the day and ordered people to come back tomorrow, as Zimbabwe's elections always take place over two days. As the guards started to close the school's gates, Mavis and Macmillan were part of a crowd that rushed up and forced their way through. A few dozen people ran up the school's drive to the polling station and demanded that they be allowed to vote.

Macmillan gave me an example of how the voting was slowed down. "Mavis was before me and the official took a long time to find her name on the voters' roll. I came next and the official started to go back to the beginning of the roll, where they have people whose names start with *A*. I said, "No, here is my name, Ngazana, right next to my aunt's before me. You don't need to go back to the *A*s; it is right here." Imagine how much time that woman wasted going through the voters' roll from the beginning for each voter. Instead of processing two voters per minute, she would only do one, or maybe even less, and that significantly reduces the number of people able to vote. It is wicked."

In fact Mavis and Macmillan were lucky. At several township polling stations, people refused to leave when the stations were closed, shouting that they must be allowed to vote. The police were called and shot tear gas into the crowds to disperse them.

The second day of voting saw the same slow-pace tactic. The MDC sought an urgent court order, and the courts ordered a third day of voting to ensure that all voters were able to cast their ballots. But less than 20 percent of the polling stations opened for the extra day.

In previous elections I had been able to go into the counting stations and watch the process of totaling and verifying the votes. I had witnessed election monitors rejecting ballot boxes that had appeared without proper identification and I had seen monitors uncover stacks of "no" votes that had been added to the "yes" pile. But in this election, which was being run by top army officers, no press were permitted to observe the counting. No independent monitors were permitted either.

At home we crowded around the television to hear the results as they were announced from each constituency. The first lot of nine constituencies were declared and Macmillan carefully wrote them down. Tsvangirai had an early lead.

But there was little cause for celebration. "Tsvangirai has lost," said Macmillan, explaining that his margins of victory in the cities were relatively small, while Mugabe had won by huge margins in the rural constituencies.

Macmillan's assessment proved to be absolutely correct. When all the votes were added up, Mugabe won by four hundred thousand.

Tsvangirai appeared absolutely stunned at a press conference the next morning. The MDC had anticipated that Mugabe would cheat, and had estimated that the government could "steal" about 20 percent of the votes, but they had never imagined voting fraud on such a massive scale.

There were dozens of rumors about people taking to the streets to protest against the results, and many looked to Tsvangirai to call for a popular demonstration. MDC insiders told me that Tsvangirai and other top party members had considered leading a revolt but felt that Mugabe's well-armed security forces would turn on any public demonstration. They felt the cost in bloodshed would be too high. "Tsvangirai is committed to achieving peaceful, democratic change," said his adviser. "He believes that is the way to bring democracy back to Zimbabwe and that is what the country needs."

The uprising did not materialize. Instead, people trudged around Harare as if in a daze, finding it hard to accept that there would be no change, that Mugabe would stay in power, and Zimbabwe would continue its downward spiral. "People are just depressed," said Mavis of the workers that she talked with on her way to work. "Everyone seems downcast and they don't want to talk or even make jokes. Everyone is very gloomy."

It was one thing for Mugabe to declare himself the winner, but the international observer groups had yet to give their seal of approval. The European Union, although banished from Zimbabwe, said they had gained enough evidence to declare the elections fraudulent. The Commonwealth had sent a large mission headed by former Nigerian leader, retired general Abdusalami Abubakar, with representatives from all fifty-four Commonwealth countries. Although many members of the mission arrived sympathetic to Mugabe, their opinions changed after they traveled across Zimbabwe and witnessed the level of violent intimidation. One Commonwealth delegate told me he had trouble sleeping after interviewing victims of torture. The Commonwealth mission declared the election to be not free and not fair; indeed, General Abubakar's report was so devastating that the Commonwealth suspended Zimbabwe's membership.

Then it was time for the judgment of the South African mission. I could not believe they would overlook the violence this time. Their mission had been attacked by Mugabe's militia and they had gathered evidence of several other incidents. On the other hand, members of the South African mission had been seen hobnobbing with Zanu-PF officials and going on shopping sprees in Harare. Would they take their observer mission seriously, or give Mugabe's reelection the political endorsement that it seemed President Thabo Mbeki desired?

I had trouble squeezing into the room at Meikles Hotel where the South African delegation was based. Journalists, diplomats, and members of human rights groups and other nongovernmental organizations all wanted to witness the South Africans' judgment. Hoots of derision greeted the South African announcement that they found the election results to be an accurate reflection of the will of the Zimbabwean people. The observers had difficulty responding to questions from the press; it was obvious that their endorsement of Mugabe's reelection had been dictated from Pretoria. Asked about the reduction of polling stations in Harare, an opposition stronghold, the team's leader replied it was probably an administrative error, prompting another round of dismissive laughter.

Emboldened by Mugabe's "victory," his supporters went on the rampage. Almost as soon as the international observers had boarded their planes to leave Zimbabwe, reports started coming in of beatings and murders of supporters of Tsvangirai and the MDC. The *Daily News* carried a horrific story of a woman who was allegedly beheaded by the youth militia in front of her daughters. The paper had an excellent record of accurately reporting incidents of political violence throughout the campaign period. I called two Harare human rights organizations and they said they were investigating the death. They told me the case appeared to be part of the trend in postelection violence in which they had confirmed murders of more than ten people. I called the police, and as usual, they refused to give me any comment.

I wrote a story about the beheaded woman for the *Guardian*. I made it clear that the husband alleged she had been killed by Mugabe's supporters but that police had not confirmed the incident. I pointed out that many others had been killed in the wave of postelection violence. All the other major newspapers and wire agencies also carried the story.

Two days later the *Daily News* announced in a long front-page article that they had been misled. The husband had apparently lied to them about his wife's beheading and had then disappeared. I was worried about my original story, and I corrected the account in a subsequent story for the *Guardian*. I was also very concerned for the reporters at the *Daily News*, whom I knew. Jonathan Moyo had been launching daily attacks on the newspaper and I feared that he would use the new severe antipress law against them. My hunch was right: on April 30, two reporters from the *Daily News* were arrested.

The next day was May 1, Workers' Day, a public holiday. At 6:55 A.M. our buzzer rang, and I went to the gate in my bathrobe. Three policemen announced that they had come to arrest me.

I had seen the government arrest so many other critics on spurious charges that I should not have been surprised, yet I could not believe it was happening to me. I told Dolores that the police were arresting me, and she phoned Beatrice while I got dressed. Still I could not believe that I was going to be forcibly taken away from my home and my wife.

Beatrice arrived within fifteen minutes. She argued with the police that she and I would come in to see them during working hours, but they were adamant that they had to take me in for questioning right away. The police frequently arrested people on holidays or during the weekend so they could hold them in jail for a few days before they appeared in court. There was nothing I could do; I got into the police Land-Rover and as the door was slammed behind me I realized I was a prisoner.

I was driven to the Harare Central, a sprawling Rhodesian building with forbidding dark hallways, small offices, and rickety benches for prisoners. I was separated from the bustling market and bus depot outside by bars on the windows. I was held in the law and order section in the upper corner of the building, where many others claimed to have been tortured. Officers Makedenge and Dhliwayo questioned me about the beheading story, which they had taken from the *Guardian*'s Web site. I explained that I had written the story, but pointed out that I did not actually state the woman had been decapitated. I had reported *allegations* that the woman had been murdered. The police were not interested in such subtleties; they just kept asking me if I would admit that I wrote the story.

Beatrice arrived at the station within thirty minutes and began challenging the police. When she spoke on her cell phone one policeman seized it from her, but she grabbed it right back. "I am not a suspect," she said. "I am a lawyer and this phone is mine. I can use it as I see fit." Beatrice had called for an urgent hearing in the courts to secure my release. The police officers assured her that they would wait with me until she returned, but as soon as her car left the parking lot they made their move. They led me along a hallway and then down several flights of stairs.

"We're taking you to the cells," said one of the officers as we went into the basement. My stomach lurched as the jail guard ordered: "Take off your shoes and socks, your belt and watch. Take off your shirt or your jersey. You are only allowed one top item of clothing in the cells."

The bars clanked behind me and I entered the chilly jail cells of Harare Central, barefoot and shirtless but with my sweater. It was a very frightening moment.

"*Psst. Psssst,* Meldrum!" somebody whispered. Looking around, I saw two young men huddled in a little closet: Collin Chiwanza and Lloyd Mudiwa, the two *Daily News* reporters who had been arrested the day before. "Stay here with us. The rest of this place is awful," said Lloyd. "How much money do you have? You will have to pay a bribe to stay here with us," said Collin. I had grabbed some money when I left my house and now Collin used it to get the prison guards to agree that I could stay with them. We stuck together in the holding cell and avoided the more crowded and filthy general cells, but even so our cell was small, with a wide bench on one side. A few other guys sat as far as possible from the stinking bucket that was our toilet. It was unimaginably smelly, cramped, and miserable.

Winter was approaching and the dark, dank jail was freezing cold. We were all barefooted and I started to feel the cold. "We've got a blanket which can keep us all warm," Collin said, showing me a large, dirty, matted rag that reeked of urine. Lloyd said it had bugs and showed little bites on his body. I vowed never to get near the thing, but as our cell became colder, I stuck my feet into it. By the time night arrived I had snuggled under it.

We talked about how we were arrested, what the police had said to us. Lloyd had written the original story and Collin had been sent out the next day to see the funeral. He had returned to the *Daily News* to tell the editors that there were no signs that the woman had been beheaded. Editor Geoff Nyarota had taken control of the story at that point. "I never wrote a word of that story!" said Collin. "I told the police I didn't write any of it but they arrested me anyway."

Lloyd said he felt terrible for having made the mistake in the first place and even worse to feel responsible for us being in jail.

"Not at all, Lloyd, you mustn't blame yourself," I told him. "You tried to check out the story and it appeared OK. The most important thing is that the law itself is unjust. It should not be a crime to make such a mistake and we should not be in jail." We talked more about journalism, other reporters we knew, the situation in Zimbabwe, how we each started in journalism, and as the hours passed, just about everything under the sun.

Although I had to surrender my shirt, shoes, belt, and briefcase, I had somehow managed to keep a copy of the *Herald*, the government-controlled daily. We looked at a short report about the arrest of Lloyd and Collin, then we came across a story that dumbfounded us. Zimbabwe had been appointed to the board of the United Nations Commission on Human Rights. We were all shocked that the UN body could allow such a prominent position to Zimbabwe, where so many recent human rights abuses had been documented.

As we discussed this outrageous news, a guard came and told us to put away the *Herald*. "You are not allowed to read the paper," he said. "You can only use it for the toilet." It cheered us hugely to be told that the government mouthpiece was only fit to be used as toilet paper.

The world became divided into two classes of people: those with shoes and those with bare feet. The people with shoes, whose footsteps echoed in the halls, were free to come and go as they pleased. Those of us who shuffled along with bare feet were prisoners.

Friendly, outgoing, and chatty, Collin entertained us for hours, telling us about his adventures at school, his work as a schoolteacher, and how he began writing articles for local newspapers. We heard about his first girlfriend and then his second. He told us how he met his wife and how he courted her. He told us all about his beloved daughter and what his wife cooked him for dinner. He went on and on and we encouraged him. Our camaraderie kept our spirits up and we laughed at silly jokes.

"Andrew Meldrum!" I suddenly heard someone call. "Andy?"

I raced to the bars. Down the hallway I could see Beatrice and Dolores. The guards were already pushing them away. "I'm fine. I'm OK," I shouted to Dolores. Beatrice had been so busy on my case that she was still wearing the same tracksuit that she had thrown on when I was first arrested at 7 A.M. We were not able to get any closer or to speak, but they left some food for us, and that little glimpse of them lifted my spirits.

At about 10 P.M., Collin yawned, said he was tired, pulled up the stinking blanket, and promptly fell asleep on the bench that we all shared. Lloyd and I talked some more as Collin snored like a hippo, and eventually we huddled under the blanket and tried to sleep. After a couple of hours Lloyd got up because he was being bitten by something and moved over to a corner.

The cold, dark hours of the early morning were the worst. I couldn't sleep at all. The walls without windows, the cramped conditions, and the stench all made me feel claustrophobic. I went to the "toilet" and cringed as my feet felt the sticky floor. I wanted to grab the cell bars and shout, "Let me out!" but I realized I could easily drive myself crazy. I just had to endure it. I clambered back under the blanket with Collin and tried to sleep.

In the morning the guards told us to come with them and handed us back our belongings. We excitedly pulled on our socks and shoes, our watches, and all our clothes. We climbed the stairs from the basement cells and became giddy when we saw blue sky through a window.

But our happiness was snatched away when we arrived at the magistrates' court and were once again taken to basement cells. We each had to wear a single handcuff and, with nearly thirty other prisoners, were ordered onto a narrow, steep staircase. The doors at the top and the bottom of the stairs were locked. We waited on those cramped stairs for two hours to appear in court. One prisoner relieved himself at the top of the stairs and his urine dribbled past us. I concentrated on the little sliver of sky I could see in the window above me.

Lloyd began acting as a jailhouse lawyer, advising prisoners on what they should do. Many had been arrested for stealing food, some were charged with swindling money in a real estate scam, several guys were in for burglaries. I asked the big muscular fellow next to me what he was in for and he said the police were waiting for the postmortem. Not knowing how to respond, I looked at him blankly.

Some graffiti scrawled on the walls asked, WHERE IS OUR CONSTITUTION? I wondered how many people huddled in the cramped stairway had benefited from their constitutional rights.

Eventually we appeared in court. The charges against Collin were dropped, since it was clear that he had not written a word of the story in question. At first it appeared that Lloyd and I would be sent back to jail, but Beatrice argued persuasively that we should be released without bail pending trial.

"This is police doing their work in the usual manner—cracking down on criminals, not journalists," said Information Minister Jonathan Moyo, commenting on our arrests on state television. "Whether they call themselves journalists, whether they are editors, reporters, Americans or anyone else, they will be held accountable. That is what the rule of law means. We have to crack down on lawlessness." In the weeks that followed, fifteen journalists and editors would be arrested and charged with criminal offences under the Access to Information and Protection of Privacy Act. Other journalists writing for the foreign media were warned that they too were to be arrested for the error of the story of the beheaded woman.

Being released was incredible; I reveled in my new-found freedom. I hugged Dolores, kissed her, and held her hand. I ran through the garden, played with our dogs, and looked up at the expansive African sky. I took a long hot bath. But even after the smell and dirt of jail had been washed away, I still had a sense of unease. That night I lay awake, berating myself for making the error over the beheaded woman. I began to worry about what was to come. I fretted and tossed and turned.

In the morning I woke feeling reinvigorated and renewed. I banished my doubts, as I knew I could not survive with them. I knew I had not committed any crime, I had done nothing wrong. I knew the government was just trying to make an example of me to cow the rest of the press. I knew many other Zimbabweans were suffering violence, torture, and hunger and the government was trying to frighten me away from reporting that. I knew I had to stand up to their bullying.

This was World Press Freedom Day and I was invited by Iden to speak at a gathering of journalists. Several people had been asked to speak, including an official of the United Nations, journalists, and leaders of civic organizations. Collin Chiwanza and I had been asked at the last minute. With all those speeches, I knew I must keep mine short.

"I have been called a terrorist, I have been jailed, I have been charged with committing a crime for which I could be sentenced to two years in jail—and I think I am a lucky guy," I said, and the crowd responded with a chuckle. "I am lucky for three reasons. First, I was lucky to have been thrown in jail with Lloyd Mudiwa and Collin Chiwanza, who helped to make the ordeal bearable. Second, I am lucky to be out of jail. Third, and most important, I am lucky to be standing up for a principle that is so important, here in Zimbabwe and around the world: press freedom."

Above, outside the holding cells of Harare's Magistrates' Court with fellow journalists Collin Chiwanza and Lloyd Mudiwa (with water bottle). We had been jailed overnight and were pleased to be out, only to be put in handcuffs and held for hours. Below, in an Internet café, Magistrate Godfrey Macheyo (right) and I watch as a police officer searches for my offending story. Macheyo had decided that he should see how the Internet actually works. *Both photographs © Howard Burditt/ Reuters*

18

ON TRIAL

My trial date was set. On June 12, 2002, I would be the first journalist tried under Jonathan Moyo's Access to Information and Protection of Privacy Act (Aippa). The trial of Lloyd Mudiwa and Geoff Nyarota, the editor of the *Daily News,* would come later.

It was a cold morning when Dolores and I drove to the magistrates' courthouse. Waiting at a red light at the junction of Herbert Chitepo and Second Streets we saw a young boy of nine or ten begging for money. Dolores will never give money but she does give food, and she handed him an orange. She watched as the boy handed it over to a teenager, who traded it for a plastic bag. The young boy began inhaling deeply from the bag—glue-sniffing. Surely, I thought, it cannot get more depressing than this.

At the courthouse all my journalist colleagues were gathered by the front steps where we would always wait before a big case. As I got out of the car they rushed toward me, cameras pointed, video cameras rolling. I don't know why I hadn't anticipated that they would want to concentrate on me, but it only hit me then. I fixed a grimly determined look on my face that became a mask I wore for the seven weeks of the trial.

I knew the round magistrates' court building well. Dolores and I had married there, and it had been the site of several political trials that I had covered. The place of our happy wedding had become the building where I had been incarcerated and now stood trial. The striking, circular building had become dilapidated and dirty. The courtrooms were scattered with broken benches and the windows were thick with dust; the fountain in the central courtyard had long ago stopped working. I could see that it would not take much to get the once handsome courthouse

227

back in shape, but like so much in Zimbabwe it would have to wait until better, more prosperous times.

Beatrice was in the courtroom, surrounded by books and documents. She was cheerful and humorous as usual, and a great support for us. Beatrice had worked for nine years as a state prosecutor and she knew the court system well. We had agreed on the strategy: she would not challenge the constitutionality of the repressive press act, since this would send the case straight to the supreme court, which was packed with Mugabe's loyalists. "We have a better chance of winning an acquittal at the magistrate level," she said. "Their case is not very strong. It is full of holes and I will point out every one."

The *Guardian* not only provided me with Beatrice's expert legal defense, they also sent out Geoffrey Robertson QC, the renowned expert on international media law, from London. He discussed the case with Beatrice and endorsed her strategy. He was only able to stay for a few days of the case, but his presence in the courtroom and his scrutiny of the proceedings helped persuade the magistrate to take the case seriously. The magistrate would hear the case and then decide the verdict and the sentence. (Zimbabwe's Roman-Dutch law system, shared with South Africa, does not use juries.)

As happens in so many of Zimbabwe's court cases, the opening of the trial was delayed from the scheduled start of 8 A.M. At 10:30 the announcement came that the trial would not start until 11:30, because the magistrate had gone home to breastfeed her baby. At 11:45 the buzzer sounded to announce her arrival and we all stood up. The door opened and out stepped the magistrate—a man, complete with full beard!

"Clearly the female magistrate didn't want anything to do with this case because it is such a hot potato," Beatrice told us later. "She went home and refused to come back, so they had to find someone else to take the case at the last minute. This magistrate was obviously grabbed and thrown in here."

I took my place in the dock where for several weeks, as accusations and arguments swirled around me, I remained, taking some notes, silently observing the ins and outs of my fate. Wooden panels boxed in the dock area, like a choir pew, and a door led off to the steep staircase where prisoners were held. Often a cold draught blew under that door, bringing me the unwelcome prison stench of stale urine. As grim as it was to be on trial, each day it was a relief to leave the courtroom through the front door a free man instead of being bundled back behind that door and taken to the cells.

The threat of jail was a nagging presence. Before and during my trial I received several warnings from people claiming to be "friends," people who had close dealings with cabinet ministers. They told me that the government intended to put me behind bars. One e-mail from a professional contact told me that "moderate" members of Mugabe's cabinet had assured him that I would be convicted and sentenced to jail, reminded me that Zimbabwe's jails are unpleasant, and said that if I knew what was good for me I would leave the country. A phone call from a journalist informed me that the government was going to "get me" through the court case and destroy my professional reputation. Another acquaintance, well connected to Zanu-PF, warned that some members of the cabinet were plotting that I should be harmed in "an accident." These were unsettling messages, to be sure, but they did not achieve the desired results. The government felt I could be frightened into fleeing the country, which would make me look guilty and make it easier to win convictions of the other journalists. Their mafialike warnings, however, only hardened my already firm resolve not to run away.

The prosecutor, Thabani Mpofu, was young, dynamic, and ambitious. From the outset he put his stamp on the case with high-volume arguments full of invective against me and insinuations against Beatrice. When asking questions of a witness, he had a way of looking over his shoulder at the public gallery. He made his points with great flourish, waving his arms and pointing his finger, usually at me. A friend attending the trial said he had watched too many American courtroom dramas.

After the first day of the trial, Dolores and I were relaxing at home when a visitor rang at the gate. It was Prosper, a young man whom Dolores had first met when she was working at the home for disabled children. He was bright and we had helped him go to school to study for his A levels. We had often visited him at that school, where he had been elected deputy head boy. After doing well in his exams, Prosper got good jobs. He was doing very well and had a flashy new company car to prove it. We had not seen him for some time and he had lots to tell us.

229

"Do you know who your prosecutor is?" he asked. "He was my room-mate at school. You used to bring us biscuits and orange squash."

Dolores had said she recognized the prosecutor but couldn't place him. Now the penny dropped: we had met him when visiting Prosper at his school. Prosper told us he was the star of the school's debating team—so that was where he developed his florid, bombastic style.

Prosper also told us that when he was driving back from a visit to his parents in a remote rural area, he stopped in the town of Chivhu to have a Coke. A group of youth militia attacked him and his passengers, saying his truck looked like an MDC vehicle. One of Prosper's passengers was beaten so badly that he had to go to the hospital. When Prosper went to the police to complain, they told him they had been given orders to allow the youth militia to do whatever they wanted.

Prosper's humorous way of describing this experience had us all gasping and then laughing in disbelief. These sorts of incidents, coupled with economic decline, were fueling opposition to Mugabe's rule.

When the trial resumed on Monday, our magistrate, Godfrey Macheyo, appeared to have new energy and new interest in the case. "This case is a very important one," he said. "Many people are closely observing this case. I took advantage of the weekend to read the new law, the Access to Information and Protection of Privacy Act. And now, having read the act, I want to step down as magistrate in this case. If the accused is found guilty, the act says I can fine him or send him to jail. But as a magistrate I can only fine him Z$7,000, so to impose a serious penalty I would have to sentence him to jail. I think this case must be heard by the high court, where the judge can impose a higher fine."

Thabani and Beatrice both jumped up to protest. Thabani argued that once I was found guilty, he would not request a huge fine or even a lengthy jail sentence. He said a small fine would suffice.

Beatrice complained strenuously. "I am extremely uncomfortable," she said, "at having any discussion about the appropriate sentence for my client before he has been found guilty. Surely this is putting the cart before the horse, Your Honor. I propose that you continue hearing this case, and if the problem of imposing a fitting sentence should arise, you can then refer the case to the high court for sentencing."

The magistrate decided to continue hearing the case, and the trial resumed.

In due course the prosecution brought the family of the dead woman to testify. It was heartbreaking. The elderly father was nearly blind; he could not hear well and did not seem to understand what was going on. The deceased woman's sister, however, knew exactly what was happening and gave a poignant account of how her sister died. "My sister was not beheaded. She died of AIDS. I know because I cared for her and she died in my arms. I buried her. I know she was not beheaded."

"So do you blame that man," said Thabani, with a dramatic sweeping gesture toward me, "for the misery that your family has suffered as a result of this story of beheading?"

The sister looked at me long and hard and then turned to the prosecutor. "No," she said. "I do not blame that man. I blame my sister's husband. He is the one who told the lie in the first place. He is the one who has caused our family so much suffering."

Although Beatrice told me that her testimony did not make much difference to the case, her words were very significant to me. To hear that she did not hold me responsible for her troubles came as a great relief.

Some light comedy was provided by the officer in charge of the rural police station in the area where the woman died. The blustering officer claimed he never saw a copy of the *Daily News* because "it is from the devil. We do not allow that paper in our area." Under stiff cross-examination from Beatrice, he said, "I don't have to answer questions from you." Beatrice insisted that he did, indeed, have to answer her questions, and the magistrate was forced to back her up.

"If I was married to you, I would divorce you," complained the policeman.

"Officer," retorted Beatrice, "I can assure you that would never happen."

A key issue in the case was the question of where my story had been published. How could the state prosecute me for a story that was published in the *Guardian* in London and that was not available in Zimbabwe? It was so difficult to find a copy of the *Guardian* in Zimbabwe that, more than six weeks after my arrest, the state still had not produced a copy of my story.

The only evidence presented by the state was a copy of the article as it had appeared on the *Guardian*'s Web site. They argued that, as it had been found and taken off the Internet in Zimbabwe, it had effectively been published in Zimbabwe. In fact, it had not yet been determined in international law where an article placed on the Internet was liable under law. Was it the point where the article was placed on the Internet, or was it every place around the world where the story was taken off the Internet? I found it fascinating how my trial spanned the considerable distance from a remote rural village, where witnesses lived in thatched mud huts with no electricity or running water, to the latest technology of cyberspace. Zimbabwe, like all of Africa, was bridging the gap between the medieval world of its rural population and the cutting-edge technology of the developed world.

There was much arguing back and forth over the Internet issue. The magistrate confessed that he did not know anything about the World Wide Web. Thabani admitted that he did not know much about it either. As so much of the case appeared to hinge on the issue, Beatrice suggested that the court should investigate how anyone can access the Internet and request to see a story. We agreed to go to an Internet café.

The judge did not have a car—this was because it had been burned by Mugabe's war veterans, angered by his ruling that "Hitler" Hunzvi had to stand trial on charges of embezzlement—and said, correctly, that he could not accept a lift offered by the defense.

It was decided we would go to the Sheraton Hotel, which was within walking distance and had a business center with Internet access. We all walked through a field—magistrate, prosecutor, defense, court officials, and public—to the glitzy, gold hotel building. In the business center the state witness, a police officer, showed how a computer could be connected to the Internet. He went to the *Guardian*'s Web site and searched for articles by me, but he failed to find the article about the beheading. I found out later that the *Guardian* had removed the article as soon as I informed them it was incorrect. Instead the prosecution found another of my articles: "My Night in Mugabe's Stinking Jail." The magistrate, prosecutor, and several others stood transfixed by their first encounter with the Internet and the array of Web sites and archives that appeared on the screen.

The prosecution wound up its case without ever calling me to the stand. Beatrice immediately called for the case to be dismissed for lack of evidence: the state had no admission from me that I had written the article, nor had it produced the offending article. An article from the Internet was not proof of publishing in Zimbabwe, she argued. The magistrate adjourned to decide whether to dismiss the charge against me or to continue with the trial.

Beatrice explained that in ordinary circumstances the case would be dismissed, but this magistrate was under considerable pressure. If he decided to continue the case, he would have to give a judgment explaining his reasons and that would show us what points to highlight in our defense.

However, when the case resumed two days later, the magistrate took the unusual step of ordering the case to continue without giving any reasons why. It deprived Beatrice of insight into what he felt were the important points of the case, but there was nothing she could do. She called an expert witness to the stand who gave further evidence about how placing an article on the Internet could not be considered actual publication in Zimbabwe.

Beatrice then decided to close the case. Thabani jumped up. "I protest, Your Honor. The defense has not put the accused on the stand." Beatrice responded that she had no need to put me on the stand. Realizing that he had failed to get me to admit to writing the article, Thabani insisted that he had the right to cross-examine me. Beatrice pointed out that "the prosecution has no right to cross-examine the witness if he has not been examined first."

The magistrate was also visibly unsettled at the prospect that I would not give any testimony. He made an extraordinary ruling that I should be called to the stand to answer questions from the prosecutor, even though I had not been sworn in as a witness.

Under questioning from Thabani I admitted that I had written the article reporting the allegation that the woman was beheaded. He flashed a smile that suggested he thought he had scored a major point. The magistrate then asked me what steps I had taken to verify the story. I replied that first of all the *Daily News* had a good record of publishing accurate stories, particularly about political violence. I said I called the police but they refused to give any comment, as they normally do. I also explained how I had gone to two human rights groups and asked them about the incident, and they said they were investigating it.

I was only on the stand for about ten minutes; then it was agreed that the prosecution and the defense would give their summations the next day. The magistrate announced that he especially wanted to hear arguments about the issue of "strict liability." A judgment of strict liability means that if someone is found guilty, there are no mitigating factors. For instance, it is often applied in drunk-driving cases; if a driver is found to have been legally intoxicated, no excuses are accepted and the full penalty is imposed.

In his closing statement for the prosecution, Thabani charged that I had written a false story, which was a crime under the Access to Information and Protection of Privacy Act. He stated simply that it was a strict liability offence: the woman was not beheaded, therefore the article was false, and therefore I must be found guilty. The magistrate questioned him further on the question of strict liability and Thabani said the law was written in a way to suggest that this was a strict liability offence. "It is not for us to decide if the law is reasonable or not," he said; "it was passed by Parliament and is therefore the law of the land."

Beatrice gave a masterful summation, dissecting the state's case against me and refuting its points one after the other. When she came to the issue of strict liability she really soared. Strict liability was used in the old racist Rhodesian regime and in apartheid South Africa to enforce racist laws. Under strict liability, if laws were broken, no matter how unreasonable they seemed, then the accused was found guilty. But, argued Beatrice, since Zimbabwe's independence and since majority rule in South Africa there had been a decided shift against strict liability offences so that now only parking violations and driving-while-intoxicated cases were judged that way. To suggest that this crime, a more serious crime carrying a jail sentence, was "strict liability" would be to go against a trend of more than twenty years. It would say that Zimbabwean law was reverting to Rhodesian law, she concluded.

We returned the next day for the magistrate's verdict. I entered the now familiar courtroom with trepidation. Beatrice had put up a strong defense and I knew the prosecution's case was riddled with holes, but the case now rested entirely with the magistrate, whose demeanor in court had been consistently favorable toward the state. What was worse, some journalists had already found me guilty because the story of the woman's beheading was false. They did not question the law at all. I was even more worried about my professional reputation than the possibility of a jail sentence.

The magistrate slowly read out his judgment from a handwritten script. He strongly criticized Beatrice for her conduct during the trial, saying she had been obstructive and too loud. He ruled that it made no difference where the article was published: it had a damaging effect on Zimbabwe's reputation and therefore I could be tried for it under Zimbabwean law. He judged that the woman had not been beheaded. It was irrelevant that I had attributed my story to the *Daily News* and had used the qualifiers "alleged" and "accused" with every mention of the crime. Following the magistrate's reasoning, I began stiffening for a guilty verdict.

Then he came to the issue of strict liability. He stated that instead of interpreting the law under strict liability, the magistrate must look at the intent of the journalist. He said I had tried to check out the story with the police and they had acted irresponsibly by refusing to give me information about the case. He said I had "acted as a responsible journalist" and therefore had not intended to publish a falsehood. The magistrate concluded, "I find the defendant not guilty of the charge."

Not guilty. Not guilty! It took a few seconds for my acquittal to sink in. I felt the weight of nearly three months' worrying lift away. I jumped out of the dock and hugged Dolores and then Beatrice. We were surrounded by people hugging us, shaking our hands, clapping me on the back. The courtroom was suddenly full of jubilation.

We moved toward the courtroom door, and I started to think about what I wanted to say to the cameras and assembled press out in front.

I was stopped by a tall man who introduced himself as Mr. Siziba. I gleefully shook his hand as I had so many others, thinking he was congratulating me. But his face was very stern. "I am from Immigration, come with me," he ordered. I looked for Dolores but she was already out of the door and surrounded by well-wishers. I turned back and found Beatrice, who immediately followed me. I pushed through the crowd and told Dolores, who was still beaming with joy, to come, too.

We were taken to a small room where Mr. Siziba showed us his identification as a senior immigration officer. He read out an order from the minister of Home Affairs that I should be deported from the country within twenty-four hours. I looked at the date on the deportation order: it had been drawn up two weeks earlier. The government had decided to get me out of the country whether I was guilty or not.

Beatrice said that we would fight the order, pointing out that I held a government permit giving me the right to permanent residence. But when the immigration officers left the room I suggested that if the government was so determined to get rid of me then maybe it was not worth fighting them any further.

"I would be uncomfortable representing you if you do not contest this," said Beatrice. "You have every legal right to stay in this country and there are nearly a million other people here with permanent residence permits. If we allow the government to take away your rights, it could affect all those others."

That was all the encouragement I needed. Beatrice set the wheels in motion immediately. We needed to apply for an urgent hearing at the high court, to prepare an affidavit, to get documents signed by immigration officials.

As we stepped out of the courtroom at last, we were surrounded by the press waiting for my comment. "My acquittal is a great victory, not only for me but for the free press in Zimbabwe. The government's action to immediately deport me highlights what the trial also exposed: that this government is suppressing a free press and trampling on its own laws to do so."

Back at Beatrice's office, my cell phone began ringing. BBC, CNN, Radio France International, New Zealand Radio—it went on and on. I scribbled out a story for the *Guardian* in my notebook. As we were on our way to lodge the appeal with the minister of Home Affairs, Dolores answered my phone and spoke to a Zimbabwean journalist with whom I had been friendly. "Tell Andy to get out of Zimbabwe now!" he urged. "The government is serious and it is dangerous." Beatrice and I laughed at this attempt to get me to give up.

When I got back home various photographers called, wanting to take pictures of me packing and preparing to leave. "I am not packing my bags or getting ready to go in any way," I said. "You can photograph me working at my computer or speaking on the phone as usual, but you won't get any photographs of me getting ready to leave."

The next day we were back in a courtroom, this time at the high court. Beatrice got the prosecution's papers and exclaimed, "Look at this! The government claims that you are a threat to national security and to public morality!"

Judge Anele Matika arrived. He had represented Zanu-PF in several legal cases before he was appointed a judge and he was widely considered to be a Zanu-PF judge through and through. But Beatrice was not worried: "The law is clear on this, there is nothing he can do."

The hearing began, and Beatrice explained that because I held a valid permit granting me the right to reside permanently in Zimbabwe, the state could not simply deport me. "The constitution of Zimbabwe states clearly that a permanent resident has all the rights of a Zimbabwean citizen. The government can only revoke the permanent residence permit under very specific circumstances, which have not been met."

The state claimed that in this case it could not, in the interest of national security, divulge the reasons it had decided to deport me. Beatrice challenged their claim, saying a meeting could be held *in camera* with just the judge, the state attorney, and Beatrice attending to hear the top-secret reasons for deporting me. "But I know the state will not agree to that because they do not have any specific reasons for trying to deport Mr. Meldrum. They are just using national security to hide the fact they have no bona fide complaints against him."

The state attorney sat mutely at her desk. Beatrice had called her bluff.

The judge said he would only need a few minutes to make a decision. Mr. Siziba and some police officers waited at the back of the courtroom to take me away. As we waited for the judge to return, I began to think I had been rash not to pack a bag or prepare in any way to leave.

The judge returned. "My hands are tied. There is nothing I can do," he said apologetically, as if he were speaking to the government instead of to us. "The constitution states unambiguously that the holders of valid permits of permanent residence have the right to live and work in Zimbabwe. If the government wants to take this measure any further, they can appeal to the supreme court."

Yet again Beatrice and I had won. This time I could smile broadly as I spoke to the press. The journalists also wanted a response from Beatrice, but when the cameras were trained on her and a journalist shoved a microphone in front of her, I saw her blanch. For the first time ever, I saw my fearless lawyer, who could argue any point in court, at a loss for words.

When we got home Mavis welcomed us with open arms and ululated with joy at the court victory. She quickly phoned her mother, who was staying up in Raffingora. Ambuya Milka had not eaten for twenty-four hours before my verdict, and had prolonged her fast when she heard that I had to go to court again to avoid being deported. When Mavis told her that the judge had said I could stay in Zimbabwe, she replied, "I'm putting on a pot for *sadza,* a big one!"

A few other older Shona people told me they, too, had fasted before my verdict was announced. The advertising department of the *Financial Gazette* newspaper had stopped to pray. We were flooded with notes, messages, phone calls, and e-mails from people all over Zimbabwe and the world. The encouragement and support helped immensely to keep our spirits up and hold our determination firm.

The newspaper and television coverage of my case had made me highly recognizable. Although the state media had consistently depicted me in the most unflattering light, whenever people recognized me they were very supportive. "You're telling the truth. Keep it up!" said an old man working at a municipal parking lot. "We are all supporting you. We know the government is wrong," said a clerk at the post office. "Tell it like it is. You are helping all of us in Zimbabwe," said a shopper at the grocery store.

The overwhelming support and encouragement I received, and the great relationship I had forged with Beatrice, made me feel more a part of Zimbabwe than ever.

Bowling for democracy. Cricket star Henry Olonga wears a black armband to protest against the Mugabe government as he bowls a delivery in Zimbabwe's opening Cricket World Cup match against Namibia in Harare, February 2002. © *Paul Cadenhead/ Reuters*

19

BACK TO REPORTING

It had been impossible to focus on other stories while I myself had been the subject of the news. Now I relished being able to step away from the cameras, get out my notebook, and start being a journalist again.

"Stop writing stories that are so critical of the government," said a close friend. "Let the other journalists do those stories and you can just write wildlife stories. That way you won't get into any more trouble and you'll be able to stay."

"I can't do that," I responded. "If I censored myself and avoided writing the tough stories, then the government would have succeeded in silencing me without even winning a court case or deporting me. I want to continue working as a journalist and that means writing about what is happening. If I were to avoid writing about torture and corruption, it would defeat my whole purpose for being here. I wouldn't be happy with myself."

My work resumed with the issue of food relief. Zimbabwe was in the grip of widespread food shortages that the government claimed were the result of a combination of Cyclone Eline, which damaged crops in eastern Zimbabwe, and a drought in other parts of the country. Agricultural experts, however, said those calamities were not sufficient to cause the widespread crop failure. They blamed the food shortages on the chaotic dismantling of the commercial farming sector and on the government's failure to provide adequate seeds and fertilizer to the small-scale farming sector, both the black peasant farmers and those blacks who had been resettled on some of the seized farms. At the same time, small-scale farmers who sold surplus maize to the Grain Marketing Board were not paid for many months, leaving them without the cash needed to put new crops in the ground. While Mugabe was confiscating white farms in the name of poor blacks, his government was neglecting the very people he claimed to be helping.

Zimbabwe, for years hailed as the breadbasket of southern Africa, was now dependent upon international food aid. To make matters even worse, there was considerable evidence that the government was preventing food from being distributed in areas that had supported the opposition. There were reports that the distribution of food aid had been stopped in Binga by Mugabe's war veterans. I decided to investigate these stories myself.

Binga is one of the most remote places in Zimbabwe, on the shore of Lake Kariba in arid Matabeleland North. It is the home of the Tonga people, who lived in the Zambezi River Valley until 1960, when the Kariba Dam flooded their area and forced them to move to higher ground. Since independence the Mugabe government has largely neglected the Tonga minority, and their areas are some of the least developed in Zimbabwe.

I made the trip with Grant Ferrett, who had moved back to Britain with the BBC and then returned to Zimbabwe as a "tourist," because the government would not issue permits to British journalists. After an eight-hour drive from Harare, we managed to miss our appointment with the MDC member of Parliament for the area, Jealous Sansole. We were tired and frustrated and the light was beginning to fade. We stopped to ask directions from the occupant of a bright red pickup truck parked beside the road. As luck would have it, it was Sansole himself. We interviewed him on the spot.

Sansole charged that the government had systematically starved his constituency in two ways: first, by restricting distribution of food through the state's Grain Marketing Board, and second, by preventing international charities from distributing food. We asked if we could see any victims of the hunger that he said was widespread. "Just go down this path," he said, pointing to a dirt trail leading from the paved road. About a hundred yards through the bush we found a clearing where a wizened, blind man was sitting with his daughter, who was boiling water over a fire.

We made our introductions and asked if they would like to speak to us. The man agreed.

"I am ashamed for you to see me like this," he said. "I cannot offer you anything. We have not had any food to eat for many days. We are eating dried leaves that we boil in water."

Some food relief had come two months earlier, but the war veterans had halted it. "We are starving," he said simply, and pulled up his tattered shirt to show the folds of an empty stomach. "I want the world to know that for us in Zimbabwe, it is like living in prison." We gave him some maize meal, sugar, and salt that we had brought.

We carried on to Binga, and next morning we viewed the storeroom where Save the Children UK had stored large amounts of a nutritious porridge intended to feed hungry schoolchildren in the area for several months. A band of local war veterans had blocked any distribution of the food because it came from Britain. We visited schools where teachers said spindly children were fainting from hunger, and we went to the district hospital, where staff confirmed that malnutrition had contributed to the deaths of more than thirty people.

"The government is trying to starve all the people of Binga," said a hospital nurse. I asked her why and she said proudly, "Because our district delivered the highest vote against Mugabe in the presidential elections."

Just a dozen men with wooden clubs and rocks were causing misery to thousands of residents. The police refused to intervene, saying it was a political matter. My stories spelled out how the Mugabe government was starving its political opposition.

Reports continued to come from all over the country that the Grain Marketing Board was withholding food from any areas that had voted against Mugabe. In areas where the GMB was selling food, war veterans and youth militia patroled the lines and threw out anyone suspected of supporting the opposition, often beating them in the process.

In many areas where the United Nations World Food Programme was distributing free food, it gave food only to people who were on lists compiled by local government officials. Human rights groups complained that the WFP did not consult local church groups, women's groups, and other nongovernmental sources to see if needy people had been left off the list.

A few months later I traveled to the Nkayi area of Matabeleland North and witnessed for myself how the government prevented people from getting food. The Nkayi camp of Mugabe's youth militia had declared this a no-go area for the MDC and whites.

First I visited a family headed by an old woman in her seventies. She was so weak from hunger that she had to crawl out of her hut, and then sat propped up against a tree. Her daughter and two grandchildren lived with her but the family had not eaten anything except wild berries for weeks. "In my whole life I have never seen such hunger," said the old woman. Within a few kilometers the Grain Marketing Board had a large depot where it sold maize meal at low prices, but "the GMB chases ordinary people away," said the grandmother. "Only the camp of youth militia and other Zanu-PF supporters can buy maize there. The rest of us must go hungry. It is wicked." Her adult daughter had a terrible cough, which the mother said was caused by her hunger. I suspected it was AIDS, exacerbated by malnutrition. Other residents of Nkayi that I spoke to told me how they had been abducted and tortured by the youth militia, showing me the scars. They said that other young men had been killed, and wanted to take me to the graves, but we heard another vehicle driving nearby and my guides were worried that the youth militia were looking for me. I headed back to Bulawayo.

As soon as I reached the city, I visited Garfield Todd, who was prime minister of Southern Rhodesia from 1953 to 1958. He had advocated a gradual process leading to majority rule and became one of the foremost critics of Ian Smith's regime during the 1960s. He was jailed and then put under house arrest, but he and his daughter, Judith, still managed to give secret support to nationalist fighters. After independence Mugabe honored his support by appointing him a senator, and later, in 1987, he was knighted by the queen.

I had first met Todd in the early 1980s. At nearly eighty, he radiated energy and an inspiring, positive outlook. He proudly showed me the school on his ranch where Mugabe had first worked as a teacher. A pregnant woman came up to him and soon he had his hands on her swollen belly, feeling how high she was carrying the baby. He told me proudly that he had helped scores of local women through childbirth.

Todd became disillusioned with the Mugabe government after watching the horrors of Matabeleland and the creeping corruption, but he remained a vital, vigorous voice in Zimbabwean politics. A month before the March 2002 presidential elections, Todd was stripped of his citizenship like thousands of Zimbabweans who were foreign-born or whose parents were born in foreign countries. Barred from voting in the election, the former premier responded in typically forthright fashion. In a letter to the *Daily News* Todd said he would not willingly agree to lose his vote, and felt bound to

> shoulder the responsibility of totally rejecting the disenfranchisement of Zimbabweans by Zanu-PF. I am horrified by the destruction of our economy, the starving of our people, the undermining of our constitution, the torture and humiliation of our nation by Zanu-PF. Just as we stood with courage against the racism of the past, so today we must stand with courage against the terror of the present. Come what may, I will be going to the polling station to claim my right, as a very senior citizen of Zimbabwe, to cast my ballot for good against evil.

On voting day, the defiant Todd stood in the polling lines, his erect bearing and thick shock of white hair belying his ninety-three years, only to be turned away by apologetic officials. He remained determinedly optimistic that good would prevail.

Now, Todd welcomed me warmly to his Bulawayo home. "I followed your trial and was very pleased when you were acquitted," he told me. The day's newspapers were spread on the table before us and we launched into discussions of Mugabe's grip on power and the victimization of the opposition. "What I will not forgive Mugabe is that he has corrupted so many good men," said Todd.

"Justice and democracy will prevail and I don't think it is very far away," said Todd as he prepared to go for his daily walk. "You can't stop the will of the people. I believe this country will get the government that it deserves."

That determined optimism about Zimbabwe's future was not shared by Ian Smith. Ever since I first arrived in Zimbabwe, he had loomed in the background of the country's consciousness. As Zimbabwe's crisis hit, Smith stepped forward to say "I told you so." Again and again he insisted that Zimbabwe's catalog of problems had been brought about by turning the country over to Mugabe.

I had interviewed Smith a few times and found him unshakable in his conviction that he was right all along, but I had been asked to interview him again and rang to request a meeting. "The *Guardian*, eh? That left-wing paper? All right. Come to my house at 8 A.M. Or is that too early for a journalist?" I assured him that I would be there at that time.

Wiry, squinty, and slightly stooped at eighty-four, Ian Smith stood in the doorway of his Harare home as I arrived on a rainy morning. "Wipe your feet," he barked at me, "I don't want you journalists bringing mud into this house."

Smith frequently railed against the press, particularly the international press, which he charged was biased against him and Rhodesia. But complain as he did, he rarely turned down an interview. He clearly enjoyed the attention and the combative interchanges. Similarly, Smith always claimed that he had never wanted to be a politician, but even his opponents credited him with craftily ruling Rhodesia with an iron hand from 1964 for fifteen years, after which he still held considerable influence.

"You're on time, I'll give you that much," he said as we sat down. The sitting room of his comfortable, but not lavish, Harare home appeared to have been frozen in time forty years ago. Photographs and memorabilia from his stint as a Royal Air Force pilot in the Second World War, and his time as Rhodesia's prime minister were on display among landscape paintings of the African bush and some African curios. The room was impeccably clean but it seemed that nothing had changed for ages, probably since Smith's wife, Janet, died several years earlier. Certainly nothing had changed in Smith's outlook. He still clung to the belief that his attempt to maintain white minority rule was right. He accepted that blacks could become members of the previously all-white Harare Club that he frequented more easily than he could accept that Robert Mugabe was now running the country. "When there are those who meet the standards of the Harare Club and mix well with members, then it is wonderful," he said tersely, showing little joy in the change. When I pointed out that he had not been seen mixing with black members he became more defensive. "I have a few black friends," he countered, "but only a few, because our culture is different. We have different ways."

He denounced Mugabe as a "gangster" who had "looted and destroyed this country's economy." But I was not interested in Smith's much quoted tirades about Mugabe and the ruin of the present; I was more curious about Smith's view of the past. When I asked him if he could have taken a more moderate, conciliatory path that would have avoided the bitter war, which took forty thousand lives, and would have allowed for better race relations after independence, Smith became riled.

"No, I could not have done things differently," he replied adamantly. "I don't apologize for what has happened. It is a twist of the truth to say that I did not take a moderate path. Absolutely ludicrous! Look here, I tried. I negotiated with the British. We were trying to develop standards, to educate the black man gradually. But we were forced by the British government to give that up."

Smith's suggestion that his Rhodesian Front government was working for a gradual achievement of majority rule was not supported by the historical record. He had conveniently forgotten his infamous vow that "never in a thousand years" would he agree to majority rule. He categorically denied any knowledge of human rights abuses, despite considerable evidence of top level orders being given to poison large amounts of clothing, resulting in the deaths of scores of ordinary rural peasants as well as some nationalist fighters. Torture, beatings, arrests, press repression were frequent occurrences in Smith's Rhodesia.

Far from being polar opposites, I see Ian Smith and Robert Mugabe as two sides of the same coin: they have used similar political cunning and brutality to maintain their rules. To my mind, they need each other. Ian Smith justifies all the wrongs of his rule by pointing to Mugabe and claiming that he was fighting against him. For his part, Robert Mugabe justifies the violence of his rule by citing Ian Smith and claiming that he is just ridding Zimbabwe of Rhodesia's past. The one cannot exist without the other.

Smith used his considerable political skills to keep Rhodesia's white population in conflict with the black majority, and Mugabe has stirred up racial animosity in order to maintain his rule. Both leaders have increased the country's racial tensions rather than given leadership toward genuine reconciliation.

In the end, I hold Smith the more culpable because he came first. He upheld a system which stripped the majority of the population of basic democratic rights and which used considerable force to keep them subjugated. Smith created the conditions so that only the most ruthless, the most violent, would succeed him: Robert Mugabe. Mugabe fought his way to the top of his party and then stayed there. He waged an unrelenting war against Smith that he knew took the lives of thousands upon thousands of his supporters. Violence corrupts. No matter how just the cause, the killing of others infects the perpetrator. Robert Mugabe paid lip service to national reconciliation in the early 1980s but when his power was challenged in 2000 he had no compunction about unleashing violence in order to maintain his grip. Zimbabwe desperately needs leadership that will break these cycles of violence and will allow for a change of government by peaceful, democratic means.

Mugabe is not alone in adopting many of the tactics of his former oppressor. Several modern African leaders have copied their colonial masters. The one-party states favored by most newly independent African countries in the 1960s and 1970s were obviously similar in structure to Eastern European communist states, with their politburos and central committees. But the African one-party states were also uncannily similar to the structure and unquestioned authority of the colonial rulers. The copying of the oppressor also works itself out at a personal level. Hastings Banda wore a three-piece suit and homburg hat throughout his long reign in Malawi's tropical heat. Jean-Bedel Bokassa wore Napoleonic satin breeches and pearl-encrusted slippers when he crowned himself emperor of Central Africa. Robert Mugabe wears expertly tailored Savile Row suits and custom-made shirts even as he excoriates the British for their colonial past and accuses the British government of plotting against him.

The Zimbabwean people increasingly began to view Mugabe as a tyrant. Throughout the closing months of 2002, the resistance to Mugabe's rule increased. The MDC called a national strike, which succeeded in shutting down all commercial and industrial activity across the country for three days. The government reacted with fury, sending the army and youth militia out through Harare's townships, beating and torturing members of the MDC.

I went to a hospital to see a woman who had been beaten by the army. Her swollen face and oozing wounds bore witness to a night of beatings, torture, and rape by a gang of soldiers. "Meldrum," she said, her face brightening. "I was hoping you would come here. You must hear my story." She told how the army men beat her with rifle butts, whipped her with the cord of her own iron, and sexually assaulted her. As she spoke she carefully watched her mother, who was sleeping in the next bed. "They forced my mother to open her legs and they pushed the barrel of an AK-47 rifle up her vagina. They shouted that was to punish her for giving birth to an MDC supporter. Now my mother is bleeding inside."

Another woman I interviewed, Deborah, was held for months at a youth militia camp outside Bulawayo. She and many other young women were raped repeatedly, and Deborah gave birth to a young daughter. "Imagine, I do not even know who the father is," she said. She discovered she was HIV-positive, and decided to tell the public about the atrocities she experienced. "I want to tell people, otherwise I will die in shame."

My conviction that my work was useful did not make the reporting any less troubling. I would return home haggard from these harrowing interviews.

Even the most ordinary things became difficult in Zimbabwe's crisis. On some occasions I got up at 4 A.M. to wait in a fuel line till 11 A.M. To get milk or butter you had to be at the supermarket when it opened at 8 A.M.

And yet the hardships made the pleasures even more prized. A good bottle of wine, a new place where we could get fresh bream, a nearby bakery that almost always had bread became little triumphs. And friends banded together more tightly. "The parties have a *fin de régime* hilarity about them," commented Iden. "People are seizing the moment."

For me, the most gratifying moments were the quiet ones. When Dolores and I would take our dogs for a walk at sunset; picking mulberries in our garden, or basil and rocket to make a salad; sitting on our veranda with friends—these were the interludes that helped me to recharge for the next round of draining news stories.

Food and fuel shortages worsened. Inflation soared to over 200 percent. Shopping for groceries was like being among a pack of panicked scavengers. (Mavis showed me how some supermarket staff would, for favored customers, hide scarce items behind the toilet paper and unpopular cereals.) Prices were skyrocketing so fast that I had to carry around a thick wad of notes the size of a brick to buy a week's necessities. With our productive garden, we were better prepared than many, and Mavis distributed extra greens to some poorer people in the neighborhood.

Mugabe stubbornly refused to alter the economic policies that had brought such ruin to what was once one of the most dynamic economies in Africa. The government had maintained a fixed official exchange rate of Z$50 to U.S.$1, yet no money was available at that rate and on the thriving black market the exchange rate was Z$5,000:U.S.$1. The disparity in rates was creating a huge distortion in the economy and Finance Minister Simba Makoni suggested moving the official rate closer to the actual rate. Mugabe sacked Makoni, calling him a "saboteur." The only one of Mugabe's nearly fifty cabinet ministers who would have any contact with me, Makoni notably said he was sorry for my troubles shortly after I was released from jail.

More and more stories of police brutality came to light. Three MDC members of Parliament were arrested and tortured by electric shock. One of them, Job Sikhala, gave gripping testimony of being shocked to convulsions and of police urinating on him.

Seventeen-year-old Tom Tawanda Spicer, who had spoken so entertainingly at numerous MDC rallies, was arrested several times. Once he was tied to a tree and beaten; on another occasion he was taken to Harare Central's law and order section, and shocked until he was unconscious. A doctor managed to see him in the police cells and recorded that his tongue was badly lacerated where he had bitten it while he was in convulsions. When I saw Tom weeks later he still had trouble grasping a coffee mug because of the damage from the electric shocks.

Zimbabwe's ongoing crisis affected every facet of national life. Playwrights and drama troupes were threatened by the CIO, and artists were thrown out of cottages as the land seizures spread. Rampant poaching of elephant, rhinoceros, and other endangered animals destroyed pioneering conservation projects that had balanced the needs of rural people with the requirements of the wildlife for open land. Even sports were affected.

Controversy blew up around the World Cup cricket tournament in February 2003. While the bulk of the tournament was played in South Africa, several preliminary matches were scheduled to be played in Harare and Bulawayo. Zimbabweans demanded that the matches be moved to South Africa to protest the worsening human rights situation, but Robert Mugabe was the patron of the Zimbabwe Cricket Union and all players were ordered to keep silent about human rights abuses. A man distributing leaflets calling for a boycott of the World Cup matches was arrested by police at a local cricket match and beaten so badly that he died of complications a few weeks later.

On the opening day of the World Cup, two of Zimbabwe's star players, Andy Flower and Henry Olonga, strode onto the pitch sporting black armbands. In a statement released to the press they said, "We are mourning the death of democracy in our beloved Zimbabwe. In doing so we are making a silent plea to those responsible, to stop the abuse of human rights in Zimbabwe. In doing so we pray that our small action may help to restore sanity and dignity to our nation."

I had known Flower, one of the world's top batsmen, for many years and found him to be unfailingly considerate to all and articulate. Henry Olonga was the first black to star on the national team. With his sporty sun-bleached dreadlocks and devout Christian beliefs, he had become an idol for many young black Zimbabweans. Olonga possesses a fine singing voice and he released a stirring anthem, "Our Zimbabwe," which became a hit and was played endlessly on state radio.

In Zimbabwe's oppressive and highly charged atmosphere, their defiant statement cut right through the blustering state propaganda that had used the cricket team and the World Cup as a publicity tool.

Once the two players had made their protest, they were pilloried by the state press. Olonga's song was pulled from the radio playlist, and officials tried to ban both of them from playing any further matches. But the pair became instant heroes. "Every now and again, amidst the gloom of our present darkness, a small light will shine, reminding us of the principles and courage still out there," wrote Iden Wetherell in the *Zimbabwe Independent*. "Just when we needed people to stand up and be counted in the struggle for freedom and justice, Andy Flower and Henry Olonga stepped forward. Now others need to follow their lead."

A few days after the protest, I interviewed Olonga on the same cricket pitch. It was completely deserted because the England team had decided to boycott the match in Zimbabwe, largely as a result of the protest by Olonga and Flower. The twenty-six-year-old Olonga revealed he had thought carefully about taking the action that changed his life.

"I have thought about the costs of making a stand and I think Christianity transcends everything else. Christians are called to speak out against evil, to speak out against things that are wrong and that are wicked. In the face of wickedness, my stand is simply that I am merely doing my duty as a Christian.

"I believe things will come right with regards to the future of the country. Everyone must realize they have to make a stand for what is right. Many issues are thrown around in this nation, but the real issues get clouded. In my opinion it's not about white or black. It's not about race. Sometimes it's not even about money. It's what is right and what is wrong."

As the World Cup tournament went on, things got decidedly tougher for Olonga. Zimbabwean cricket officials threw him off the team bus and prevented him from wearing the team uniform. He received death threats and was followed by men believed to be agents of the CIO. He went into hiding and eventually sought asylum in Britain, where he works as a cricket commentator.

In the same month as the World Cup cricket tournament was played, the treason trial of MDC leader Morgan Tsvangirai opened. On the first day, I went to the historic high court building on Samora Machel Avenue in the center of Harare. Ordinarily it is relatively easy to attend a court case: you need only show identification and be dressed "properly," which for men means a jacket and tie and for women a dress or skirt below the knees, although frequently women wearing trousers are permitted. But for the opening of Tsvangirai's trial the doors were firmly shut and there were dozens of police ordering people away. The state prosecutors, the defendants, and their lawyers were the only ones allowed in. Leading diplomats had come, including the American ambassador, Joseph Sullivan, to see if Tsvangirai was given a fair hearing; the press corps had turned out in force, including many who had flown up from South Africa; there were also more than a hundred MDC supporters. But the police were forcefully pushing all these people away from the entrance. Diplomats, reporters, photographers, members of Parliament stumbled into one another as police tried to push the crowd into the street.

The police ordered us to get in a single-file line before they would allow us in. As we were forming the line, two police plucked me out and one began shoving me very brusquely with a truncheon and shouting at me. I lost my balance and fell to my knees. When I got up he shoved me down again and I had to struggle not to turn around and fight back. They pushed me all the way to the end of the line, shouting the whole time. The incident was filmed and photographed.

Two Zimbabwean journalists were arrested and put in a police van. When I went over with a German diplomat to see if they were all right the police threatened the embassy official and tried to put me inside the van, but I pulled away.

It was chaotic, but the police succeeded in preventing the first day of the trial from being open to the public. The high court judge, however, realized that the trial would not be viewed as fair unless diplomats, press, and public were able to attend. The next day, with only a few difficulties, we were all allowed to attend.

The state charged that Tsvangirai and two other top MDC officials had conspired to have Robert Mugabe assassinated by former Israeli intelligence agent Ari Ben Menashe, who was working as a "political consultant" in Canada. The main evidence against Tsvangirai was a videotape that was secretly filmed by Ben Menashe at a meeting the two had in Montreal. The grainy and largely inaudible tape was played over and over again in the trial. It did not show Tsvangirai contracting

255

the murder of Mugabe; it showed Ben Menashe asking Tsvangirai leading questions about the elimination of Mugabe. Tsvangirai responded that his party wanted to remove Mugabe "through democratic means." Tsvangirai may have been naive and incautious to have gone to the meeting, but he was clearly not guilty of treason.

Ben Menashe admitted on the stand that he had a contract with the Zimbabwean government, which he said owed him in excess of U.S.$100,000. It was also reported that Ben Menashe had been involved in several dubious grain-import schemes with other African governments, where he received money but the grain was never delivered.

The evidence against Tsvangirai was so weak that top Harare lawyers were surprised that the case was taken to court at all. Nevertheless Morgan Tsvangirai and two key MDC officials were on trial for their lives, and the government was forcing the MDC to spend valuable time, energy, and considerable amounts of money on the case. In the process the government showed how it controlled large parts of the police and judicial system.

John Makumbe the day after he was assaulted by police in May 2003. Typically he joked about his bruises. "You have the entire Rainbow Nation on my face! I am black, blue, red, yellow, white, every color you can think of!" © *Michele Mathison*

20

EXPULSION

Events seemed to be building to a climax, although no one was sure which way things would go.

One night Dolores received a phone call saying that some of her work colleagues and several civic leaders, including John Makumbe, had been arrested and were being held at the police station in the smart Borrowdale suburb. We put aside our dinner and drove out to see what was going on. We hoped the presence of a journalist would encourage the police to behave properly.

It was a cool, moonless night. As a result of the fuel shortages there was very little traffic and we reached Borrowdale quickly. The police had broken up a meeting of civic leaders at a church, arresting several church leaders. John had arrived late for the meeting and been arrested as he entered. When he protested that he had not done anything, he was put in handcuffs. Then he was hit in the face several times.

When we arrived at the police station, there were a number of people at the entrance, and some of Dolores's workmates recounted what had happened. Across the counter I could see about twenty people being held by police. John was sitting in the middle, his face badly swollen. I waved to catch his attention and he smiled. A policeman charged around the counter and grabbed my arm. "So these are your friends? You want to be with your friends? Then go in there," and he shoved me toward those who had been arrested.

"No, thanks, I'll stay where I am," I said and started to walk back toward the station's entrance. The policeman shouted at me to stay where I was, next to two lawyers who were trying to represent those arrested. Clearly the Borrowdale station had been transformed into a Zanu-PF outpost.

"You haven't done a thing, they can't arrest you," said Irene Petras of Zimbabwe Lawyers for Human Rights. I agreed, but added that lots of people were being arrested for no good reason these days. Then we heard the police intercom crackle: "That journalist is here. Meldrum is here." The policeman ordered me to stay exactly where I was until the officer in charge came to see me. One lawyer stood in front of me to separate me from those arrested.

The lawyers demanded to know why the police had arrested John Makumbe and the others. The police said they would have charges later.

After about ten minutes the officer in charge arrived and took me out to the dark parking area. "I know what you are up to!" he shouted. "You were making MDC signals at people we arrested. You were trying to have an MDC rally at our station!" I said I had not. The man's face twisted into a contortion of rage and as he shouted spittle flew from his mouth. "I know what you are trying to do and we will get you for this!" He leaned closer to me and I thought he was about to hit me. "Get away from here! I order you to leave here or I will arrest you. Get away now!"

I walked to my car, shaken by his fury but not wanting to show it. Dolores rushed over and we drove back home. Those arrested were not released until hours later.

The next morning John Makumbe was exultant. "Look at my face!" he exclaimed at a press conference. With his irrepressible humor, he managed to make a joke of the mottled bruises across his cheeks and eyes. "I am a rainbow nation all in one. Black, white, yellow, red, purple, it is all here on my face!" he proclaimed, and everyone chuckled. John continued in a humorous vein, joking that nowadays you couldn't even go late to a church meeting without getting arrested.

Then, still smiling, he struck a serious note. "We can laugh about what the police are doing but we know it is wrong. The repression in Zimbabwe has become a threat to everyone. More and more people are going to be arrested and there is going to be violence and more people are going to be hurt. We already know people have been tortured and

260

murdered. All of us demanding our democratic rights need to be ready to be arrested. I, for one, am not afraid and I know there are many others like me."

John was brief and to the point, as always, but I found myself unexpectedly moved. I admired his courage but at the same time I was worried that he would be more seriously hurt. I dreaded the thought of interviewing him about torture that he had endured; I did not want to report that he was arrested or missing. I felt a surge of emotion at the events in which we were all caught up. Mugabe had largely dismantled the great Zimbabwean democracy, but Zimbabweans were still insisting on their democratic rights. Their resistance brought increased state repression, which in turn brought more resistance: it was a terrible yet inspiring cycle in which people from all walks of life were banding together to insist that democracy and the rule of law be restored to their country.

When the conference was over I went up to John and we hugged. "Many people don't want to hug an albino," he joked.

"I'm not worried about that," I replied, "I'm worried about your safety."

He waved off my concern, changing the subject. "What do you think of my face?" he asked, holding up his head for the cameras like a movie star. "It couldn't be better if I had put on makeup! I want everyone to see this."

A couple of days later, May 4, it was World Press Freedom Day and I was again asked to speak at the UN-sponsored event. It was a sparkling sunny day, in the Harare Gardens park. When I got up to speak, I said I could not believe that a year had passed since I had been jailed: "So much has happened since then, but it seems to have been squeezed into a short space of time." I told the crowd I was proud to be the first journalist to have been tried under the government's notorious Access to Information and Protection of Privacy Act, popularly known as Aippa. "I am proud that I won acquittal and that none of the more than fifteen journalists tried under that law has been convicted. To Aippa I say, '*Aiwa!*' [a Shona word for 'no']. I am proud that we journalists in Zimbabwe are doing our duty to report on corruption and human rights abuses, to hold this government responsible for its actions."

261

Banners at the gathering proclaimed the theme of the meeting—"The media we have is not the media we need"—and I picked up on that slogan. "Things cannot stay as they are. There is change in the air. Some day, very soon, Zimbabwe will have the media it needs. It will have the respect for human rights that it needs and it will have the democracy it needs."

Nearby the press event, in another part of the park, the Harare International Festival of the Arts was being held. The idea of enjoying a cultural jamboree in the midst of Zimbabwe's crisis was disconcerting, but the entertainment was invigorating, and many of the performances highlighted social and political issues.

"Face to Face" was an art exhibit curated by Raphael Chikukwa, well known for assembling stimulating exhibits of Zimbabwean artists. He stands out in Harare for wearing colorful shirts in African fabrics and traditional African hats, beads, and bracelets. He looks to many people like a spirit medium or traditional healer. They are not far wrong, because Raphael acts like a cultural medium with a mission to make art speak to all Zimbabweans about their lives, to express for Zimbabweans and international audiences alike what the country is experiencing. "Face to Face" is an exhibit which makes us face up to the realities of Zimbabwe today," Raphael told me. "The days are gone when we can do a pretty exhibit about the Zambezi or about wildlife. Art must deal with the issues that are affecting people in Zimbabwe today."

In a small booth a metal sculpture of a life-size human figure sat in a chair, as if bound to it. A canvas bag covered its head. Next to it was a box with a large red button labeled PRESS, and when it was pushed the figure's head moved slowly from side to side. Scattered about were copies of the *Daily News*, the *Herald*, the *Zimbabwe Independent*, and other local newspapers. This chilling sculpture brought to mind the torture of journalists.

An installation by Berry Bickle displayed enlargements of the *Daily News*, showing articles and letters to the editor. In the corner was an old television broadcasting videos of the state Zimbabwe Broadcasting Corporation, nicknamed the Dead Broadcasting Corporation for its deadening repetition of state propaganda. On a school desk were copies of the government's new Aippa law, the Public Order and Security Act, and the constitution. There was an old typewriter with paper in it and a large blackboard on the wall to encourage people to write what they felt. "Down with repression, forward with freedom!" said one.

A huge painting depicted the hubbub of activity at a Zimbabwean hospital, with people waiting in lengthy lines, guards smoking, nurses giving injections, people on the verge of collapse in wheelchairs. Using cartoonlike figures, the painting portrayed a squalid vision of the hospital that was at the same time somehow humorous and full of life. There was an assemblage of an Air Zimbabwe jet crashing into the Reserve Bank of Zimbabwe, the shiny new office tower of the state's central bank. Another installation featured a mobile of tattered clothes hanging over a pile of battered pots and pans. The final piece was outside the gallery, in the park. A metal sculpture of a mangled skeleton lay in a shallow grave, surrounded by a few candles.

This was no decorative exhibit to distract the viewer from events in Zimbabwe. These were works designed to force those who attended the show to witness what was happening in Zimbabwe.

That weekend the government announced that South African president Thabo Mbeki and Nigerian president Olusegun Obasanjo were jetting into Harare the next day, Monday, May 5. The state media said the two leaders were coming to mediate in the dispute between Zimbabwe and Britain, but everyone knew their visit was to press Mugabe toward some resolution of the country's ongoing crisis.

When Zimbabwe was suspended from the Commonwealth in March 2002, after the group found that Mugabe's reelection had been marked by violence, Obasanjo, Mbeki, and Australian prime minister John Howard were appointed to monitor the situation in Zimbabwe and make suggestions. A year after the suspension, the troika consulted and Mbeki and Obasanjo proposed that the suspension be lifted and Zimbabwe be readmitted to the Commonwealth. The Australian leader pointed out that state violence had increased, repression against the press had stepped up, and undemocratic laws remained in place. These were all the points that Mugabe had been advised to correct in order to gain readmittance to the Commonwealth.

Obasanjo and Mbeki were coming to Harare now to see if they could persuade Mugabe to make some progress on any of the issues. They needed some concrete sign of progress in order to argue for Zimbabwe's readmittance.

First they met with Mugabe at State House and then went to the Sheraton Hotel to meet Morgan Tsvangirai. Mugabe would not countenance allowing the opposition leader to cross the threshold of his offices. So the leaders of Africa's two most powerful countries went to a hotel to carry out their mission to try to find a solution to Zimbabwe's crisis.

I dashed over to the hotel to see if the leaders would say anything. Near the entrance to the hotel complex I saw about three hundred demonstrators. Men and women were singing and holding up placards: MBEKI AND OBASANJO, HELP THE SUFFERING PEOPLE OF ZIMBABWE; PLEASE TELL MUGABE TO GO NOW, WOMEN ARE BEING TORTURED. I scribbled down the slogans and was just stepping forward to speak to a few people in the crowd, when suddenly the police came charging across the street, waving truncheons and grabbing demonstrators. Some of those arrested were women with babies on their backs.

When I got to the hotel itself, I joined a large crew of journalists; the usual suspects of the Harare press corps had been joined by South African and Nigerian journalists who had come with their presidents. Thabo Mbeki uttered a few words to the effect that he and Obasanjo had come to encourage the process of dialogue between Zanu-PF and the MDC. It seemed like an innocuous statement to the South African journalists, but to the Zimbabweans it directly contradicted Mugabe's explanation of their visit as an effort to mediate between Zimbabwe and Britain over the land dispute.

"It appears as if this country is sitting on a keg of gunpowder," said Obasanjo after the meetings. He confirmed that the two leaders had wrested an agreement from Mugabe that his party would begin negotiations with the MDC. By meeting Tsvangirai and publicly stating their intention to foster negotiations between Mugabe and the opposition, the two African leaders were putting significant pressure to bear upon Mugabe. If they were to maintain such pressure, Robert Mugabe would eventually have to enter into negotiations with the opposition. This could be a significant turning point in Zimbabwe's history. It was cause for hope.

Iden agreed with me. "It may be a halting step but this is nonetheless the first step in the movement toward a democratic government," he said when I called him for a comment. "It may be a protracted and messy process, but it has now begun. The visit of the two leaders represents a significant chink in the hitherto solid armor of African solidarity protecting Mugabe. If those African leaders succeed in getting Mugabe to the negotiating table, he will be hostage to a political process that he does not control. The process will inexorably lead him toward a new round of elections, under free and fair conditions, and that will spell the end to his rule and the rule of his party. In other words this could be the beginning of the end."

This was not overoptimism. South Africa had effectively pressed Ian Smith to the negotiating table with Robert Mugabe and Joshua Nkomo, resulting in the elections that gave birth to independent, majority-rule Zimbabwe and brought Robert Mugabe to power. History could be repeating itself if South Africa, with help from Nigeria, were to press Mugabe to hold fresh elections that would allow a peaceful, democratic change of power.

"They're telling Mugabe to go!" said a young man, sharing a *Daily News* with two others. (Times were so tight that people often split the cost of a newspaper and then passed it around. A million people read the *Daily News*, according to surveys.) Gas lines also buzzed with the news. "Obasanjo says Zimbabwe will explode if Mugabe doesn't step down," said a taxi driver, only slightly exaggerating the Nigerian leader's words. People were smiling as they talked about change, clenching their fists as if to grasp it.

The *Guardian* foreign desk asked me to write a piece about life in Harare's crisis. I felt a renewed enthusiasm and set about interviewing people and describing scenes of the political and economic crisis that had spilled over into every aspect of life. It was this article that I was finishing when the buzzer announced that someone was at our gate. I asked Dolores if she would answer the intercom so that I could finish the story.

Breathless with shock and suppressed panic, she came to tell me it was someone from Immigration. We both knew that meant trouble. Determined that I would not let any immigration agent stop me from completing my story, I rattled away on the keyboard to finish the last two paragraphs. It would be the last story I wrote in Zimbabwe. It appeared in the *Guardian* the next morning:

In Harare these days you never know where you are going to end up when you take a taxi. A dozen passengers crammed into a taxi van recently complained angrily among themselves about Zimbabwe's high inflation, critical fuel shortages, and the police who shoved them when they were stopped at roadblocks.

When one man tried to defend the police, a woman retorted: "The police are just Mugabe's dogs." The rest of the passengers cheered. When the taxi stopped, the man jumped out and ran to some nearby police officers. He identified himself as an off-duty policeman and ordered them to arrest the passengers. They were jailed overnight and charged for insulting police, a crime under the Public Order and Security Act.

For many months horror stories have been emerging from Zimbabwe about the suffering inflicted by President Robert Mugabe. Newspapers have been filled with accounts of political corruption, rapes, and beatings. But behind these stories lie the daily hardships felt by the capital's 1.7 million people.

What was once a thriving city has descended into a place of empty supermarkets, gas lines, and blackouts.

In the past week the longstanding fuel shortages have taken a turn for the worse. Hundreds of vehicles spend entire days and nights in fuel lines in Harare. "We used to laugh at Zambians because of all the shortages they had. Now they are laughing at us because it is much worse here," said a salesman. "We never thought it would get this bad."

A few months ago Mr. Mugabe's motorcade of more than twenty vehicles, including two trucks full of armed soldiers, passed a fuel line on Samora Machel Avenue in downtown Harare. The president was met by jeers and hoots of derision. Some people threw empty cans. The soldiers later returned and beat up many of those in the line. A law has also been passed declaring it illegal to make derogatory comments or gestures to the presidential motorcade.

Harare's new mayor, Elias Mudzuri, tried to improve city services; garbage collections were organized and crews sent out to fill potholes. But Mr. Mudzuri, elected by nearly 80 percent of Harare's voters, belongs to the opposition party, the Movement for Democratic Change (MDC). Last week the Mugabe government sacked him, accusing him of incompetence and corruption. Mr. Mudzuri has been barred from his office and has gone into hiding after receiving threats.

At first glance, the supermarket in central Harare appears well-stocked and busy. But on closer inspection, rows and rows of toilet paper are displayed. "That is where there should be salt and that is where there should be sugar, but those items are out of stock so they put up toilet paper," said Idah Mandaza.

"And mealie meal [maize meal, Zimbabwe's staple food] and cooking oil and soap, they have all been replaced with toilet paper. But we can't eat loo paper. Either basic things are not available or I can't afford them. I never thought it would come to this."

For Mrs. Mandaza, Zimbabwe's inflation of 228 percent and 12 percent decline in GDP are not dry economic statistics. They are the harsh facts of life that she, her family, and everyone in Zimbabwe grapple with daily.

Mrs. Mandaza, fifty-three, is proud of her job as the assistant production manager in a Harare factory. But by the time she pays for travel to and from work and her rent for a small two-roomed house, more than half of her salary is gone. "I'm lucky, I have two sons and they both have jobs. But I still must be very careful when I shop. I support my mother and my sister, plus I help my brothers in the rural areas. There is just not enough money," she said.

Zimbabwe's once thriving middle class is struggling to get by, but the poor are desperate. Growing numbers are begging and rummaging through rubbish bins. The disparity in wealth has widened after two years of economic crisis.

"In forty years working as a doctor, I have never seen so many cases of malnutrition, particularly among children," said a general practitioner. "It used to be that I would only see signs of kwashiorkor [a form of malnutrition caused by inadequate protein intake] in children from the rural areas. Now I see it in city children."

The United Nations estimates that nearly one million urban Zimbabweans do not have enough food. In total, more than seven million of the country's twelve million people are threatened with starvation, according to the government. Just a few years ago Zimbabwe was extolled as the breadbasket of Africa.

An unruly commotion erupts in the supermarket as people rush to the bakery section where bread is put on the shelves. After a few minutes of shoving and grabbing, the bread is gone. One woman was knocked down in the scuffle.

There used to be a similar rush when milk and other fresh dairy products were delivered. But for two weeks there have not been any milk deliveries. A dairy farm that supplied 40 percent of Harare's milk has been overrun by Mr. Mugabe's supporters, according to local newspaper reports.

The supermarket no longer puts its rare deliveries of maize meal or other scarce items on sale in the store. After some miniriots in which shelves were knocked down, the scarce goods are sold at the back of the store where deliveries are made. People wait in line there for hours.

Zimbabwe's once respected police are now widely feared for arbitrary arrests, beatings, and torture. In the past two months ten high-profile Zimbabweans, including three members of Parliament and one lawyer, have accused police of torturing them with electric shocks. Medical examinations have confirmed injuries consistent with their harrowing accounts. Most were released without charges.

Last month more than 250 opposition supporters had to be hospitalized after men dressed in army uniforms raided their homes and beat them.

But not everyone is gloomy and depressed. "The worse things get, the sooner we will have a change," said one motorist waiting for fuel. "The more angry people get, the sooner they will press Mugabe to go."

He pointed to the visit to Harare on Monday of South Africa's president Thabo Mbeki and his Nigerian equivalent Olusegun Obasanjo. "Do you think they came to congratulate Mugabe on doing such a good job? No, they came to tell Mugabe he must go. The pressure is mounting and change is in the air. I can feel it."

Even as Mugabe's security agents were at my gate, I concentrated on completing and transmitting this story. Despite the difficulties swirling around us, I believed the words of those I had interviewed: change for the better in Zimbabwe was not far off.

By the time I had succeeded in e-mailing the story, Dolores had come back to the house. She said she had told the men I was not at home. She recognized the leader of the group as Evans Siziba, the immigration agent who had tried to deport me after my trial. She said other men were with him. We agreed that we knew too many people who had been taken away under such circumstances and then been tortured. I was not going to turn myself over to them. Dolores phoned Beatrice, who said she would come right over, and then went back to the gate with our dogs.

I grabbed a sweater and my cell phone. I went out the back and, using the stepladder, scaled the wall and dropped down to the other side.

Luck was on my side as I moved through the chilly night undetected. When my friend came to pick me up, I lay on the floor of his car as he drove past four government vehicles at our gate, including a van with blacked-out windows. He saw that Beatrice had arrived. I was relieved that our fearless, feisty lawyer would be there to help Dolores.

During those first days when I was on the run, I kept hoping against hope that the situation could be resolved and my life would return to normal. Beatrice and I communicated by cell phone. "We must try to get your situation on a legal footing," she said. "You have every legal right to be here and we must just get the government to obey its own court rulings." She planned to go back to the courts to get an order that immigration and other agents must leave me alone.

At first Immigration claimed they did not know anything about agents coming to my house, but soon they told her that they did indeed want to see me and ordered her to bring me to their offices.

Two executives from the *Guardian*, including the head of the paper's legal office, flew in from London to try to assist Beatrice. They went with her to Immigration but as soon as they asked a question about my case, the authorities ordered them to leave the country within twenty-four hours.

By then it was the weekend, and a demonstration was being held by a group called Women of Zimbabwe Arise (Woza). Despite constant reports in the state's *Herald* newspaper that government agents were closing in on me, I was determined to see it. The women gathered in the heart of Harare at Africa Unity Square, which is flanked by the Parliament building, the Anglican cathedral, and the *Herald*'s offices. I sat in a car very nearby and listened to their singing. NO TO TORTURE, NO TO VIOLENCE, YES TO PEACE read one of the placards. Surprisingly the police did not break up the gathering or arrest the women. I was glad I watched the event, even from a distance: the women's optimism boosted my own.

I had arranged to meet Beatrice that afternoon and I walked across the park and down an alley to the back entrance of an office block; Beatrice went in the front door. We agreed that we should try to get the government officials to state why they wanted to see me.

"You must show the government that you are not in hiding. You should make strategic appearances," said Iden, and we decided that the large diplomatic reception to mark Europe Day on Monday would be a perfect opportunity. It would be packed with ambassadors and journalists, so if anyone came to arrest me there would be a lot of high-powered witnesses.

I was feeling quite upbeat that day. I enjoyed the reception. But when I left, I received a phone call warning me not to go back to the house where Dolores and I had been staying as some men were hanging around.

Dolores was trying to continue working, so my friend Michele Mathison picked me up and took me out to a small lodge on the outskirts of Harare. It was unnerving to be forced to pack up and go at a moment's notice, and neither Dolores nor I slept well. And the next morning things changed again. The hotel manager said he was not comfortable with us staying there any longer.

Someone I knew in the police reached me on my cell phone. He wanted to meet. I was suspicious at first, but he told me he had been hounded out of the force, accused of supporting the MDC. He had been an assistant inspector, but recently he had been summarily fired, plus he had been beaten and his house burned down. He was now living apart from his wife and children to prevent them from suffering because of his reputation. He confirmed what I had heard from other police officers that many stations had been taken over by rabid supporters of

Mugabe. "These men are poorly educated and they have not passed any of the exams that we must take to get promotions," said the former officer. "They do not want to see any professionalism in the force, they just want Zanu-PF. It is shameful for those of us who were trying to do a good job." He said that police were ordered not to assist any victims of violence by the war veterans or youth militia. I asked him what would bring back professionalism on the force. "A change of government," he said. "A change of government is the only thing that can help the police force." It was the last interview I would do in Zimbabwe.

Once again I found myself in the position of having become the news, as I had been during my trial. I was not able to write and file stories. Continually moving from place to place was wearing and I felt it was just a matter of time before Immigration, the police, or the CIO caught up with me. And I felt I was putting others around me at risk, too.

"You are doing a great job," said John Makumbe when he reached me on the phone. "You are making them so uncomfortable, like they are sitting on something that makes them itch and when they scratch it, it stings," he said, breaking into such infectious laughter that I joined in. "Everyone can see that Jonathan Moyo is afraid of you, and even Mugabe, too. That's why they want to shut you up. You have showed them up."

When I said I thought they would eventually succeed in kicking me out of the country, John responded, "Don't worry, we will get you back here soon. You are a key part of the press and that is part of civil society. We all have our part to play in getting this country back to democracy. You are doing your bit, Brother."

When I hung up the phone Dolores said she knew it was John Makumbe because he got me to laugh, which I hadn't done for days. "He called me Brother," I told her. "I really like that."

It was the early evening and Michele Mathison took me to Beatrice's office. She said she thought I would have to go to Immigration the next morning. "I know they want to arrest you and expel you. I will get a court order to prevent that," she said.

"Look, Beatrice," I said, "go ahead with the court action, but we both know the government will probably ignore it." We talked about other options: staying on in this limbo, seeking the protection of the U.S.

271

embassy, quietly leaving the country on my own. None of them seemed right. By going to Immigration with my lawyer I was trying to make this cat-and-mouse game a legal process.

That night I insisted that we go home. Our house had not been under surveillance for several days and I wanted to go there more than any place on earth. We got a rapturous welcome from our dogs and I delighted just in feeding them dinner as usual. Our veranda, our bed, our bath glowed like mystical, mythical places, and I was in a kind of state of grace, enjoying every moment among my surroundings.

We slept very well that night and the morning dawned bright and fresh. I walked in my garden, picking the first limes, pulling some weeds, looking at the start of a new palm frond. I tried to absorb every tree, shrub, and flower through my pores, to make a permanent record in my mind of how everything looked, smelled, and felt.

I looked up and saw Mavis running toward me. She hugged me and began shaking and sobbing. "They can't take you away, they can't," she said. I could feel my eyes filling up.

"Mave, they can't take away our friendship," I said with a scratchy throat. "That is never going to change. It will only get stronger."

Dolores did not want to go to Immigration with me. She did not want to see the journalists or any of the government agents. She drove Beatrice and me to the immigration office but did not stay. Michele went ahead to Immigration, where he would be filming events for the BBC. Iden reached me on the phone and said, "Tell those goons that I expect to have our Friday lunch with you, and if they stop that they will have to answer to me!"

Driving through the center of Harare to Linquenda House, I thought about how much the city had changed. The buildings were the same, though shabbier, but the big difference was that the pavements were much more busy. Every street corner had makeshift stands selling tomatoes, onions, apples, and bananas. People were buzzing about. On closer inspection I could see the poverty in the ragged clothes and the look of hungry desperation. We drove past Robert Mugabe's offices in the old colonial building, the only office building bearing a fresh coat of paint. Soldiers with automatic rifles kept pedestrians away and prevented anyone from parking nearby.

We went past the MDC's offices in Harvest House on Nelson Mandela Avenue and I saw the usual group of young supporters hanging out by the entrance to offer a bit of security to the opposition leaders inside. The young men could do that because they did not have any jobs. I knew injured men and women were there as usual, getting referrals to doctors who were willing to treat them.

We drove up to Linquenda House and Beatrice pointed out police vehicles, CIO cars, and military trucks—she recognized their license plates. We went inside and took the rickety elevator up to the fifth floor. Officials from the U.S. embassy were there, but they were not permitted to sit in our meeting with the chief immigration officer.

That meeting seemed to go well. I answered his questions and agreed to bring some of my articles in for him to see. For an instant I almost believed that we could sort things out. But then Beatrice and I were referred over to Evans Siziba, and instantly everything felt much more sinister. Before I knew it Siziba had announced I would be deported from the country. As we walked out of his office, Beatrice and I were surrounded by police.

"You cannot call this deportation," said Beatrice. "Deportation suggests a legal process and this is completely illegal. You must not say you were deported."

When we reached the ground floor I was pleased to see the Harare press corps out in force. I knew this was my only chance to highlight the issues. "I have been declared a prohibited immigrant and am being expelled from the country. This is not the action of a government—" and at that the police grabbed me and started pulling and pushing me away. I was determined to make a statement about what was going on and kept speaking: ". . . that is confident of its own legitimacy." I could see all my press colleagues, Angus Shaw of Associated Press, Cris Chinaka of Reuters, Jan Raath of the *Times*, photographers Howard Burditt and Aaron Ufumeli. I wanted to stop all the commotion and go over and rejoin them, to report on something happening to somebody else. But

273

from the angry force of the police officers grabbing and dragging me, I knew that was not possible. I couldn't see Beatrice anywhere; she had been pushed away from me. We were getting close to a waiting car and I knew I had to keep up with my statement. "These are the actions of a government that is afraid of a free press and afraid of critical and independent reporting!"

There was more I wanted to say—that the government was afraid of the press because it was highlighting the real issues of hunger and poverty and human rights abuses; that the government was trying to muzzle the press, but in this day and age of the Internet and fax machines and radio their efforts were bound to fail; that as sure as the sun comes up in the morning, Jonathan Moyo and Robert Mugabe would fail to control the news; that the real news will get out no matter what they do—but before I could say anything more I was bundled into a car and driven away. Beatrice and the journalists tried to get the number of the license plate, and the U.S. officials tried to follow the car, but it sped off too fast.

While I was being held in the basement of the airport, Beatrice went to the high court and obtained a ruling ordering the action against me to be halted. She delivered it to the various airlines, and South African Airways and British Airways refused to carry me as it would be an illegal action. The state-owned Air Zimbabwe was the only airline prepared to collaborate in my illegal deportation.

Dolores rushed to the airport. A car matching the description of the vehicle that took me away was parked at the front. They waited and waited. Finally a journalist saw me being led through the immigration offices and told Dolores and Beatrice where I was.

Dolores called out my name and I turned to see her far down the passageway. Then I saw Beatrice charging through the security, waving the sheaf of papers that was my court order. "Stop! Stop! This is illegal. Here is the court order!" shouted Beatrice. I struggled to break free from the men escorting me and started running toward Beatrice and Dolores. The officers called for more security and once again I was surrounded and dragged away, this time to the Air Zimbabwe plane. I was shoved on the plane and then to my seat.

As the plane took off and Harare became just a cluster of twinkling lights, I was still charged with adrenaline from the struggle. I thought about how different this departure was from my arrival. I knew that, as much as it tried, the Mugabe regime could not keep me out of Zimbabwe. The country was a part of me and I knew I would be coming back.

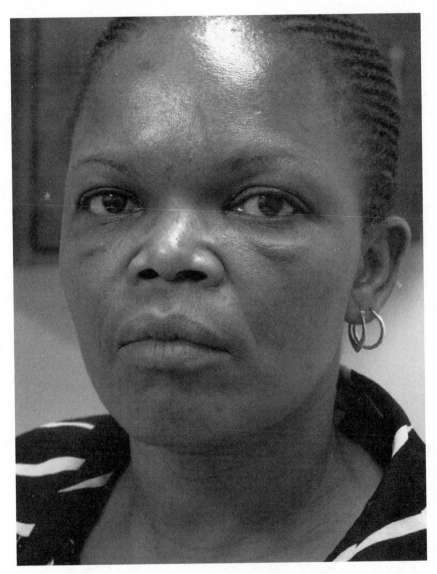

My valiant lawyer, Beatrice Mtetwa, after she was assaulted by police in October 2003. She typed up assault charges and served them on the perpetrators. Beatrice's fearless advocacy of press freedom and human rights in Zimbabwe remains an inspiration to me. © *Michele Mathison*

EPILOGUE

Since I was thrown out of Zimbabwe, the change that seemed so imminent has remained elusive. Robert Mugabe is still president. His regime has tightened its repression of the press, its control of the police, and its violence against anyone voicing criticism or suspected of supporting the opposition.

Three weeks after I was expelled, Evans Siziba and other "immigration officers" came back to our house looking for Dolores. She was not at home at the time and she stayed away. Like me, Dolores had every legal right to stay in the country, and Beatrice sought court protection for her, but the government was determined to get her out. The period when government agents were looking for her was agonizing for me, much worse than when I had been in the same situation. I was in London and there was little I could do from there. The three of us decided that we should press for her legal rights to be upheld, but that she should leave Zimbabwe of her own accord to avoid being arrested and held captive as I had. She flew out two days after Siziba came to our house, and I met her at Heathrow Airport.

After a flurry of interviews with the international press, I got back down to work, first writing some articles about Zimbabwe from London. Through Amnesty International I met a Zimbabwean policeman who had been granted political asylum in Britain. He told me in great detail of torture and murder carried out by police in his area—Mataga. This man, who had been twice honored as "officer of the month," was deeply troubled by the violence he witnessed. The new commander of his station turned on him and called him a traitor and his gun was taken from him. Knowing this was the prelude to torture, he fled Mataga and eventually sought asylum in Britain. The interview added to my bulging dossier on the debasement of Zimbabwe's police force.

I also wrote an article about Harare police officer Henry Dowa, identified by several victims as perpetrating torture in the Law and Order section of Harare Central. Far from being reprimanded for such acts, Dowa was rewarded by being seconded to the United Nations' peacekeeping force in Kosovo. Redress, a British-based organization which assists torture survivors, informed the UN that an officer with documented allegations of torture against him was working on their force, urging the UN to arrest Dowa and see that he was brought to trial according to the UN convention against torture. Sadly the UN declined to take action against Dowa, citing insufficient funds. He was sent back to Zimbabwe where he has been seen in Harare driving a police Land-Rover, wearing his trademark *gudza* hat and continuing to carry out illegal and brutal acts.

If Jonathan Moyo and the government thought they would mute my voice by expelling me, they were mistaken. I may not be in Zimbabwe but now I have a more prominent platform.

Dolores and I resettled in Pretoria, South Africa, and I am working for the *Guardian* and the *Observer*, covering Zimbabwe and other events in the continent. There are estimated to be more than two million Zimbabwean refugees in South Africa, many of them survivors of violence and torture. One torture survivor (whom I interviewed in Harare) fled Zimbabwe and is now living a precarious existence as an illegal immigrant in South Africa and sleeping in a city park. Dolores is working with a project to help some of those refugees find a more stable existence and begin healing from the trauma they have experienced.

Mercedes Sayagues and her daughter Esmeralda live nearby and we see a great deal of each other. Mercedes works as a freelance journalist and remains well informed, perceptive, and impassioned about Zimbabwe, AIDS education, and many other things. She is our most stimulating and rewarding friend in our exiled existence.

Michele Mathison drove our car down to South Africa with some of our belongings and our dogs. That delivery gave us a start and we have made the best of our new life here, determined to carry on what we had been doing before. Michele is working as a freelance cameraman in Zimbabwe and creating sculptures and art installations.

In September 2003 police armed with AK-47 rifles marched into the newsroom of the *Daily News* and closed the paper. After six weeks the courts ruled that the banning of the *Daily News* was illegal, and the spirited staff immediately put out an edition with a banner headline proclaiming triumphantly WE'RE BACK! Police stormed back into its newsroom the next day and closed it again. It is by far the most popular newspaper in the country and the only daily paper to report independently on events. Many acts of violence and intimidation against ordinary Zimbabweans went unreported while it was closed. Beatrice Mtetwa and the paper's own lawyer, Gugulethu Moyo, won four court orders for the paper to be able to resume publication, which it finally did in January 2004. But the paper's resuscitation was short-lived. By February the supreme court, packed as it is with Mugabe's cronies, gave a ruling that forced the paper to close down.

One evening, as Beatrice was driving home, thieves attempted to hijack her car. Neighbors witnessing the incident called the police and they arrived relatively promptly, but when the officers recognized Beatrice they stopped pursuing the thieves and turned on her instead. Claiming that she had been driving while intoxicated, they arrested her. "The tables have turned," said one officer to Beatrice. "You are no longer a lawyer, you are a suspect, and you will see what it is like."

Incensed by the fabricated allegation against her, Beatrice demanded to be given a breathalizer test or to be taken to a doctor for a blood test. The police took her away in their vehicle and an officer began punching her. The assault intensified when they arrived at the Borrowdale police station, where the officer beat her with his fists and choked her until she nearly passed out. He kicked her when she fell down. Several other police officers stood by and watched the lengthy assault.

Beatrice was released without charges after three hours. She went immediately to a doctor to document the violent abuse she had suffered. She had two black eyes and severe bruising on her arms, ribs, and legs. She could not speak for two days as a result of the strangulation. On the third day she returned to the police station to file charges of assault, complete with medical evidence.

In December 2003, Beatrice won the Human Rights Lawyer of the Year award, presented in London by the British organizations Liberty and Justice. The *Guardian* ran a story about the honor on the front page, with a color photograph of Beatrice's bruised face, taken by Michele Mathison just after her assault. "Can you imagine, my one time on the front page and they show a photo of me looking my worst!" Beatrice said, chuckling. "A British lawyer asked someone at the *Guardian* if the black marks around my eyes were tribal markings. I said, 'Tell them yes: everyone in Zimbabwe is getting markings like that.'"

Jonathan Moyo was so annoyed by the award that he said in the *Herald*, "It is a meaningless award given only because she represented Andrew Meldrum in court."

John Makumbe continues to be a dynamo powering Zimbabwe's civic organizations in their demands that the Mugabe government should respect basic democratic freedoms and human rights. In November 2003, John was arrested along with forty other civic leaders when they attempted to stage a demonstration in central Harare. They were held in jail for two days. "It was great!" enthused John afterward. "They didn't know what to do with us and so they put us in one big room. We all got to know each other very well and we all got along together. It was like a retreat to build solidarity."

And when police came to take away Raymond Majongwe, leader of the Zimbabwe Progressive Teachers Union, who had been tortured earlier in 2003, Makumbe and the others stood together and refused to let the guards separate Majongwe from the rest.

I reminded John that he had told me things would have to get worse before they got better, and asked him, "How much worse? Is there a light at the end of the tunnel?"

"Sure there is a light at the end of the tunnel," he responded. "The only problem is that Mugabe keeps building more tunnel!"

Mavis has continued to be the greatest friend we could have. She has scrupulously looked after our house and garden, and tells me that the avocado and lime trees we planted are now producing fruit and that my palms and acacia trees are flourishing. This pleases me tremendously, even though I cannot be there.

Mavis's mother, Milka, came to live with her in the cottage. When she heard I had been kicked out of Zimbabwe she said, "This is one more thing that makes me mad at Mugabe and Jonathan Moyo. I thought

Anderoo would bury me. But now I know I will see him in heaven."
Mavis looked after her well and made sure she was comfortable, but
in October she suffered a massive stroke and died two days later. Mavis
organized her mother's funeral and burial in the rural Seke plot that she
had farmed for nearly all of the ninety years of her life. I wrote a short
eulogy that Michele read out at the funeral.

Iden Wetherell gave many interviews at the time of my ejection.
He said he felt like he was speaking about a colleague who had just died:
"Andy went out the way he would have wanted to: making a fuss and
calling attention to the burning issues in Zimbabwe."

Iden wrote a column the week after I was expelled entitled "Not
over yet": "The government of President Robert Mugabe, signaling to
the world its contempt for its own judiciary, has added Meldrum's name
to the roll call of foreign correspondents evicted for reporting unpalat-
able home truths about the malignant regime that tyrannizes this once
promising nation." He described how immigration agents, Air Zimbabwe, and other arms of the government blatantly ignored court orders
when they abducted me and forcibly put me on a plane to London.

> The obvious message the government is sending here—wittingly
> or unwittingly—is that nobody in Zimbabwe today is safe from ar-
> bitrary arrest, illegal abduction, and deprivation of their rights . . .
> Let's hear no more complaints about the bad press that Zimbabwe
> gets abroad; that it is all a conspiracy. This was a spectacular own
> goal by Mugabe's minions who are determined to get even with their
> detractors and will use any means to do so. It is no secret that Andy
> caused deep embarrassment to the regime when he was acquitted
> in the first landmark test of the vicious Access to Information and
> Protection of Privacy Act last year. Meldrum's abduction and de-
> portation will simply add to the sense of terminal insecurity that
> now hangs palpably over this government. It is understandably wor-
> ried about the truth getting out. But Meldrum's removal certainly
> won't help. Rather it will reinforce the determination of all profes-
> sional journalists—as distinct from the state's public relations
> officers—to go on exposing Zimbabwe's lawless rulers as the ma-
> levolent despots they are. And when democracy and rule of law are

restored—no longer a distant prospect—all those deported under Zanu-PF will be welcomed back as veterans in the battle for freedom of expression, just as those deported by the Rhodesian Front were in 1980. I suspect Meldrum's absence won't be as long as his kidnappers had hoped.

Iden and I remain in regular contact. Even though we are not having our Friday lunches together, we generally speak on that day and discuss the week's events. After the closure of the *Daily News,* Jonathan Moyo said his next target would be Iden's paper, the *Zimbabwe Independent.* On January 10, 2004, police arrested Iden, news editor Vincent Kahiya, and chief reporter Dumisani Muleya and held them in jail for two nights. They were charged with criminal defamation of Mugabe for reporting that Mugabe and his wife had commandeered an Air Zimbabwe jet for a personal holiday and shopping trip in Asia. Their last-minute use of the state airline's Boeing 767 jet reportedly caused the floundering corporation to lose significant amounts of money and wreaked havoc on the scheduled flights. The government does not dispute the main facts of the story, but claims Mugabe chartered the plane. Jonathan Moyo said that "if one detail of the story is wrong then those journalists face two years in jail."

Iden and his talented, brave staff have continued to produce a world-class paper with plenty of hard-hitting news stories, biting satirical comment, and analysis that puts Zimbabwe's current crisis in its historic context.

Thabo Mbeki did not maintain the pressure he had so promisingly applied on Mugabe in May 2003. Instead he repeated Mugabe's assertion that Zimbabwe's crisis is the fault of the country's land issue, and failed to mention anything about torture, human rights abuses, perversion of the democratic system, and suppression of the free press. He pressed for Zimbabwe to be readmitted to the Commonwealth, despite the fact that no progress could be reported on any of the complaints for which Zimbabwe had been suspended in March 2002.

Commonwealth secretary-general Don McKinnon has worked hard to atone for his failure to take a decisive stand against Mugabe's state violence in the June 2000 parliamentary elections. Realizing that Zimbabwe will be the issue that defines his tenure at the helm of the Commonwealth, McKinnon skillfully outflanked the efforts of Mbeki to get Zimbabwe readmitted, by leading the Commonwealth to stand up for its democratic principles and to refuse to be divided along racial lines. The Zimbabwe issue made the organization stronger and increased its stature. Mbeki, on the other hand, has seen his reputation for leading African opinion badly dented and his support for democracy seriously questioned.

Mbeki continues hotly defending his "quiet diplomacy" toward Mugabe, saying Zimbabwe's problems will be solved by a "government of national unity" or some sort of coalition between Zanu-PF and the MDC. I disagree. Zimbabwe's fiscal implosion, which has seen the country's economy lose half its value in the four years since 1999, is the result of Mugabe's policies, and as long as he wields power the country's sharp decline will not be stopped. The solution to Zimbabwe's crisis is much more simple: free and fair elections. Without government manipulation of the voting process and state violence against the opposition, democracy will put Zimbabwe firmly on the path to better governance.

It was therefore significant when the Southern African Development Community, the regional body of fourteen nations including Zimbabwe, passed a new charter for democratic elections in August 2004. It calls for elections to be held without any fear of violence, covered by a free press, and administered by an independent commission. Zimbabwe meets none of these criteria. Pressure from Zimbabwe's southern African neighbors will be difficult for Mugabe to ignore.

If Thabo Mbeki and others in South Africa cannot accurately assess and criticize the atrocities Mugabe is perpetuating in Zimbabwe, then there is cause for worry that South Africa may follow the same path. This point was enunciated by Desmond Tutu, the retired Anglican archbishop of Cape Town. "Human rights are human rights and they are of universal validity or they are nothing," said the Nobel Peace Prize laureate, speaking about Zimbabwe in January 2004. "There are no peculiarly African human rights. What has been reported as happening in Zimbabwe is totally unacceptable and reprehensible and we ought to say so, regretting that it should have been necessary to condemn erstwhile comrades. The credibility of our democracy demands this. If we are seemingly indifferent to human rights violations happening in a neighboring country, what is to stop us one day being indifferent to that in our own?"

Despite all the high hopes in 1980 that the new Zimbabwe would avoid the problems that have plagued other African nations—ethnic violence, a stultifying one-party state, corruption, economic decline, and a leader who dismantles democracy in order to cling to power—each of these problems has been inflicted on the country by Robert Mugabe and Zanu-PF. Mugabe's rhetoric against whites and the former colonial power, Britain, make it appear that the country's deepening problems are a reaction against the years of colonial domination and white minority rule. Perhaps they are, but Mugabe has tried hard to stir up an antiwhite hatred that is not felt by the ordinary Zimbabwean. Inside Zimbabwe, Mugabe's antiwhite stance is viewed by most as a smoke screen to hide his much baser motive to maintain his power at all costs.

From a distance it may appear to some that Zimbabwe's descent from democracy was inevitable, but from within the country we saw that at each step there were many who tried to influence Mugabe's decisions and to encourage the country down a different route.

Zimbabwe will one day restore its democracy and a new government will resurrect respect for human rights and a free press. Sound economic management will put the country back on the path toward prosperity and equitable development. When all this will be achieved, however, I cannot say. It is not known how many Zimbabweans will be beaten, tortured, and killed in the struggle to regain their freedoms. But I am absolutely sure that the country will return to its democratic ideals and Zimbabwe will once again be a beacon for all of Africa. And after having fought for their rights, Zimbabweans will guard them jealously. The Zimbabwean electorate will emerge from the struggle strengthened and considerably wiser.

I am very lucky to have lived in Zimbabwe through this time. The twenty-three years I spent there enriched my life and gave me a sense of purpose. This account may suggest that those years were dominated by turmoil and oppression, but that is not the case. My life in Zimbabwe was full of joy and laughter and great friendships. And my professionalism benefited tremendously. I came to Zimbabwe young and full of ideals about liberation and multiracial democracy. Those ideals were challenged, threatened, and forged by trial, and remain intact. I came to Zimbabwe to report on the aspirations of its people. That goal has not changed. It is the Mugabe government that changed when it placed its own power above the welfare of Zimbabwe's people.

I know now how violence corrupts. Those who use violence, even for a just cause such as ending Rhodesia's minority rule, often find it too easy to employ violence again for less noble purposes. Robert Mugabe and his Zanu-PF party now revel in using violence to maintain their power. Violence has infected the very principles that they once championed.

As a journalist I have learned to shy away from making excuses for the failings of any government. I am determined to expose torture, state violence, corruption, and repression wherever I see them. That is not an onerous burden; it is a privilege. In this modern world, where so many question the meaning of life, I am honored to be able to stand up for human rights, press freedom, and democracy. I know they will win in the end.

December 2004